University of Michigan Studies
HUMANISTIC SERIES
VOLUME XXVII

ATHENIAN FINANCIAL DOCUMENTS OF THE FIFTH CENTURY

ATHENIAN FINANCIAL DOCUMENTS OF THE FIFTH CENTURY

BY

BENJAMIN DEAN MERITT

UNIVERSITY OF MICHIGAN

ANN ARBOR

UNIVERSITY OF MICHIGAN PRESS

1932

PRINTED IN THE UNITED STATES OF AMERICA

AT THE HARVARD UNIVERSITY PRESS

CAMBRIDGE, MASSACHUSETTS

TO

JOHANNES KIRCHNER

In Friendship and Esteem
and in
Recognition of his Lasting Contributions to
Greek Epigraphy

FOREWORD

SOME years ago, while studying in the Epigraphical Museum at Athens, I became convinced that careful scrutiny of the texts of several inscriptions already published might yield additional evidence for the financial history of Athens in the fifth century. The class of documents to which I wished to devote particular attention included the records of expenditures of the Athenian state from moneys borrowed from the treasury of Athena. Most of these inscriptions are in Athens, but several important fragments are now in Paris and London. I am indebted to Professor Étienne Michon for placing at my disposal every possible facility for study when I visited the Louvre Museum in December of 1929, and to Mr. H. B. Walters, keeper of Greek and Roman antiquities in the British Museum, for generously furnishing to me squeezes and photographs of the documents under his care.

During the course of the investigation I have had the advantage of discussing many problems with Messrs. H. T. Wade-Gery and J. K. Fotheringham at Oxford, and with Messrs. A. B. West, W. B. Dinsmoor, and W. S. Ferguson in this country. To Dr. Fotheringham I am especially grateful for suggestions about the Athenian calendar, many of which I have adopted, though the views set forth in the last chapters of this volume have also been considerably influenced by Mr. Dinsmoor's recent book on the archons of Athens. A satisfactory analysis of the documents from the later years of the fifth century could hardly have been made without the help of Mr. Ferguson's study of the treasurers of Athena.

I have endeavored to present accurate drawings of most of the inscriptions recorded in this volume. All the drawings have been made with the aid of squeezes on which the letters were marked with pencil. These penciled squeezes were then traced on drawing paper with India ink, and restorations were added in red. The drawings thus prepared were reduced to zinc plates by the photoengraver's process and thus made available for publication. The photographs in the text and at the end of the volume give a measure of control over the text as presented in the drawings. It must always be remembered, however, that no photographic reproduction in a book is as clear as the original. In doubtful cases a final test of the accuracy of the text can be made only by direct comparison with the stones themselves. In the transcription of the Greek epigraphical texts the symbols employed are those now in use in the *Supplementum Epigraphicum Graecum*.

Mr. Homer Thompson and Mr. Oscar Broneer, of the American School of Classical Studies at Athens, have secured for me excellent photographs of many of the documents, and have given freely of their time to verify readings from the stones themselves. I wish here to express my gratitude to them, and also to Mr. G. P. Oikonomos, director of the National Museum in Athens, and to Mr. A. Philadelpheus, director of the Epigraphical Museum, for their constant assistance and courteous generosity in allowing the publication of these texts. My own work at the museum in Athens has always been greatly facilitated by the unfailing loyalty and devotion to his trust of the phylax Stavros. Every epigraphist will wish him, as I do, χρόνια πολλά.

Permission to publish the documents in Paris was granted by the authorities of Les Archives Photographiques d'Art et d'Histoire, and the documents in London were generously placed at my disposal by Mr. H. B. Walters. To Mr. Humfry Payne, director of the British School of Archaeology at Athens, I am indebted for permission to use a photograph of one of the pages of the notebook of Sir William Gell written in 1805. It is a pleasure to acknowledge financial aid from the funds at the disposal of the Institute of Archaeological Research of the University of Michigan for studies in the humanities, without which this book could not have been prepared. Finally, I wish to express gratitude to my departmental colleagues, Professors Campbell Bonner, John G. Winter, and Henry A. Sanders, who have assisted me with good judgment and sound criticism while the book was in press. For aid and helpful suggestions I am also indebted to the editor of this series, Mr. E. S. McCartney.

BENJAMIN D. MERITT

UNIVERSITY OF MICHIGAN
June 7, 1932

CONTENTS

LIST OF PLATES

(All plates are to be found at the end of the book)

LIST OF FIGURES IN THE TEXT

LIST OF ABBREVIATIONS

A.J.A. = American Journal of Archaeology

Anz. Ak. Wien = Anzeiger der phil.-hist. Klasse der Akademie der Wissenschaften in Wien

Ath. Mitt. = Mitteilungen des kaiserlich deutschen archäologischen Instituts. Athenische Abteilung

B.S.A. = The Annual of the British School at Athens

Berl. ph. Woch. = Berliner philologische Wochenschrift

Cl. Phil. = Classical Philology

Cl. Quart. = Classical Quarterly

Cl. Rev. = Classical Review

Cornell Stud. Cl. Phil. = Cornell Studies in Classical Philology

E.M. (These letters refer to the inventory of inscriptions in the Epigraphical Museum at Athens)

F.H.G. = Fragmenta Historicorum Graecorum

Harv. Stud. Cl. Phil. = Harvard Studies in Classical Philology

I.G. = Inscriptiones Graecae

J.H.S. = The Journal of Hellenic Studies

Jahresh. d. öst. arch. Inst. = Jahreshefte des österreichischen archäologischen Institutes in Wien

Num. Chron. = The Numismatic Chronicle

Pauly-Wissowa = Paulys Real-Encyclopädie der classischen Altertumswissenschaft. Neue Bearbeitung unter Mitwirkung zahlreicher Fachgenossen, herausgegeben von Georg Wissowa

Pauly-Wissowa-Kroll = Paulys Real-Encyclopädie der classischen Altertumswissenschaft. Neue Bearbeitung, begonnen von Georg Wissowa unter Mitwirkung zahlreicher Fachgenossen, herausgegeben von Wilhelm Kroll

Ph. Woch. = Philologische Wochenschrift

Rev. arch. = Revue archéologique

Rev. des ét. anc. = Revue des études anciennes

Rh. Mus. = Rheinisches Museum für Philologie

S.E.G. = Supplementum Epigraphicum Graecum

Sitzb. Ak. Berlin = Sitzungsberichte der preussischen Akademie der Wissenschaften

Sitzb. Ak. München = Sitzungsberichte der philosophisch-philologischen und historischen Classe der k. b. Akademie der Wissenschaften zu München

Trans. Am. Phil. Assoc. = Transactions of the American Philological Association

ATHENIAN FINANCIAL DOCUMENTS OF
THE FIFTH CENTURY

CHAPTER I

THE TRIBUTE ASSESSMENT OF 428/7 B.C.

SINCE the publication in 1898 of Ferguson's epoch-making treatise on the Athenian secretaries [1] everyone who has studied the chronological problems connected with Athenian inscriptions has found his task made easier because of the results of Ferguson's investigation. The fact that the secretaries of the Council held office in rotation in such a way that the official tribes were represented in this office according to a traditional order has made possible, for example, a degree of certainty in building up the framework of Hellenistic history that would otherwise have been unattainable.[2] Without question the office of the secretary of the Council is the most important of those discussed in Ferguson's original work, but it was observed also that even as early as the fifth century a certain tendency had made itself manifest toward the adoption of cycles whereby other secretaries held office in rotation, representing the official tribes of Athens in a certain fixed order or sequence. The secretaries of the joint treasury boards of Athena and of the Other Gods were represented in the reverse of the official order of tribes from 403/2 to 390/89. Shorter sequences, which did not endure for a complete cycle of ten years, are found for the secretary of the treasurers of Athena from 434/3 to 430/29, and from 416/5 to 413/2.[3]

At the time when Ferguson's monograph was published there was no way of determining a cycle of rotation in the office of the secretary of the board of *hellenotamiai*. More recent studies, however, have served to fix the relative chronological order of the

[1] W. S. Ferguson, "The Athenian Secretaries," *Cornell Stud. Cl. Phil.*, Vol. VII, 1898.

[2] For the most recent discussion of the chronology of this period, see W. B. Dinsmoor, *The Archons of Athens in the Hellenistic Age*, Cambridge, Massachusetts, 1931.

[3] Ferguson, *op. cit.*, pp. 72–73. In Ferguson's recent volume, *The Treasurers of Athena*, pp. 9–10, there is presented a table showing that the secretaries of the treasurers of Athena held office in the reverse of the official order of tribes from 411 to 407/6, and that from 406/5 to 386/5 the secretaries of the combined board of treasurers of Athena and the Other Gods continued to hold office according to the same sequence.

tribute lists from 439/8 to 432/1, in which the secretaries of the hellenotamiai are mentioned. Fimmen's contributions in 1913 gave a disposition of the various fragments which was in the main correct, though important changes have been made since that time.[1] It is apparent that for a brief period the secretaries of the hellenotamiai were chosen from the tribes in the reverse of the official order, probably for the decade 439/8–430/29. The evidence is as follows:[2]

DATE	DOCUMENTS	NAME OF SECRETARY	TRIBE	
439/8	S.E.G., V, 16; I.G., I², 347	Ἐργόφιλος . . . . ⁹ . . . .ος	(Antiochis)	X
438/7	S.E.G., V, 17; I.G., I², 348	– – – – [Ῥαμ]νόσιο[ς]	Aiantis	IX
437/6	S.E.G., V, 18; I.G., I², 363	[Ἀριστόφ]υλος (?) – – –	(Hippothontis)	VIII
436/5	S.E.G., V, 19; I.G., I², 364	– – – – Αἰχ[σονεύς]	Kekropis	VII
435/4	S.E.G., V, 20; I.G., I², 365	Θοίνιλος . . . ⁷ . . . Ἀχαρνεύς	Oineis	VI
434/3	S.E.G., V, 21; I.G., I², 366	Προτόνικος ἐκ Κεραμέον Ἐπιχάρος	Akamantis	V

---

[1] D. Fimmen, "Die attischen Tributquotenlisten," *Ath. Mitt.*, XXXVIII (1913), 231–238; A. B. West, "The Place of *I.G.*, I, 256 in the Lapis Secundus," *A.J.A.*, XXIX (1925), 180–187; *S.E.G.*, III, 27; West, "Supplementary Notes on the Place of *I.G.*, I, 256," *Cl. Phil.*, XXI (1926), 250–254; B. D. Meritt, "The Reassessment of Tribute in 438/7," *A.J.A.*, XXIX (1925), 292–298. The inscriptions are given in the *Corpus* as *I.G.*, I², 206–213. For the most recent revised publication cf. *S.E.G.*, V, 16–23.

[2] For the sake of reference to the *Corpus* we give the following table of comparison between the first volume of *Inscriptiones Graecae* (*editio minor*) and the fifth volume of the *Supplementum Epigraphicum Graecum*:

S.E.G.	I.G., I²		S.E.G.	I.G., I²
V, 16	= 206		V, 26	= 222
V, 17	= 207		V, 28	= 218
V, 18	= 208		V, 29	= 214 + *I.G.*, I², 215
V, 19	= 209		V, 30	= 223
V, 20	= 210		V, 34	= 220
V, 21	= 211		V, 35	= 221
V, 22	= 212		V, 36	= 219
V, 23	= 213		V, 37	= 224
V, 25	= 216 + *I.G.*, I², 217 (*I.G.*, I², 231)			

433/2	S.E.G., V, 22	Φιλε . . . . $\overset{10}{.}$ . . . . εκτο . . . . $\overset{10}{.}$	(Leontis)	IV
432/1	S.E.G., V, 23	[. .]μοχάρες Μυρ[ρ]ιν[όσι]ος	Pandionis	III
431/0	------	-----------	(Aigeis)	II
430/29	------	-----------	(Erechtheis)	I

It is not possible to demonstrate from this table alone that the cycle was continuous for the entire period of ten years, for the *demotics* of the secretaries in 439/8, 431/0, and 430/29 are unknown; but the fact that the partial cycle of secretaries of the treasurers of Athena came to an end in 430/29 makes it seem probable that the cycle of secretaries of the hellenotamiai continued to that same year and came to an end at the same time. We do not know the reasons for abandoning the cycles, but the same causes were probably operative in both cases and should doubtless be associated with the outbreak of the Peloponnesian War and possible administrative readjustments at that time.[1]

If this arrangement of the cycle for secretaries of the hellenotamiai is correct, we can no longer date in 430/29 the quota list from tribute paid to Athens by her allies which has come down to us as *S.E.G., V, 25*.[2] The first line of this document contains in part the name of the secretary of the hellenotamiai and his demotic Φυλάσιος. For the secretary cycle it is necessary that the secretary in 430/29 should belong to tribe I (Erechtheis), while the demotic Φυλάσιος shows that the secretary named in *S.E.G., V, 25* belonged in fact to tribe VI (Oineis). The opening lines of this inscription each contain forty-nine letters, thus yielding the restoration ['Επὶ τês . . $\overset{\pm 6}{.}$ . . καὶ εἰκοστês ἀρχês hêι . $\overset{\mp 5}{.}$ . .]ιππος Φυλάσιος | [ἐγραμμάτευε - - - - etc.]. It is impossible to restore the date of this inscription as ['Επὶ τês τριακοστês ἀρχês - - -] because then no restoration could be found for the name of the secretary of the hellenotamiai with eighteen letters ending in - - ιππος. Any restoration of the date as of the thirtieth year (425/4) or later is likewise impossible because the quotas listed in the document itself do not agree with the amounts of tribute assessed for this later period which are still preserved in the as-

[1] Ferguson, *The Treasurers of Athena*, p. 10, note 1.

[2] For this proposed date cf. West, "Methone and the Assessment of 430," *A.J.A.*, XXIX (1925), 440–444; also *S.E.G.*, III, 29; Meritt, "A Revision of *I.G.*, I², 216," *A.J.A.*, XXXI (1927), 180–185.

sessment decree *I.G.*, I², 63. A comparison of the Island panels in *I.G.*, I², 63 and *S.E.G.*, V, 25 will show at a glance that these two inscriptions cannot belong to the same assessment period. It becomes at once apparent, therefore, that the only date which can be given to *S.E.G.*, V, 25, now that it has been excluded from 430/29 by the secretary cycle which ends in that year, must lie between the years 429/8 and 426/5.

We must, in fact, examine again the evidence for the date of this inscription in the light of our knowledge of the other quota lists representing tribute paid during the early years of the Archidamian War, and in the light of the narrative of Thucydides as it affects the Bottic cities named in this inscription.

The quota lists *S.E.G.*, V, 28 and *S.E.G.*, V, 29 are the first to engage our attention. Professor West and I had assigned *S.E.G.*, V, 28 to a different assessment period from *S.E.G.*, V, 25, and to a later date,[1] including it, in fact, in the same assessment period with *S.E.G.*, V, 29.[2] It was then discovered that *S.E.G.*, V, 28 contained within itself some evidence that the inscription belonged to the first year of an assessment period, so that *S.E.G.*, V, 28 was assigned to 427/6, while *S.E.G.*, V, 29 was dated in 426/5. The date of the assessment was assumed to be 427/6.[3] The chronology of the fragments assigned to this period may be illustrated in the following table:

430/29	Assessment	*S.E.G.*, V, 25 (*I.G.*, I², 216/31)
429/8		*S.E.G.*, V, 26 (*I.G.*, I², 222)
428/7		
427/6	Assessment	*S.E.G.*, V, 28 (*I.G.*, I², 218)
426/5		*S.E.G.*, V, 29 (*I.G.*, I², 214/5)
425/4	Assessment	*I.G.*, I², 63

A comparative study of these various documents shows, however, that *S.E.G.*, V, 28 has a much closer affinity to *S.E.G.*, V,

---

[1] West and Meritt, "The Athenian Quota List, *I.G.*, I², 216," *A.J.A.*, XXIX (1925), 434–439.

[2] West καὶ Meritt, "Ὁ Φορολογικὸς Κατάλογος *I.G.*, I², 218," Ἀρχ. Ἐφ., 1925–26, p. 64; Meritt and West, "A Revision of Athenian Tribute Lists, Part II," *Harv. Stud. Cl. Phil.*, XXXVIII (1927), 59–67.

[3] West καὶ Meritt, "Ὁ Φορολογικὸς Κατάλογος *I.G.*, I², 218," Ἀρχ. Ἐφ., 1925–26, pp. 46–66, especially p. 46; Meritt and West, "A Revision of Athenian Tribute Lists, Part II," *Harv. Stud. Cl. Phil.*, XXXVIII (1927), 48, 59 note 1, 64–66; W. Kolbe, "Die Kleon-Schatzung des Jahres 425/4," *Sitzb. Ak. Berlin*, 1930, p. 334, prefers the date 429/8.

25 than to *S.E.G.*, V, 29. In fact the difference between *S.E.G.*,
V, 28 and 29 is in one particular so fundamental that they cannot
longer be attributed to the same period. We discover in the very
fragmentary Hellespontine panel of *S.E.G.*, V, 29 two names
which make their appearance for the first time in the tribute
lists: Σεριστειχι̂(ται) (Col. II, line 11) and [Σο]μβία (Col. II,
line 15). Where there are only six Hellespontine names preserved, it is striking that two of them belong to cities which have
not been represented before, but which do appear again in later
lists. That they were not present in *S.E.G.*, V, 28 is now definitely known, for the complete Hellespontine panel has been
there restored. The conclusion must be that these names were
present in *S.E.G.*, V, 29 by virtue of an assessment which had not
been in effect at the time of *S.E.G.*, V, 28. To the two names
already mentioned we may add also Βέσβικος, now listed in the
main panel of the Hellespontine list in *S.E.G.*, V, 29, Col. II,
line 13. The fact of an assessment after *S.E.G.*, V, 28 and before
S.E.G., V, 29 means of course that the two documents belong,
not to the same, but to different assessment periods.

On the other hand our recent studies of *S.E.G.*, V, 25 and
S.E.G., V, 28 have shown certain points of marked similarity
which indicate that these two inscriptions must now be dated
in the same assessment period. The realization that *I.G.*, I², 231
is part of the same document with *I.G.*, I², 216 brings to our
attention in *S.E.G.*, V, 25 a group of Hellespontine cities making
partial payments which is almost the exact duplicate of that
found in *S.E.G.*, V, 28, lines 44–53. The similarity is so close
that it will be well to represent the two appendices side by side:

S.E.G., V, 25, IV, 2–10		*S.E.G.*, V, 28, III, 44–53	
[ΔΓ]	Χαλχεδόνιοι	[Δ]Γ	[Καλχεδόνιοι]
– – ΔН	Δαρδανῆς	[Δ]ΔΔНН	[Κυζικενοί]
– – ΔΔΓ	Λαμφσακενοί	[Η]ΔΔΔΔΓ[Н –]	[Λαμφσακενοί]
[X]ΡНΙΙΙ	Βυζάντιοι	ΔΔΔНН	['Ελαιόσιοι]
– – –	'Αβυδηνοί	ΔΔΔΔΓΙ[ΙΙΙ]	['Αβυδενοί]
– – – ΙНН	Παριανοί	ΡΗΗΗΔΓ[– –]	[Βυζάντιοι]
– Δ –	Μαδύτιο[ι]	ΡΙ ΔΙНН[– –]	[Παριανοί]
[Δ]ΔΔНН	'Ελ[α]ιόσιο[ι]	ΔΔΔНН	[Μ]αδύτιοι
[ΡΙ]ΔΔНН	Κυ[ζ]ικενοί	ΔΔΔΔН[– –]	[Δ]αρδανῆς
		ΔΔΓΗ[– –]	['Α]λοποκοννέσιοι

In both inscriptions the partial payments recorded in the appendices may be added to the partial payments listed in the main panels to give figures representing a round sum of tribute.

We may add to these points of likeness the probable restorations in the lacunae of *S.E.G.*, V, 28, Cols. II and III of the appendices found in *S.E.G.*, V, 25 at the bottom of Cols. I and IV.[1]

Instead of lists differing widely in character, as heretofore supposed, we have therefore two lists which show a marked similarity of arrangement, and which reflect the same peculiar phases of imperial management. These similarities indicate that the two lists belong to the same assessment period.

It may be further observed that the amounts of tithe recorded in *S.E.G.*, V, 25 agree in every case with those recorded in *S.E.G.*, V, 28. The slight differences in the composite totals of Hellespontine payments are not significant. The tithe of Tenedos in 25 was HHℙΔΔΔΓHⱵ; in 28 it was HHℙΔΔΔΓIII. In the latter case the numeral on the stone may well have been a stone-cutter's error for HHℙΔΔΔΓHⱵ. Cyzicus in 25 paid 900 drachmae; in 28 it paid 890 1/3 drachmae. The assessments were evidently the same. I suggest that the irregular figure in 28 was occasioned by the fact that Cyzicus paid actually in staters of Cyzicene gold, which did not yield quite the desired value when converted into Attic silver. It is particularly significant

---

[1] We note at this point that Kolbe, *Sitzb. Ak. Berlin*, 1930, p. 336, note 1, proposes to restore the name Σαμοθρᾱικες in the lacuna of Col. II, in *S.E.G.*, V, 28, lines 38–42, with a quota of 400 dr., so that the total quota for this year (600 dr.) may be the same as in the period before the war. Cf. *S.E.G.*, V, 20, Col. VI, line 13; *S.E.G.*, V, 23, Col. II, line 65. This suggestion is to be rejected. The Thracian panel of *S.E.G.*, V, 28 is complete, and shows no sequence of irregular partial tithes, as does the Hellespontine panel of the same year, which Kolbe cites to support his claim. Moreover, in the case of Θραμβαῖοι and Αἰγάντιοι (*S.E.G.*, V, 28, Col. II, lines 25–26), the irregularities in payment were recorded in the main panel itself. We must suppose that such would have been the case also with Samothrace, had any irregularity existed. It is hardly permissible to assume a special appendix (of one name only) to contain an extra quota for this city, after first assuming that such a quota existed. For whatever reason, there were some noticeable reductions in Thracian tribute after the opening of the war. I suggest that the reduction may have been allowed in return for services to fleets or armies in the field. Not only was the tithe of Samothrace reduced from ℙH to HH, but that of Aineia was reduced from HHH to ΔΓHIIII. Cf. *S.E.G.*, V, 23, Col. II, line 54; *S.E.G.*, V, 28, Col. II, line 20.

that not only the composite totals, but also the individual payments for Chalcedon are the same in both inscriptions.

The prescripts also must be restored according to the same formula, which so far as is known occurs only in these two inscriptions and differs from that used earlier (*S.E.G.*, V, 23) and later (*S.E.G.*, V, 30 and 34).

We have already observed that the internal evidence of *S.E.G.*, V, 28 shows it to belong to the first year of an assessment period. The fact that Πυγελῆς paid current tribute and only arrears in ἐπιφορά (*S.E.G.*, V, 28, Col. I, lines 45–46) is the indication that current ἐπιφορά was not expected from them.[1] In fact, there is no record of current ἐπιφορά in the entire document, although two of the panels of cities from which ἐπιφορά had been collected (Thrace, Hellespont) have been preserved in their entirety, and although a large part of the Ionic list also has been preserved. It is a safe assumption that at the time of the assessment preceding *S.E.G.*, V, 28 the collection of ἐπιφορά was abandoned. If we are to assign *S.E.G.*, V, 28 and 25 to the same period, it follows that there can also be no record of ἐπιφορά in 25. Professor West and I had restored one such item in 25, III, 33, but the restoration is conjectural, [. . .⁶. . .ἐπιφορᾶ]s, and may be definitely rejected now as incorrect, in view of the other evidence we have adduced in favor of the close connection between *S.E.G.*, V, 28 and 25. We should restore rather [. . . . . ἀπὸ Καρία]s, on the analogy of [Πελειᾶ]ται ἀπὸ Καρίας (28, I, 18), or some such name as [Χαλκεᾶται Κᾶρε]s, on the analogy of Αὐλιᾶται Κᾶρες (*S.E.G.*, V, 1, Col. VI, line 13). *S.E.G.*, V, 25 and 28 therefore both belong to the first assessment period in which the ἐπιφορά was abandoned.

There remains the troublesome problem of the prescripts of the appendices in Col. I of *S.E.G.*, V, 25. As our inscriptions are at present restored, the prescript [πόλες αὐταὶ φόρ]ον | [ταχσάμεναι] of 25, I, 34–35 must correspond to the prescript ταῖσδ[ε ἔτ]αχσαν hοι τάκται | ἐπὶ Κρ[. . .]ο γραμματεύοντος of 28, III, 54–55, and the prescript [ταῖσδε πό]λε[σιν h]οι | [ἰδιôται φόρ]ο[ν ἔ]τ[α]-χ[σαν] of 25, I, 43–44 must correspond to the prescript ταῖσδε h[ε] βολὲ καὶ hοι πεντακόσιοι | καὶ χίλ[ιοι ἔτ]αχσαν of 28, III, 60–61.

---

[1] Cf. *S.E.G.*, V, 28, and commentary *ad loc.*

The prescripts of *S.E.G.*, V, 25 have been restored in such a way as to make them agree as closely as possible with the prescripts of similar appendices in earlier years (*S.E.G.*, V, 21, Col. VI, lines 5–6, 18–21; *S.E.G.*, V, 22, Col. II, lines 76–77, 89–92; *S.E.G.*, V, 23, Col. II, lines 68–70, 76–79). It was because of these prescripts, in fact, that *S.E.G.*, V, 25, was originally assigned to an earlier date than *S.E.G.*, V, 28,[1] with the further assumption that the two inscriptions belonged to different assessment periods.[2] But this was before the discovery of the striking points of similarity between *S.E.G.*, V, 25 and 28, listed above, and before the discovery of fundamental differences between 28 and 29. We must now see whether the prescripts in question in 25, depending largely upon restoration, can be interpreted in such a way as to give a closer approximation in sense to those of 28.

The prescript in lines 34–35 of *S.E.G.*, V, 25 causes little difficulty, for the preserved letters may be readily incorporated in the restoration:

$$[\tau a \hat{\imath} \sigma \delta \epsilon \ \check{\epsilon} \tau a \chi \sigma a \nu \ \tau] \grave{o} \nu$$
$$[\phi \acute{o} \rho o \nu \ \mathit{h} o \iota \ \tau \acute{a} \kappa \tau a \iota \ \grave{\epsilon} \pi \grave{\iota}]$$
$$[\mathrm{K} \rho \iota \tau \acute{\iota} o \ \gamma \rho a \mu \mu a \tau \epsilon \acute{\upsilon} o \nu \tau o \varsigma].$$

This restoration has, indeed, even a slight advantage over that which I have proposed elsewhere,[3] in that the letters restored extend to the left beyond the margin of the column of names a distance of seven letter spaces, instead of six, and so agree in their disposition with the preserved letters of the prescript in lines 51–52.

The badly weathered condition of the stone makes the determination of readings in some parts of *S.E.G.*, V, 25 very difficult. It may be that the letters which I have previously read in line 34 as ON are in reality OI, in which case the restoration can be made to conform word for word with that in *S.E.G.*, V, 28, Col. III, lines 54–55:

[1] West and Meritt, "The Athenian Quota List, *I.G.*, I², 216," *A.J.A.*, XXIX (1925), 434–439.

[2] West, "Methone and the Assessment of 430," *A.J.A.*, XXIX (1925), 441, note 3; Meritt and West, "A Revision of Athenian Tribute Lists, Part II," *Harv. Stud. Cl. Phil.*, XXXVIII (1927), 48.

[3] Meritt, "A Revision of *I.G.*, I², 216," *A.J.A.*, XXXI (1927), 181.

$$[\tau a \hat{\iota} \sigma \delta \epsilon \ \check{\epsilon} \tau a \chi \sigma a \nu \ h] o \iota$$
$$[\tau \acute{a} \kappa \tau a \iota \ \grave{\epsilon} \pi \grave{\iota} \ K \rho \iota \tau \acute{\iota} o]$$
$$[\gamma \rho a \mu \mu a \tau \epsilon \acute{\upsilon} o \nu \tau o s].$$

In lines 43–44 there is evidently not room for the entire formula used in 28, III, 60–61: $\tau a \hat{\iota} \sigma \delta \epsilon \ h \epsilon \ \beta o \lambda \grave{\epsilon} \ \kappa a \grave{\iota} \ h o \iota \ \pi \epsilon \nu \tau a \kappa \acute{o} \sigma \iota o \iota$ $\kappa a \grave{\iota} \ \chi \acute{\iota} \lambda \iota o \iota \ \check{\epsilon} \tau a \chi \sigma a \nu$, and some compromise must be adopted which will give the same meaning in other words; but it must be remembered at the same time that the entire formula of the earlier lists is likewise too long for the restoration of this passage: $\pi \acute{o} \lambda \epsilon s \ h \grave{a} s \ h o \iota \ \grave{\iota} \delta \iota \hat{o} \tau a \iota \ \grave{\epsilon} \nu \acute{\epsilon} \gamma \rho a \phi \sigma a \nu \ \phi \acute{o} \rho o \nu \ \phi \acute{\epsilon} \rho \epsilon \nu$. In fact, to bring the reading of the lines in question into conformity with this earlier phraseology we were compelled to restore: $[\tau a \hat{\iota} \sigma \delta \epsilon \ \pi \acute{o}] \lambda \epsilon [\sigma \iota \nu$ $h] o \iota \ [\grave{\iota} \delta \iota \hat{o} \tau a \iota \ \phi \acute{o} \rho] o [\nu \ \check{\epsilon}] \tau [a] \chi [\sigma a \nu]$, with the word $\grave{\iota} \delta \iota \hat{o} \tau a \iota$ of seven letters appearing where the *stoichedon* order of the inscription required properly a word of six letters.[1] There was also considerable change in the wording if not in the sense of the passage. It is impossible to make the wording of these lines agree either with the earlier inscriptions or with *S.E.G.*, V, 28; and yet the letters LE in the second and third letter spaces from the left margin of the column of names may be integrated as part of the word $\beta o \lambda \acute{\epsilon}$ (cf. *S.E.G.*, V, 28, Col. III, line 60) just as satisfactorily as with the word $\pi \acute{o} \lambda \epsilon \sigma \iota \nu$ now restored. The verb $\check{\epsilon} \tau a \chi \sigma a \nu$ appears in both 25 and 28, though not in the earlier corresponding prescripts. If we assume that the stone-cutter condensed the formula of *S.E.G.*, V, 28 as much as possible, we might read in the lines in question the following restoration:

$$[\tau a \hat{\iota} \sigma \delta \epsilon \ \beta o] \lambda \acute{\epsilon}, \ [\chi \acute{\iota} \lambda \iota] o \iota,$$
$$[\pi \epsilon \nu \tau a \kappa \acute{o} \sigma \iota] o [\iota \ \check{\epsilon}] \tau [a] \chi [\sigma a \nu].$$

Other suggestions which yield a less perfect parallel with *S.E.G.*, V, 28 are

$$[\tau a \hat{\iota} \sigma \delta' \ \grave{\epsilon} \ \beta o] \lambda \grave{\epsilon} \ [\kappa a \grave{\iota} \ h] o \iota$$
$$[\pi \epsilon \nu \tau a \kappa \acute{o} \sigma \iota] o [\iota \ \check{\epsilon}] \tau [a] \chi [\sigma a \nu],$$

or perhaps

$$[\tau \acute{a} \delta \epsilon \ h \epsilon \ \beta o] \lambda \grave{\epsilon} \ [\kappa a \grave{\iota} \ h] o \iota$$
$$[\pi \epsilon \nu \tau a \kappa \acute{o} \sigma \iota] o [\iota \ \check{\epsilon}] \tau [a] \chi [\sigma a \nu].$$

[1] Cf. West and Meritt, "The Athenian Quota List, *I.G.*, I², 216," *A.J.A.*, XXIX (1925), 435.

In both of the restorations last suggested, it must be assumed that the words καὶ χίλιοι were omitted through inadvertence of the stone-cutter. On the whole, I am inclined to favor the first suggestion, namely, that we have, for whatever reason, a condensed form of the prescript of S.E.G., V, 28, but with all the essential elements retained.

However our decision may rest with regard to this prescript and the nature of the restorations proposed, I do not believe that the differences here noted between S.E.G., V, 25 and 28 are sufficient to justify assigning them to different assessment periods as before, when we consider the cumulative evidence of other observations pointing to the separation of 28 from the period of 29, and to its close connection with 25. Perhaps a more suitable restoration for lines 43–44 of 25 will yet be found. In the meantime I do not regard the anomaly, if one really exists, as anything more serious than the different classification of Ἀλοποκοννήσιοι in the two documents (25, IV, 21 and 28, III, 53). We may note in passing that even this name, spelled with Ο in the fifth letter space, offers a slight support for the association of the two documents.

We thus find that S.E.G., V, 28 must be assigned to the year 430/29. It was, in fact, the first list of the assessment period beginning with the Panathenaia of 430. The secretary of the hellenotamiai, whose name has not been preserved, must have belonged to the tribe Erechtheis (I), in conformity with the secretary cycle. S.E.G., V, 25 belongs to the same period, and must be assigned to some year earlier than that of the assessment which regulated the payment of tribute recorded in S.E.G., V, 29. It is possible, I believe, to determine the date of this assessment, and also to give exact dates to S.E.G., V, 25 and 29.

The next assessment following the date of S.E.G., V, 29 was that of 425/4, the record of which has been in large part preserved in I.G., I², 63. This last decree of assessment was passed during the prytany of Oineis, which was the fourth prytany of the year when Stratokles was archon.[1] As a matter of fact there were two decrees, but we know that they were passed during

---

[1] I.G., I², 63, lines 3, 34, 54–57; Meritt, *The Athenian Calendar in the Fifth Century*, pp. 26 and 91. The name of the tribe Aigeis has been heretofore restored in lines 3 and 34.

different prytanies, for the restoration of the prescript in line 3 cannot be made the same as that in line 55. Professor West informs me that he discovered during his study of this document in Athens in the summer of 1929 that fragments *b* and *c* must be separated by two more letter spaces than are at present represented in the *Corpus*. It is physically impossible that the two fragments be juxtaposed as required by the now accepted restorations. This discovery necessitates changes, of course, in the restorations of lines 3–8, and, of especial importance to us now, shows that the name of the secretary of the Council when Oineis held the prytany was [. . .⁵ . .]ον rather than [. . .]ον. It is highly probable that the small fragment E.M. 6862, now published in *I.G.*, I², p. 32, should be so placed in its relation to the other fragments of the inscription that the secretary's name in line 55 may be restored as [. . .]ιπ[πος]. This allows the following restoration of the prescript of the second decree in lines 54–55: ἔδοχσ[εν] τε͂ι βολε͂ι καὶ το͂ι δέμοι, Α|[ἰγεὶς ἐ]πρυτάνευ[ε, . . .] ιπ[πος ἐγραμμάτευε, . . .⁷ . . .]ορος ἐπεσ[τάτε], Θόδιππος εἶπε· – – –.¹

Since the secretary's name was different in line 3, the name of the tribe to be restored in lines 3 and 34 must be Oineis, rather than Aigeis.²

Now, subsequent to the passage of this decree in the fourth prytany, word was sent out to the various cities in the tributary districts to report back to Athens during the month of Maimakterion. The determination of amounts of tribute from the allies was to be made by a special court during the month of Posideion.³ The tribute would fall due, as usual, at the Greater Dionysia in Elaphebolion in the spring of 424.⁴ The decree outlines the procedure of assessment and adjudication, and provides strict penalties for delay (lines 4–22).

Beginning with line 26 of this inscription there are provisions for the assessment of tribute at the Greater Panathenaia.⁵ These lines cannot be interpreted as part of the arrangements for assess-

---

¹ Professor West and I are preparing a new text of this decree.

² The name Oineis should also be restored in *I.G.*, I², 324, lines 18–19. This change has been made in the text as given on page 138, below.

³ Meritt, *The Athenian Calendar*, p. 90.

⁴ Scholia to *Acharnians* of Aristophanes, 378, 504.

⁵ It is impossible to avoid this interpretation, as attempted by W. Bannier, "Zum neuen ersten Bande der attischen Inschriften," *Rh. Mus.*, LXXVII (1928), 273–276.

ment in 425/4, for not by any possibility could these assessments be introduced at the Greater Panathenaia of 426/5, more than a year before. Furthermore, it is unbelievable that assessments declared in 425/4 should have been held in abeyance until the next Greater Panathenaia of 422/1. The whole tenor of the document is that the present assessments, those of 425/4, should be carried to completion as speedily as possible. Lines 26–33 refer rather to the necessary procedure for subsequent assessments, and indicate an attempt on the part of the authors of the decree to return to the long-established custom of regular assessments in Panathenaic years. So far as we know, the assessments from 454/3, when the treasury of the Delian League was moved from Delos to Athens, down to 430/29, with one exception only (443/2), had been made in the third year of the Olympiad, which was the year of the Greater Panathenaia at Athens.[1]

During the early years of the war the Athenians were faced with the necessity of making reassessments in other than Panathenaic years. *I.G.*, I², 63 itself represents an extraordinary assessment, made in order that the tribute moneys might be sufficient for the expenses of the war (cf. lines 19[?], 46). The provision of the decree, therefore, for regular assessments at the time of the Greater Panathenaia is not only a safeguard for the future, but also a rebuke to the politicians of the previous year (426/5) for failing to carry out a reassessment at the proper time. We may be certain that there was no reassessment of tribute in 426/5, and since failure to carry out an assessment then would hardly have laid the politicians open to charges of neglect if there had been an assessment in the previous year, we get our first indication that there had been no reassessment since 428/7.

The text of *I.G.*, I², 63, lines 26–33, should be restored in conformity with the observations above, as follows:

26   [- - - τὸ δὲ λοιπὸν ἀποφαίνεν τῆσι π]όλ[ε]σι περὶ τô φ[όρο πρὸ
        τôμ Παναθεναίον τ]ôμ με[γ]-

[1] Meritt, "Tribute Assessments in the Athenian Empire from 454 to 440 B.C.," *A.J.A.*, XXIX (1925), 247–273; *idem*, "The Reassessment of Tribute in 438/7," *A.J.A.*, XXIX (1925), 292–298; E. B. Couch, "An Interpretation of the Prescript πόλες αὐταὶ φόρον ταχσάμεναι in the Athenian Tribute Lists," *A.J.A.*, XXXIII (1929), 502–514, especially p. 502, note 1.

27 ἀλον· ἐσ[άγεν δὲ τὲν πρυτανείαν ἥτις ἂν] τυ[γ]χάνει πρυτ[ανεύοσα
    τὰς τάχσες κατὰ Π]αναθ[έ]-

28 ναια· [ἐὰν δὲ hοι πρυτάνες μὲ τότε ἐσάγο]σι ἐ[s] τὸν δῆμον κ[αὶ τὲμ
    βολὲν καὶ τὸ δικαστ]έριον

29 περὶ τô [φόρο καὶ μὲ τότε χρεματίζοσι ἐ]πὶ σ[φ]ôν αὐτὸν ὀφ[έλεν
    hεκατὸν δραχμὰς hιε]ρ[ὰ]s τê-

30 [ι 'Α]θενα[ίαι hέκαστον τôμ π]ρ[υτάνεον κα]ὶ τô[ι] δεμοσίοι h[εκατὸν
    καὶ εὐθύνεσθαι χιλί]ασι

31 [δρα]χμê[σι hέκαστον τôμ πρ]υτά[νεον· κα]ὶ ἐάν τις ἄλλος δι[δοî
    φσêφον τê]σι [πόλεσι μ]ὲ êναι τ-

32 [ὰς] τάχσ[ες κατὰ Π]α[ναθένα]ια τὰ μ[εγάλα] ἐπὶ τês πρυτανεί[ας
    hέτις ἂν πρ]ότε [πρυτα]νεύει ἄτ-

33 [ι]μος ἔσ[το καὶ] τὰ χ[ρέματα] αὐτô δ[εμόσι]α ἔσ[τ]ο καὶ τês θεô
    [τὸ ἐπιδέκατο]ν – – – – – –.

There are far-reaching consequences in the provisions embodied in these lines, for they give us evidence that reassessments
of tribute in subsequent years were to be made in 422/1, 418/7,
414/3, etc., instead of in the years 421/0, 417/6, 413/2, etc., as
has been assumed to date.[1] Nor is there any reason to believe
that this was not the case. West has shown the probability of a
new assessment with general lowering of the tribute after the
Peace of Nicias in 421,[2] but this was an exceptional occasion
which could not have been foreseen in 425/4. In all probability
this assessment of 421 followed as a result of the proposals made
to the Council and the Demos and the Court at the Panathenaic
festival of 422. We have learned that actual proclamation of
assessment was followed by a period of deliberation and adjudication. If we assume that a new assessment was announced at the
Panathenaia of 422, there was still considerable time before the

[1] Meritt and West, "A Revision of Athenian Tribute Lists, Part II," *Harv. Stud.
Cl. Phil.*, XXXVIII (1927), 49–50.

[2] West, "Aristidean Tribute in the Assessment of 421 B.C.," *A.J.A.*, XXIX
(1925), 135–151; West and Meritt, "Cleon's Amphipolitan Campaign and the Assessment List of 421," *A.J.A.*, XXIX (1925), 59–69.

amounts of tribute could all be determined and embodied in a law. It was at precisely this time that the Athenians and Spartans were directing their efforts toward peace after the death of Cleon and Brasidas at Amphipolis in the late summer of 422.[1] It would have been impossible to impose a heavy war assessment upon the allies at a time when everyone was eager for peace, and we must concede that any definitive settlement of amounts of tribute was postponed until after peace was assured. This means, of course, that the decree of assessment, following the initial proposals at the Panathenaia in 422, was not passed until the spring of 421, as West has argued. There is, therefore, no real inconsistency between the provisions of *I.G.*, I², 63 that there should be an assessment immediately after the Panathenaia of 422 and the fact that the assessment actually was voted early in the following year. The negotiations for the peace, which was ratified in Elaphebolion of 422/1 (Thuc. V, 19), were sufficient reason for the delay.

The next reassessment fell at the Greater Panathenaia of 418, and following this the next reassessment in order, according to the decree passed in 425/4, was due at the Panathenaia of 414. At this time, however, the Athenians thought that they could realize a larger income from their subject states by the imposition of a 5 per cent tax. I suggest that instead of the reassessment of 414/3, the necessary machinery for collecting this tax was prepared and set in motion.

It has been generally assumed from the narrative of Thucydides (VII, 28, 4), that this tax was first levied in 413. Demosthenes had sailed from Athens with reinforcements for Sicily in the midwinter of 414/3. His departure is definitely dated in the seventh prytany of the year by the record of expenses for his expedition in *I.G.*, I², 297, lines 11–13 (cf. below, p. 89). We also learn from *I.G.*, I², 328 that this prytany coincided approximately with the month of Gamelion.[2] Certain Thracian mercenaries had reached Athens too late to join the expedition, and the Athenians had sent them home again because of the expense of maintaining them. It is in this connection that Thucydides

---

[1] Thuc. V, 10, 9–11; V, 14, 1.

[2] Meritt, *The Athenian Calendar*, p. 93.

describes the ravages of the war on Attica and the heavy expenses
they were forced to meet. His words are significant: (VII, 28,
4): δι' ἃ καὶ τότε ὑπό τε τῆς Δεκελείας πολλὰ βλαπτούσης καὶ τῶν ἄλλων
ἀναλωμάτων μεγάλων προσπιπτόντων ἀδύνατοι ἐγένοντο τοῖς χρήμασιν.
καὶ τὴν εἰκοστὴν ὑπὸ τοῦτον τὸν χρόνον τῶν κατὰ θάλασσαν ἀντὶ τοῦ
φόρου τοῖς ὑπηκόοις ἐποίησαν, πλείω νομίζοντες ἂν σφίσι χρήματα οὕτω
προσιέναι.

When Thucydides says that the 5 per cent tax was levied
"at about this time" his words may with propriety be taken as
the equivalent of "instead of the assessment of 414/3." The
Thracian mercenaries were sent home at least a month, perhaps
almost two months, before the time for the payment of tribute
at the Dionysiac festival in Elaphebolion. It is evident in any
case that the Athenians were not collecting tribute in 414/3;
the logical assumption is that they did not intend to do so, and
that no program for reassessment of the empire had been introduced at the previous Panathenaia. Since this was the time for
proposing a new assessment, according to the provisions of *I.G.*,
I², 63, it is evident that the Athenians then gave up the idea of
collecting tribute and resorted to the new tax instead.

In order to determine more exactly the time of the reassessment which intervened between 430/29 and 425/4 we must
study more closely the quota list *S.E.G.*, V, 29. Although preserved in very fragmentary condition, it is clear that the Ionic
panel of names followed immediately after the Hellespontine
panel at the end of Col. II. When we study the assessment decrees of 425/4 and 421 we discover that immediately following
the Hellespontine panel there were listed the cities of the Lesbian
peraia known as Ἀκταῖαι πόλες (*I.G.*, I, 543 and *I.G.*, I², 64, lines
80–100, fragments yz").[1]

---

[1] I cannot agree with Kolbe, *Sitzb. Ak. Berlin*, 1930, pp. 342–345, that *I.G.*, I², 63
and 64 are copies of the same document. The documents are similar, as he claims,
but not identical. Names from one may be used in the restoration of the other, but
the similarity is no greater than that between *S.E.G.*, V, 12 and 13, which are from
different years. Furthermore, the physical aspects of the stones are entirely different,
in width of column and in the form, shape, and spacing of letters. Both inscriptions
were found on the Acropolis, though we learn from *I.G.*, I², 63, line 24, that one of the
two copies of the assessment of 425/4 was to be set up in the bouleuterion. Cf. West,
"Two Assessments of the Athenian Empire," *Metropolitan Museum Studies*, III (1930–
31), 174–193.

These cities were taken over by Athens at the time of the subjugation of Lesbos in the spring of 427 (Thuc. III, 50, 3; IV, 52), and made directly subject to her; we should expect to find them included in the quota lists subsequent to this time. If the disposition of the assessment lists of 425/4 and 421 is any criterion, the names should appear immediately after the Hellespontine panel. Since there is no room for the record of the Aktaian cities in *S.E.G.*, V, 29, we may assume with some probability that these cities did not pay tribute in the year in which this inscription must be dated. In other words, *S.E.G.*, V, 29 must be given a date earlier than 427/6. Since it is later than *S.E.G.*, V., 25 and 28, both of which follow the assessment of 430, the only year to which it can be assigned is 428/7. The assessment which differentiates *S.E.G.*, V, 25 and 28 from *S.E.G.*, V, 29 must also have been the assessment of 428. If this is true, *S.E.G.*, V, 28 may be assigned definitely to the year 430/29 and *S.E.G.*, V, 25 definitely to the year 429/8.

This assignment of *S.E.G.*, V, 29 to 428/7 is borne out also by the evidence of irregularity in the payment of tribute by Notion in this inscription. So far as our records show, the tribute of Notion was always 2000 drachmae, which yielded a quota of △△△⊢⊢II. In *S.E.G.*, V, 29, Col. III, line 15, however, the quota appears as the abnormally low sum of ⊢IIII. The reason for this is to be sought in the disturbances at Notion recorded by Thucydides (III, 34) in the year 428/7, and his account gives further support to our dating of *S.E.G.*, V, 29 in this year. According to Thucydides, the loyal Colophonians who had settled at Notion after the capture of Colophon by the Persians in 430 became engaged in civil strife with the citizens of Notion proper, who were joined also by Medizing Colophonians. The loyal Colophonians summoned aid from the Athenian general Paches, who quelled the disturbance. But Notion had evidently been hostile to Athens and in open revolt for the greater part of the year 428/7. I believe that this fact is reflected in the quota list *S.E.G.*, V, 29 in the low quota from Notion. The quota from the loyal Colophonians at Notion was the same in 428/7 as later.[1]

[1] For a different account of the disturbances at Notion, to my mind less satisfactory, cf. Meritt and West, "A Revision of Athenian Tribute Lists, Part II," *Harv. Stud. Cl. Phil.*, XXXVIII (1927), 58–60.

It may also be said that 428/7 was the logical year for a reassessment of tribute, because in this year Athens was badly in need of money to meet the heavy expenses entailed in the struggle against Mytilene. Thucydides describes this necessity (III, 19, 1) and states that in this year for the first time the Athenians levied a direct tax of 200 talents. He also says that they sent out twelve ships under Lysikles and four other generals to collect tribute from the allies. The Athenians must have known that a difficult financial crisis was ahead as early as the spring of 428, for Lesbos revolted from Athens immediately after the incursion of the Peloponnesians into Attica in this year (Thuc. III, 2). There was consequently plenty of time, after the need for a reassessment became manifest, to prepare the new schedule of tribute for presentation at the Panathenaic festival in Hekatombaion. Even after the new assessment, which I believe we may now concede took place in this year, the long siege necessitated the ἐσφορά and an expedition had to set forth to collect tribute from the subject states.

It is a noteworthy fact that these expeditions which set out for the collection of tribute are mentioned by Thucydides only in 430/29, 428/7, and 425/4. Now since we know that there were reassessments of tribute in 430/29 and 425/4, the fact of a tribute-collecting expedition in 428/7 lends support also to our thesis that there was a reassessment of tribute in this year as well.

The expedition of Melesander (Thuc. II, 69) left Athens in the early winter of 430/29. We have observed that except in special cases the assessments were proclaimed at the Panathenaic festival in Hekatombaion, that is, in the latter part of summer. Normally, the adjudication of individual cases would be completed by early winter. Though the *terminus ad quem* for the payment of tribute seems to have been the Dionysiac festival, the Athenians in war time probably needed tribute money as soon as they could get it, and made attempts to collect from the allies as soon as the amounts of tribute were known. Melesander's expedition falls into place perfectly in this chronological scheme. In years of new assessments, the difficulty of making collections must have been increased by the unwillingness of subject states to pay heavier taxes. In these years the expeditions were powerful enough to engage in military enterprises worthy of the attention of the historian. There were doubtless tribute-collecting ships in every year during the period of the war, but in years of new assessment the forces sent out for this purpose must have been more than usually strong.

The expedition of Lysikles in 428/7 was also sent out from Athens in early winter (Thuc. III, 18, 5; III, 19), after the assessment of tribute at the Panathenaic festival. In 425/4 we find that tribute-collecting ships under Aristeides were at Eion on the Strymon River in the winter (Thuc. IV, 50), and that tribute-collecting ships under Demodokos and Aristeides were engaged in the Hellespont, while Lamachos had proceeded to the Pontos, in the early summer of 424 (Thuc. IV, 75). The activities of tribute collection extended in this year later than usual, but we know also that the assessment was particularly severe and that the new levy was not proposed until the fourth prytany. The adjudication of claims was not completed until after the month of Posideion and at the earliest the ships could not have left Athens before Gamelion. The fact that they were still occupied in the early summer is in part explained by this late departure from Athens.

I contend that there is a direct connection between these expeditions mentioned by Thucydides and the new assessments of tribute in the Athenian empire. They give additional confirmation to our proposal that the reassessments took place in 430/29, 428/7, and 425/4.

If we now rearrange the table of dates for the inscriptions of this period given above on page 6 so that it will agree with the conclusions reached in our argument thus far, we get the following result:

430/29	Assessment	*S.E.G.*, V, 28
429/8		*S.E.G.*, V, 25
428/7	Assessment	*S.E.G.*, V, 29
427/6		
426/5		
425/4	Assessment	*I.G.*, I², 63

There is no longer room for *S.E.G.*, V, 26 in the assessment period from 430 to 428, and we cannot assign it to the same period with *S.E.G.*, V, 29 because of differences in the tithe of

Clazomenae. Neither can the document be assigned to 431/0, because in this period the Erythraeans and their dependent cities paid together as a "syntely" (*S.E.G.*, V, 22, Col. I, lines 48–49; *S.E.G.*, V, 23, Col. I, line 40). In the first lines of *S.E.G.*, V, 26 we find that B[o]υθειὲς and Ἐλαιόσιοι Ἐρυθραίον are listed separately. The document is also excluded from the two assessment periods 425/4–423/2 and 422/1–419/8 by the fact that

FIG. 1. *S.E.G.*, V, 26 (left) and a fragment of *I.G.*, I², 310 (right)

the members of the Milesian syntely paid separately in *S.E.G.*, V, 26 and as a group in *I.G.*, I², 64, lines 11–12 and *S.E.G.*, V, 34, Col. I, lines 63–65.[1] There remains the possibility of dating the inscription between 418/7 and 414 where we have no other evidence for the quota of Clazomenae or the payments of the Milesian syntely. Wilhelm's argument for a date early in

[1] Cf. Meritt and West, "A Revision of Athenian Tribute Lists, Part II," *Harv. Stud. Cl. Phil.*, XXXVIII (1927), 62.

the war on the basis of letter forms is hardly convincing.[1] The writing is distinctly different from that of *I.G.*, I², 310, with which Wilhelm compares it, especially in the case of the letter lambda, and I very much doubt whether letter forms alone can be used to distinguish between the years 429/8 and 418/7. I have no hesitation in assigning the document to one of the years of the last assessment of the Athenian empire, unless perhaps we prefer to assume an irregular payment by Clazomenae within a period. In this case one of the years 427/6 or 426/5 is also available.

We must still consider the implications of West's argument that *S.E.G.*, V, 25 belongs in the year 430/29 because of its connection with the well-known Methone decree (*I.G.*, I², 57) and disturbances in Bottice recorded by Thucydides (II, 79).[2] So far as the epigraphical evidence is concerned, the date 429/8 is just as satisfactory as 430/29 in that Methone in this year (*S.E.G.*, V, 25, Col. I, line 53) paid only the ἀπαρχή due to Athena from the tribute, by virtue of the privileges granted in the first Methone decree (*I.G.*, I², 57, lines 29–32). The only necessity is that the date of *S.E.G.*, V, 25 should be subsequent to the date of the first Methone decree. West has demonstrated clearly that the first Methone decree was passed in one of the winter months of an Attic year not long before the Dionysiac festival. This is evident from the fact that an embassy was to be sent to Methone and the court of Perdikkas, to stay until they agreed or disagreed, with time in case of failure for a return embassy to reach Athens before the Dionysia (*I.G.*, I², 57, lines 16–27). The year of the decree was also a year in which Athens and Perdikkas were on friendly terms.

We have now proved that *S.E.G.*, V, 25 cannot be later than 429/8, and consequently the Methone decree must be dated in the winter of either 429/8 or 430/29. In fact, the only possible date is 430/29, because in the autumn of 429 Perdikkas had come to an open break with Athens (Thuc. II, 95). Perdikkas was friendly with Athens in 431/0 (Thuc. II, 29), but the first decree for Methone cannot be dated in 431/0, because the pres-

[1] A. Wilhelm, "Urkunden des attischen Reiches," *Anz. Ak. Wien.*, XLVI (1909), 51; Meritt and West, *op. cit.*, XXXVIII (1927), 63, note 1.

[2] West, "Methone and the Assessment of 430," *A.J.A.*, XXIX (1925), 440–444.

ence of Athenian soldiers in Potidaea (*I.G.*, I², 57, lines 27–28) shows that the decree belongs after the fall of Potidaea in the winter of 430/29.

The embassy from Methone to Athens in this winter was probably one of many which came to plead before the Athenian people on the subject of their assessment at the Panathenaia of 430.[1] I assume that the case of the Methonaeans was left *sub iudice*, or perhaps reopened for favorable consideration after the general assessment had been passed. A chronological table best illustrates the sequence of events:

430		General reassessment of the Athenian empire introduced at the Panathenaia (cf. p. 14, above).
430	Autumn	Adjudication of tribute assessments (cf. p. 19, above).
430	Autumn	Final decree of assessment passed, probably including also the assessment of Methone (*I.G.*, I², 57, lines 8–9: ἡὸν τοῖς προτέροις Παν[αθ]ε[ναίοις] ἐτετάχατο φέρεν).
430	Early winter	Expedition of Melesander to collect tribute assessed (Thuc. II, 69; cf. p. 19, above).
430/29	Winter	Fall of Potidaea (Thuc. II, 70).
430/29	Winter	Embassy from Methone reopens their case for special privileges in tribute assessment, and receives a favorable vote from the Demos (*I.G.*, I², 57, lines 29–32).
430/29	Winter	Embassy from Athens to Methone and Perdikkas perhaps two months before the Dionysia.
429	Spring	Methone pays only an ἀπαρχή from the tribute at the Dionysiac festival (*S.E.G.*, V, 28, Col. II, line 35).

West has argued, however, that in view of the fact that the Athenian forces suffered a severe reverse before the Bottic stronghold of Spartolos in the summer of 429, it is possible that Bottic cities did not pay tribute at the Dionysiac festival of 429/8, as indicated in *S.E.G.*, V, 25, Col. I, lines 40 and 42.[2] This depends

---

[1] Cf. *I.G.*, I², 57, lines 8–9; τοῖς προτέροις Παν[αθ]ε[ναίοις].

[2] West, "Methone and the Assessment of 430," *A.J.A.*, XXIX (1925), 442.

of course on how complete was the evacuation of Bottice by Athenian troops and how well outlying Bottic communities were able to withstand pressure from Athenian forces located at Potidaea and elsewhere on the Thermaic Gulf. In *S.E.G.*, V, 25 we find that Pleume and Aioleion are recorded as paying tribute. There is this indication, only, that 430/29 is perhaps a better date for *S.E.G.*, V, 25 than 429/8. But it must be remembered that Aineia remained faithful to Athens even after the revolt of Bottice and Chalcidice in 432. It paid its normal quota of tribute in 432/1 (*S.E.G.*, V, 23, Col. II, line 54) and the name appears again later in *S.E.G.*, V, 25, Col. I, line 24. Aineia was located on the western border of Bottic territory near the westernmost point of the Macedonian Peninsula,[1] and it is probable that there were Athenian garrisons in Aineia as well as in Potidaea during both the years 430/29 and 429/8. There was also a center of Athenian influence at Dikaia, which should be located on the coast of the Macedonian Peninsula between Aineia and Potidaea.[2] We learn from *S.E.G.*, V, 25, lines 55–56, that Dikaia received from Athens the same concession that was granted to Methone and Haison, namely, that she should remit each year only the one-sixtieth part of her assessed tribute, which was consecrated to the goddess Athena. It may well be that the Athenians with three footholds along the edge of Bottic territory were able to collect the tribute from some smaller towns, like Aioleion and Pleume, even in 429/8.

The first lines of *S.E.G.*, V, 25 may now be restored:

[Ἐπὶ τῆς ἕκτης καὶ εἰκοστῆς ἀρχῆς ἧι . . .⁵ . .]ιππος Φυλάσιος | [ἐγραμμάτευε – – – – – – – – – –].

This date, 429/8, which has been found necessary for *S.E.G.*, V, 25, makes it clear that the cycle of secretaries of the helleno-

---

[1] For the site of Aineia, cf. Col. W. Leake, *Travels in Northern Greece*, III, p. 451; M. Δημιτσᾶς, Τοπογραφία τῆς Μακεδονίας, pp. 361 ff.; A. Struck, *Makedonische Fahrten, I: Chalkidike*, p. 35; S. Casson, *Macedonia Thrace and Illyria* (Oxford Univ. Press, 1926), pp. 85 and 87; Herodotus, VII, 122–123; *I.G.*, IV², fasc. 1, no. 94, lines 9–14.

[2] West, *op. cit.*, p. 444, located Dikaia on the western shore of the Thermaic Gulf. Cf. also *Cambridge Ancient History*, Vol. V, Map 5 (facing p. 173). But the correct location is indicated by *I.G.*, IV², fasc. 1, no. 94, lines 10–14, where the following towns are named in geographical order: Αἴνεια, Δίκαια, Ποτείδαια, Καλίνδοια, Ὄλυνθος.

tamiai which lasted throughout the decade from 439/8 to 430/29 did not continue later into the period of the war. If the cycle were to be continued after 430/29, the secretary for 429/8 should have been a representative of the tribe Antiochis. The demotic of the secretary in *S.E.G.*, V, 25 has been preserved, however, as Φυλάσιος, belonging to the sixth tribe (Oineis), and cannot be made to agree with any continuation of the earlier cycle. We have already noted that the partial cycle of secretaries for the treasurers of Athena came to an end also in 430/29.

CHAPTER II

TREASURERS OF ATHENA FROM 443 TO 430 B.C.

THE discovery that there was a cycle in the reverse of the official order of tribes for the hellenotamiai beginning in 439/8 and continuing until 430/29 raises also the question of whether there may have been a cycle of similar nature for the treasurers of Athena earlier than 434/3. Ferguson's study, already mentioned, revealed the following partial cycle for the secretaries:

434/3	Κράτες Ναύπονος Λαμπτρεύς	*I.G.*, I², 232, 233, 256, 257, 276, 277, 295, 352	Erechtheis	I
433/2	Εὐθίας Αἴσχρονος Ἀναφλύστιος	*I.G.*, I², 232, 233, 256, 257, 276, 277, 295	Antiochis	X
432/1	Ἀπολλόδορος Κριτίο Ἀφιδναῖος	*I.G.*, I², 233, 234, 235, 257, 258, 259, 277, 278, 279	Aiantis	IX
431/0	Δίογνις Ἰσάνδρο Περαιεύς	*I.G.*, I², 234, 235, 258, 259, 278, 279	Hippothontis	VIII
430/29	Θέολλος Χρομάδο Φλυεύς	*I.G.*, I², 236, 237, 260, 261	Kekropis	VII

Earlier than 435/4 documentary evidence is less abundant, though some significant additions to our knowledge have been made. Fragment *U* of the building accounts of the Parthenon has been identified by Dinsmoor as part of *I.G.*, I², 347, the record of the year 439/8. Lines 11–12 of this inscription contain an item of receipts from the treasurers of the goddess:

$$[\pi\alpha\rho\grave{\alpha} \ \tau\alpha\mu\iota\hat{o}\nu \ h\omega\iota \ \tau\grave{\alpha} \ \tau\hat{e}s \ \theta]\epsilon\hat{o} \ \dot{\epsilon}\tau\alpha\mu\dot{\iota}\epsilon\upsilon o\nu$$
$$[h\omega\hat{\iota}s \ .. \ ^5 \ .. \ \dot{\epsilon}\gamma\rho\alpha\mu\mu\dot{\alpha}\tau\epsilon\upsilon]\epsilon \ \Lambda\alpha[\kappa]\iota\dot{\alpha}\delta\epsilon s$$

If the partial cycle discovered by Ferguson is to be carried back to 439/8 the orderly sequence of tribal representation demands for 439/8 a secretary from Oineis (VI). These conditions are fulfilled by the discovery of the new name in fragment *U*, for the deme Lakiadai does in fact belong to Oineis. It seems clear that we may postulate an unbroken cycle from at least 439/8 to 430/29.

The most recent studies of the expense accounts of the Samian War (*I.G.*, I², 293) indicate also that a grant of money was received and expended in 440/39 from the treasurers of the preceding year for whom Epicharinos (?) of Peiraeus was secretary. The reading of *I.G.*, I², 293, lines 13–14, is as follows:

$$\pi\alpha\rho\grave{\alpha} \ \tau\alpha\mu\iota\hat{o}[\nu \ \grave{\epsilon}\pi\grave{\iota} \ T\iota\mu o\kappa\lambda\acute{\epsilon}os \ \mathring{\alpha}\rho\chi o\nu\tau os \ ho\hat{\iota}s \ {}^{\prime}E\pi\iota\chi\alpha\rho \ (?)]$$
$$\hat{\iota}\nu os \ \Pi\epsilon\rho\alpha\iota[\epsilon\grave{\upsilon}s \ \grave{\epsilon}\gamma\rho\alpha\mu\mu\acute{\alpha}\tau\epsilon\upsilon\epsilon \ - - - - - - - - - - - -]$$

This text again confirms the existence of the secretary cycle, for a secretary from the tribe of Hippothontis (VIII) is required for the year 441/0, and the deme Peiraeus does in fact belong to Hippothontis.

Whether or not we agree that this restoration is correct, it is highly probable that this early cycle, which we now know to have existed at least as early as 439/8, began with the tribe Antiochis in 443/2. This seems the more likely because the cycle of the hellenotamiac secretaries appeared in the reverse order of tribes from X to I inclusive.

Ferguson was able to show in his study of the Athenian secretaries that there was a continuous cycle, in reverse order, for the secretaries of the treasurers of Athena and the Other Gods covering a period of perhaps twenty years.[1] He proposed that the cycle began with Akamantis in the year 406/5 and continued until 387/6. Until recently it has remained obscure why this particular cycle should begin with the fifth tribe rather than with the tenth, but later studies have thrown new light upon this problem. Dinsmoor has shown that *I.G.*, I², 254 belongs in the year 409/8 rather than in 408/7.[2] Here we find that the secretary of the treasurers of Athena was from the deme Eleusis (line 281), which belongs to the eighth tribe, Hippothontis. We may infer that the secretaries of the treasurers of Athena were chosen according to a cycle after the reorganization of the government under the Five Thousand in 411 in such a way that the treasurer for 411/0 belonged to Antiochis (X), for 410/9 to Aiantis (IX), for 409/8 to Hippothontis (VIII), etc. This cycle,

[1] Ferguson, "The Athenian Secretaries," *Cornell Stud. Cl. Phil.*, VII (1898), 72–73.
[2] Dinsmoor, in *The Erechtheum*, edited by J. H. Paton, p. 649, note 1.

which finds its justification in *I.G.*, I², 254 (now dated in 409/8), was merely continued without interruption in the choice of secretaries for the joint board of treasurers of Athena and the Other Gods after the amalgamation of these two boards. Ferguson now informs me that *I.G.*, I², 255, lines 323–331, should be dated in 405/4, reading ἐπὶ ᾽Αλεχσίο ἄρχοντος in line 323 and making other changes in the text, the most significant of which is the new reading [φσεφισαμένο τô δέμο ἐπὶ Κ]αλλίο ἄρχοντος in line 329. The treasure of Athena was given over to the hellenotamiai in 405/4 in accordance with a vote of the people made during the previous year 406/5. It will be noted that the secretary from Leukonoe in line 327 belongs to the fourth tribe Leontis, and so falls into place in the secretary cycle.[1]

Just as was the case in the hellenotamiac board of earlier date the cycle began, therefore, not with the fifth tribe as previously supposed, but with the tenth tribe, in 411/0. We have evidence in *I.G.*, I², 298 that the secretary of the treasurers of Athena during the rule of the Four Hundred in 411 was Εὔανδρος ᾽Ε[ρι]θαλίωνος Εὐωνυμ[ε]ύς of the tribe Erechtheis (I). Perhaps it was the purpose of the oligarchic faction to continue the cycle with the sequence I, II, III, etc., in direct order in subsequent years. We do not know. It seems improbable that they should have commenced a cycle in reverse order, such as we actually find, with tribe I. I assume, rather, that the Moderate Democracy reversed the decision of the Four Hundred and instituted the cycle in reverse order with the tenth tribe in 411/0.

There is one other example in the sequence of secretaries for the prytanies of the year 408/7 to illustrate the rotation of tribes from X to I in the fifth century. This was recognized by Ferguson some time ago,[2] and is supported by the evidence of *I.G.*, I², 374.[3] The secretary who gave his name to the year appears in *I.G.*, I², 118 as Εὐκλείδης, when Antiochis was the prytanizing tribe. The apparent conflict between this interpretation and the reading of *I.G.*, I², 313, line 175, is due only to faulty res-

[1] Ferguson, *The Treasurers of Athena*, pp. 8–15.

[2] Ferguson, "The Athenian Secretaries," *Cornell Stud. Cl. Phil.*, VII (1898), 26. note A.

[3] Lines 105–106, 115, 185–186, 272, 343.

toration in the latter document. I suggest that Dorotheos, who
now appears in *I.G.*, I², 313 as first secretary of the Council in
the year of Euktemon, was in fact the secretary of the treasurers
of Athena, and that the passage in question be restored as
follows: [1]

> τᾰμίαι[s ἱιερὸν χρεμάτον τῆς 'Αθεναίας]
>
> ἐπὶ Εὐκ[τέμονος ἄρχοντος καὶ ἐπὶ]
>
> 175   Δοροθέο [γραμματεύοντος παρέδομεν]
>
> κατὰ φσέ[φισμα τὸ δέμο ἀργύριον]
>
> ℎυποθεμ[ένοις χρυσίον τὸ ἐν τôι]
>
> 'Οπισθοδ[όμοι ἐν κοίτει χαλκêι]
>
> ἐκ τῆς τε[τάρτες θέκες]

In every case where we find in reverse order a complete cycle,
or more, the cycle began with a representative of the tenth tribe,
Antiochis. It seems a reasonable conclusion that the cycle of
treasurers of Athena which we have been able to outline from
439/8 (VI) to 434/3 (I) should also begin with the tenth tribe
in 443/2. I assume that such was the case and that this cycle
may be used as a chronological framework for dating certain
unassigned documents from this period of Athenian history.
That the cycle was not in use before 443/2 is shown by the appearance of the name 'Εχσέκεστος 'Αθμονεύς in *I.G.*, I², 340, lines
45–46 and 48–49, which must be dated in 446/5. The cycle here
requires a secretary from the tribe Pandionis (III), but the
deme Athmonon belongs to Kekropis (VII).

---

[1] Ferguson, *The Treasurers of Athena*, p. 27, note 1.

CHAPTER III

THE ACCOUNTS OF THE GOLD AND IVORY STATUE

DURING the early years covered by the financial inscriptions of
the fifth century the board of treasurers who handled the moneys
of Athena is described in various ways. In the building accounts
of the Parthenon and Propylaea they appear regularly as
ταμίαι hοι τὰ τῆς θεõ ἐταμίευον,[1] and in the records of treasures
kept in the Pronaos, the Hekatompedon, and the Parthenon they appear as hοι ταμίαι τõν hιερõν χρεμάτον τῆς Ἀθεναίας.[2]
There can be no question as to the identity of these two boards,
for the treasurers of 434/3, whose secretary is known, are recorded in the building inscriptions with one formula and in the
treasure records with the other. The expense accounts of the
Athenian state describe the board as ταμίαι hιερõν χρεμάτον
τῆς Ἀθεναίας,[3] employing a phraseology which does not differ in
any essential detail from that of the treasure records. Toward
the end of the century (in 408/7) we find the same board listed
as ταμίαι τῆς θεõ.[4] Where the record was not a publication of
the board of treasurers itself, there was a tendency to shorten
the formula, as in the examples just cited. In the reckonings of
the *logistai* for the quadrennium from 426/5 to 423/2 the treasurers of the sacred moneys of Athena are referred to simply as
hοι ταμίαι.[5] The addition of the name of the chief treasurer
was not necessary merely to show that the board had control
over the moneys of Athena, but rather to distinguish the board of
one year from that of earlier or later years. In a similar way the
designations ταμίαι ἐκ πόλεος or ταμίαι, which appear in the
records of overseers of the gold and ivory statue of Athena, can
be interpreted only as referring to the treasurers of Athena.[6]
Aside from the quite evident propriety that the treasurers of
Athena should pay the expense for Athena's most magnificent
statue there was no other financial board at Athens, except the

[1] *I.G.*, I², 340, 342, 347, 352, 364, 366.   [2] *I.G.*, I², 232–288.
[3] E.g. *I.G.*, I², 295, 296.   [4] *I.G.*, I², 374, lines 117 and 187.
[5] *I.G.*, I², 324, lines 2, 16, 25, and 36. For the corrected reading of line 1 of this
inscription cf. Plate XII.   [6] *I.G.*, I², 355, 358, 359, 360.

hellenotamiai or the *kolakretai*, which could on any hypothesis have been called upon to expend the sums necessary for the gold and ivory statue. Both the hellenotamiai and the kolakretai are listed as such in our financial records, and cannot, of course, be confused with the ταμίαι *par excellence*.

This identification of the ταμίαι or ταμίαι ἐκ πόλεος with the ταμίαι ℎοι τὰ τῆς θεῶ ἐταμίευον is supported also by certain epigraphical considerations. The secretary of the treasurers of Athena is known from *I.G.*, I², 340 to have been Ἐχσέκεστος Ἀθμονεύς in the year 446/5. The name Ἐχσέκ[εστος] appears also in one of the expense accounts of the gold and ivory statue, *I.G.*, I², 361, where the restoration as given in the *Corpus* must be substantially correct. At present, lines 1 and 2 of this inscription are restored to read [λêμμα παρὰ ταμιôν ἐκ πόλεος (?) ℎοῖς] Ἐχσέκ[εστος ἐγραμ|μάτευε Ἀθμονεύς – – – – – – ἀγάλμ]ατι [χρυσôι – –]. There is an uninscribed surface of stone above these lines, so that it is certain that no part of the introductory formula immediately preceded line 1. We are dealing with an inscription which contains approximately forty-two letters in each line, somewhat more than the other documents of this group. The preamble of *I.G.*, I², 355 contains only thirteen letters on a line, though the stone is wide enough to accommodate seventeen. The text of *I.G.*, I², 356 consists of lines of approximately fourteen letters; *I.G.*, I², 358 has lines of exactly fourteen letters, although here too the stones might have accommodated several more letters except for the fact that the left margin was reserved for numerals. *I.G.*, I², 359 has about twenty-one letters in each line, and *I.G.*, I², 360 has twenty-eight. It is evident that *I.G.*, I², 361 should be restored with as short a line as possible, in order to effect a reconstruction of the inscription similar to that of other documents in the same category. This has been effected, in my estimation, by the present restoration. A further criterion of the width of the stele may be gained from lines 3–4, where sufficient room must be left for the name of the secretary of the Council and his demotic, in addition to the words πρôτος ἐγραμμάτευε.

In this inscription, certainly, any restoration of the formula [λêμμα παρὰ ταμιôν ℎοι τὰ τῆς θεῶ ἐταμίευον ℎοῖς] Ἐχσέκ[εστος ἐγραμμάτευε] is improbable, because it would necessitate a length of line of approximately fifty letters, and leave approximately twenty-three letters for the name of the secretary of the Council and his demotic. But even if the restoration is possible, we should then have the anomaly of expenses for the gold and ivory statue paid in one year by the ταμίαι hοι τὰ τῆς θεῶ ἐταμίευον and in other years by the ταμίαι or ταμίαι ἐκ πόλεος. This is a real anomaly only if one considers the two boards as distinct. To avoid this horn of the dilemma the longer restoration could be made here only on the assumption that the two boards were identical. On the other hand, if we adhere to the present restoration of the *Corpus*, we find Exekestos appearing as secretary of the ταμίαι ἐκ πόλεος in *I.G.*, I², 361 and as secretary of the ταμίαι hοι τὰ τῆς θεῶ ἐταμίευον in *I.G.*, I², 340, both inscriptions belonging on the evidence of content to the same period in Athenian history. To avoid this other horn of the dilemma, one must again assume that the two boards are identical.

It is at once apparent, therefore, that the secretary cycle may be used to date, either exactly or approximately, those records of the overseers of the gold and ivory statue of Athena which have preserved the name of the secretary of the treasurers from whom the money was received, but it will be useful first to make several general observations about the relative dates of these accounts. The evidence to be considered is the size and shape of the stones and the character of their contents.

I.G., I², 361 may be dated definitely in 446/5, during which year Exekestos was secretary of the treasurers of Athena. This is the only one of the records of the overseers to which a definite date can so far be given, and it falls earlier than the time of introduction of the secretary cycle. The earlier accounts seem to have been cut on *stelae* somewhat larger than the later ones. On the evidence of this physical characteristic alone we might arrange the inscriptions which belong certainly to this category in the following order: *I.G.*, I², 361, 360, 359, 358, 356, 355, and 355a. It will be observed that in the three earlier documents the ταμίαι are regularly listed as ταμίαι ἐκ πόλεος and that in the later records they are listed simply as ταμίαι. This slight change toward simplicity of expression is just that which might be expected as familiarity and lack of meticulous care led to abbreviation. Similarly we find the treasurers listed in *I.G.*, I², 360 with name and demotic; in *I.G.*, I², 359 with name, patronymic, and demotic; in *I.G.*, I², 358 with name and demotic, though here the demotic was not always added; and in *I.G.*, I², 355 with the name alone. With the same chronological arrangement of the stones, we find again a tendency to simplification and abbreviation. We shall also find support for this general arrangement of the stones in the study of the secretaries and their relation to the cycle.

The first approach to this problem may be made with *I.G.*, I², 359. The money received by the overseers was listed as λêμμα παρὰ ταμιôν ἐκ πόλεος [hοῖ]s Δεινία[s] Εὐάγος Φ[ι]λάιδες ἐ[γρ]α-μ[μά]τευε. The deme Philaidai belongs to the second tribe, Aigeis. Consequently the inscription must be assigned to the year 435/4 if it is to fall within the period of the cycle. Otherwise it must be dated in one of the years prior to 443/2, though not in 446/5. A date so late as 435/4 is out of the question for this inscription, which records heavy expenses of approximately thirty-four talents for gold, implying that there was still considerable work to be done on the statue. Since Pheidias had so far finished his work that the statue was ready for dedication at the Panathenaia of 438/7,[1] we cannot reasonably assume so large an outlay for new material three years later. It seems probable also that the overseers of the statue ceased to keep separate accounts after the dedication, at which time they delegated their responsibilities to the overseers of the Parthenon. Surplus gold and ivory which had been purchased by the old board was disposed of by the overseers of the Parthenon. Amounts received from the sale of this material make their appearance among the receipts listed by these overseers in the years following the Panathenaia of 438.[2] If this interpretation of the epigraphical evidence is correct, then it is impossible to date any of our records of expense for the gold and ivory statue later than 439/8.

In lines 4–6 of *I.G.*, I², 359 the name of the secretary of the Council appears in the formula of date ἐπὶ τês βολês [hêι Οἰ]όνι-[χ]ος ᾿Αλοπεκêθεμ πρôτος ἐγραμμάτευε. If the inscription is to

----

[1] See R. Schöll, "Der Prozess des Phidias," *Sitzb. Ak. München*, 1888, pp. 1–53, for an interpretation of the evidence of the scholiast on the *Peace* (605) of Aristophanes (*F.H.G.*, I, 400, 97 [Müller]).

[2] *I.G.*, I², 348, 349, 352. Cf. Dinsmoor, "Attic Building Accounts," *A.J.A.*, XXV (1921), 244.

be dated in 435/4, then the name of this secretary must also be restored in *I.G.*, I², 351, line 56 and in *I.G.*, I², 365, line 2, the building accounts of the Parthenon and Propylaea respectively.

The present restoration of the *Corpus* gives the secretary's name in *I.G.*, I², 351 as [. . . .⁸. . . .]A[ς], followed by the doubtful Π of π[ρῶτος ἐγραμμάτευε]. The first publication of the fragment by Woodward [1] indicates that he saw no traces of letters at all in the line where the secretary's name is now given. Dinsmoor's first publication recorded here only a diagonal stroke, like the right-hand stroke of A,[2] followed, after one letter space, by the upper stroke of what may have been the letter Π. The diagonal stroke has now been read in the *Corpus* as alpha, followed after an interval of one letter space by a doubtful pi. The readings in this line are certainly subject to question. Mr. Homer Thompson wrote to me from Athens as follows, under the date of June 30, 1930: "In line 56, midway between the epsilon and gamma of line 55, there is the trace of a stroke hard to explain otherwise than as the top of the hasta of iota. Beneath the second nu, though slightly to the left, the circle of an omicron is marked both by indentation and by rust stain. I can find no trace of Dinsmoor's diagonal stroke to the left where the surface is deeply worn. To the right of the omicron the surface is worn and scratched; a sigma may have once been there. The next letter to the right is completely obliterated by a deep sinking in the stone which has also carried away the lower part of the tau above." According to Thompson's description, the name of the secretary might possibly be read [– – –]Ι . . . Ο– –, of which the iota is the only letter that seems certainly to belong to the name. Even this letter is doubtful. On the basis of such questionable evidence only negative conclusions can at present be drawn from a comparison of *I.G.*, I², 359 and 351.

In *I.G.*, I², 365 the name of the secretary of the Council has been indicated by ten letter spaces on the basis of a stoichedon line of thirty-eight letters. Line 5 can be made to contain thirty-eight letters instead of forty-three by omitting the word τοῦτο

---

[1] A. M. Woodward, "Some New Fragments of Attic Building-Records," *B.S.A.*, XVI (1909–10), 190.

[2] Dinsmoor, "Attic Building Accounts," *A.J.A.*, XVII (1913), Plate IV, facing p. 72, line 68.

from the phrase λ[έμματα τô ένιαυτô τούτο τάδε]. Such an omission finds its justification in the record of the following year (*I.G.*, I², 366), where we read merely λ[έμματα τ]ô ένι[αυτô τάδε]. There is even so the possibility that the lines of this prescript ended with complete words or syllables, so that the name Οίόνιχος might be restored in line 2 followed by two uninscribed spaces. But a strict adherence to the stoichedon order necessitates a name of ten letters for the secretary, and makes the restoration Οίόνιχος impossible.

While it must be admitted that the comparative study of *I.G.*, I², 351, 359, and 365 does not prove definitely that *I.G.*, I², 359 cannot be dated in 435/4, it seems possible on the basis of the other evidence outlined above to carry the inscription back to an earlier date, before the introduction of the secretary cycle, and consequently earlier than 443/2.

The inscription containing accounts for the gold and ivory statue and now preserved as *I.G.*, I², 358 is in need of particular study. In many places the text of the document must be changed, for more can be read from the stone than has been published hitherto. I give in Figure 2 a photograph of the stone as it is now preserved in the Epigraphical Museum at Athens, and in Figure 3 a facsimile drawing showing the restorations in red and the letters still legible in black. It may be noted that the restoration of the *Corpus* in lines 17–18 for the treasurer [Κρι]τίας Πε[ρ]α[εύς] is no longer tenable. The deme Peiraeus belongs to the eighth tribe Hippothontis, and this tribe is already represented by the treasurer Λ[άχε]s: Κ[οιλεύς], whose name appears earlier in lines 13–14. In view of the fact that the treasurers were chosen one from each tribe the restoration of the demotic Πε[ρ]α[εύς] was in any case subject to suspicion. This is all the more true since in the fifth century the regular spelling of the word was Περαιεύς and not Περαεύς. The letters still preserved make necessary the restoration of the demotic Πε[ρ]γασε̂[θ]εν. The name of the treasurer should be restored as [Κ]λυτίας, rather than [Κρι]τίας. Following the demotic Πε[ρ]γασε̂[θ]εν, there appears the name of the next treasurer, Πετραî[ο]s, without demotic. Every letter of the name is perfectly clear on the stone, except the penultimate omicron; there can be no doubt about the restoration. We must reject the suggested [Μενέ]στρατ̣[ο]s of the *Corpus*.

Further corrections in the accepted text are also possible. In line 12 the initial letters are ΔΑΘ, which must be combined with the other letters which follow from the same word to give

Fig. 2. Photograph of *I.G.*, I², 358

the demotic [Κυ]δαθ[εν]α[ιε]ύς. It is evident now that the name of the secretary bearing this demotic appeared in line 11 and consisted of eight letters. The initial letters of line 11 belong to

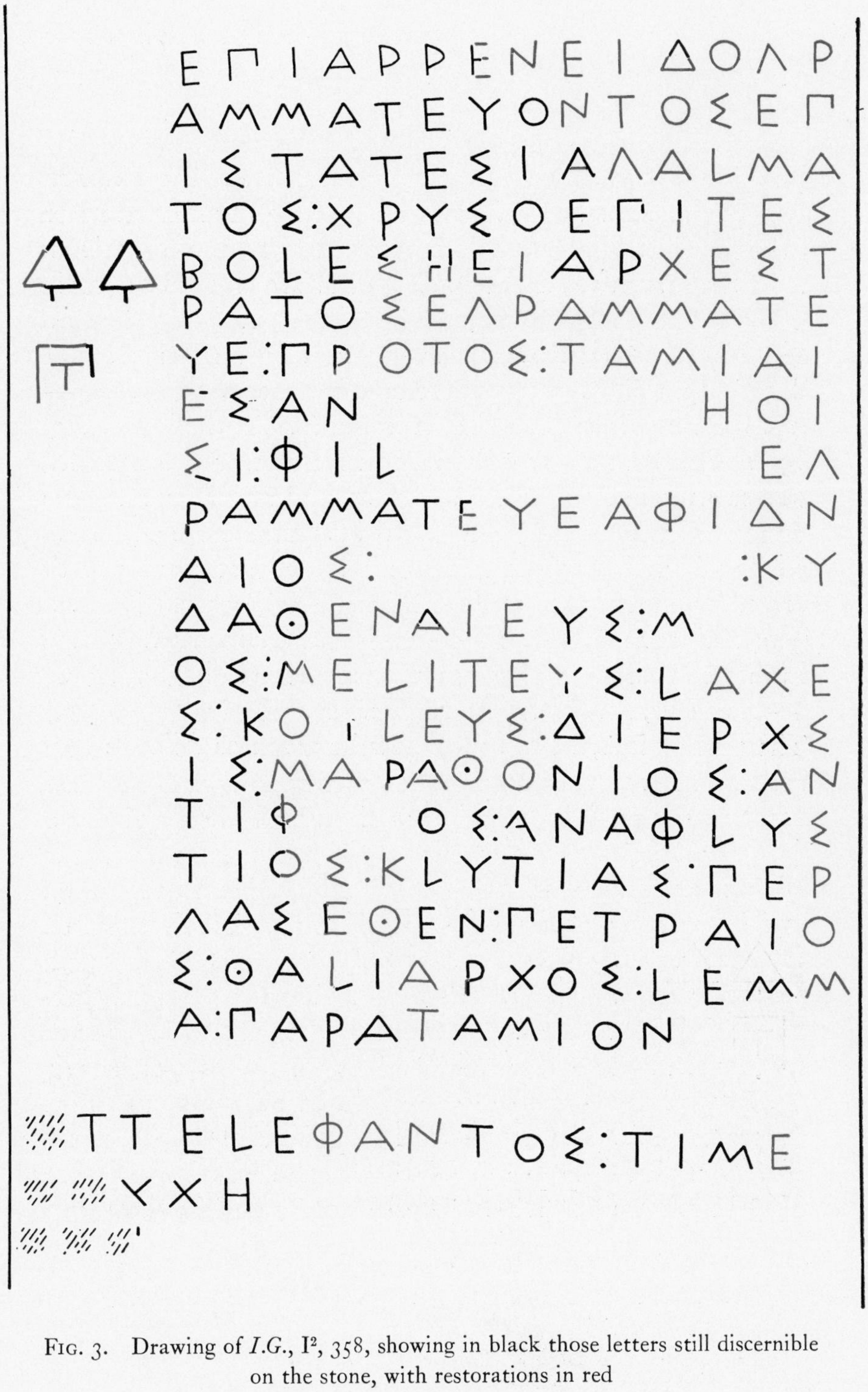

ΕΓΙΑΡΡΕΝΕΙΔΟΛΡ
ΑΜΜΑΤΕΥΟΝΤΟΣΕΓ
ΙΣΤΑΤΕΣΙΑΛΑΛΜΑ
ΤΟΣ:ΧΡΥΣΟΕΓΙΤΕΣ
ΒΟΛΕΣΗΕΙΑΡΧΕΣΤ
ΡΑΤΟΣΕΛΡΑΜΜΑΤΕ
ΥΕ:ΓΡΟΤΟΣ:ΤΑΜΙΑΙ
ΕΣΑΝ   ΗΟΙ
ΣΙ:ΦΙL   ΕΛ
ΡΑΜΜΑΤΕΥΕΑΦΙΔΝ
ΑΙΟΣ: :ΚΥ
ΔΑΟΘΕΝΑΙΕΥΣ:Μ
ΟΣ:ΜΕLΙΤΕΥΣ:LΑΧΕ
Σ:ΚΟΙLΕΥΣ:ΔΙΕΡΧΣ
ΙΣ:ΜΑΡΑΘΟΝΙΟΣ:ΑΝ
ΤΙΦ   ΟΣ:ΑΝΑΦLΥΣ
ΤΙΟΣ:ΚLΥΤΙΑΣ:ΓΕΡ
LΑΣΕΘΕΝ:ΓΕΤΡΑΙΟ
Σ:ΘΑLΙΑΡΧΟΣ:LΕΜΜ
Α:ΓΑΡΑΤΑΜΙΟΝ

ΤΤΕLΕΦΑΝΤΟΣ:ΤΙΜΕ
ΥΧΗ

FIG. 3. Drawing of *I.G.*, I², 358, showing in black those letters still discernible on the stone, with restorations in red

[37]

the demotic of the secretary of the treasurers. There is only one legitimate restoration, after the word [ἐγ]ραμμάτε[υε] in lines 9–10, and we supply ['Αφιδν]αῖο[s].

The new readings shown in our photograph and facsimile copy in lines 8–11 are particularly significant. Homer Thompson has written to me from Athens after an inspection of the stone: "Of the first letter in line 8 I detect the right tip of a horizontal bar. In the fourth place the strokes of N are clear and certain." We may restore with confidence ἐπὶ [τês] βολês hê[ι] 'Αρ[χέστ]ρατο[s ἐγραμμάτε]υε: πρ[ôτος: ταμίαι] êσαν – – –.[1] The word ταμίαι is now displaced from lines 8–9, and the usual formula hoîs – – – – ἐγραμμάτευε may be substituted in its stead. At the beginning of line 9 the preserved iota belongs to the relative pronoun hoîσι, written here as in I.G., I², 311, lines 10 and 17. I detect also on the squeeze the tip of the lower stroke of sigma before the iota. It is more difficult to fill the lacuna in line 8, but I suggest that the restoration should be [– – ἐν ἀρχêι hoî]|σι: Φιλ[. . .⁷. . . ἐγ]|ραμμάτε[υε 'Αφιδν]|αῖο[s – – – – – –].[2] The secretary of the treasurers of Athena had a name of ten letters beginning with Φιλ – –, such as, for example, Φιλ[οκράτες].

The text of I.G., I², 358 may now be given as follows:

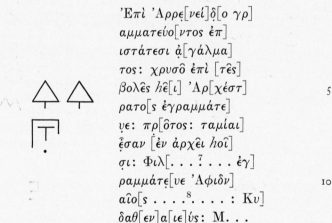

'Επὶ 'Αρρε[νεί]δ[ο γρ]
αμματεύο[ντος ἐπ]
ιστάτεσι ἀ[γάλμα]
τος: χρυσô ἐπὶ [τês]
βολês hê[ι] 'Αρ[χέστ]   5
ρατο[s ἐγραμμάτε]
υε: πρ[ôτος: ταμίαι]
ệσαν [ἐν ἀρχêι hoî]
σι: Φιλ[. . .⁷. . . ἐγ]
ραμμάτε[υε 'Αφιδν]   10
αῖο[s . . . .⁸. . . . : Κυ]
δαθ[εν]α[ιε]ύs: Μ. . .

_____

[1] I do not believe it possible to restore lines 7–9 of I.G., I², 358 [– –Λ]υσαν[ίας ἔρχε: ταμία]ι Φιλ – –. The first letter of line 8 seems clearly Ε rather than Υ, though only a small tip of the upper right stroke is preserved.

[2] The restoration suggested by Bannier (Ph. Woch., 1925, p. 863): [– – ταμίαι ἐ]σα[ν ἐν τôι ἐνιαυτô]ι Φιλ[– – –] is thus shown to be impossible.

οs: Μ[ελιτε]ύs: Λ[άχε]
s: Κ[ο]ι[λεύs:] Διερχ[σ]
ιs: [Μα]ρα[θό]νιος: Ἀ[ν]   15
τίφ[. .]ος: Ἀναφλύ[σ]
τιο[s: Κ]λυτίας: Πε[ρ]
γασε͂[θ]εν: Πετραῖ[ο]
s: Θαλί[α]ρχος: λε͂μ[μ]
α παρὰ [τ]αμιο͂ν   20

[▨]Τ Τ   ἐλέ[φαν]τος: τιμ[έ]
[. .]ΧΧΗ
[▨ ▨]▨¹

The tentative chronological arrangement of these records
which was suggested on page 32 indicated that *I.G.*, I², 358
should be assigned to a date about midway between the earliest
and latest documents of the group. The possible limits are
447/6, when work on the Parthenon was commenced, and 439/8,
after which the overseers of the statue turned over their accounts
to the overseers of the temple. The approximate date for *I.G.*,
I², 358 is, therefore, 443/2, if the issue is to be decided purely
on the evidence of physical characteristics of the stone and manner of recording the names of the secretaries. The exact date
may be determined as 442/1, however, by the application of the
secretary cycle, which demands in this year a representative of
Aiantis (IX). Since the secretary of the treasurers whose name
appears in our inscription was from the deme Aphidnai, which
belongs to Aiantis, we may with confidence assign the inscription to this year. The somewhat careless record of the names of
the treasurers and the narrow width of the stone argue against
a date earlier than 443/2, when the secretary cycle was not in
effect.

We find, therefore, that Archestratos was first secretary of
the Council in 442/1 and that the treasurers of Athena were
eight in number, listed in the following order:

[. . . .⁸. . . . Κυ]δαθ[εν]α[ιε]ύs   III
Μ[. . .]ος Μ[ελιτε]ύs   VII
Λ[άχε]s Κ[ο]ι[λεύs]   VIII
Διερχ[σ]ις [Μα]ρα[θό]νιος   IX

'Α[ν]τίφ[. .]ος 'Αναφλύ[σ]τιο[ς]   X

[Κ]λυτίας Πε[ρ]γασê[θ]εν   I

Πετραî[ο]ς   ?

Θαλί[α]ρχος   ?

Their secretary was Φιλ[. . . ? . . . 'Αφιδν]αîο[ς] (IX).

In the text of *I.G.*, I², 343, as given in the *Corpus*, the fifth line of Col. III exhibits also the demotic ['Αφι]δναîος in such a position that one might be led to construe it possibly as the demotic of the secretary of the treasurers of Athena. It would then be tempting to assign *I.G.*, I², 358 to the same year (443/2) and to restore the name 'Αρχέστρατος for the secretary of the Council in *I.G.*, I², 343, line 76. But the transcript of *I.G.*, I², 343 in the *Corpus* is misleading in this particular, for the letters of the demotic ['Αφι]δναîος in Col. III, line 5, and in fact all the lines from fragment *D*, are cut in larger characters than the rest of the inscription and belong, not to *I.G.*, I², 343, but to the end of the prescript of *I.G.*, I², 339. The correct disposition has been given by Dinsmoor (*A.J.A.*, XVII [1913], 62). It would be, of course, entirely gratuitous to assume that 'Αρχέστρατος of *I.G.*, I², 358 should be identified with – – – – – – ος of *I.G.*, I², 343, line 76.

Another of the records of the overseers of the statue which gives the name of the secretary of the treasurers of Athena is preserved as *I.G.*, I², 355. The chronological scheme indicated above suggests a relatively late date for this document, certainly later than 443/2. Consequently it was within the period when the cycle of tribal rotation was employed in determining the secretaryship. In lines 4–8 we read: [λ]êμμα: παρὰ ταμιôν: ho îς Δεμόστρατος: ἐγραμμάτευε: Χσυπεταόν.

The deme Xypete belongs to the seventh tribe Kekropis, and this inscription may be definitely dated according to the secretary cycle in the year 440/39. Certain apparent difficulties which seem to militate against this date will be discussed in the following chapter.

We have found that the inscription cut on the broadest stele (*I.G.*, I², 361) is definitely dated in 446/5 by the prosopographical evidence of the secretary's name, 'Εχσέκεστος, and that another inscription cut on a relatively broad stele (*I.G.*, I², 359) may be definitely dated earlier than 443 by the secretary cycle. These inscriptions both name the treasurers as ταμίαι ἐκ πόλεος. With them is to be associated closely in point of time a third record (*I.G.*, I², 360), which also is cut on a broad stele, which names the treasurers as ταμίαι ἐκ πόλεος and which gives the list of treasurers with name and demotic. *I.G.*, I², 359 gives the names of the treasurers with both patronymic and demotic, while the narrower stele *I.G.*, I², 358 lists some of the names with demotic only, and some without demotic. A definite date late in the series has been determined for *I.G.*, I², 355, which is cut on a narrow stele, like *I.G.*, I², 356 and 358, which lists the treasurers by name alone and which agrees with *I.G.*, I², 358 in referring to the board merely as ταμίαι.

We may take as established, therefore, the following chronology for the records of the overseers of the gold and ivory statue of Athena:

I.G., I²		*I.G.*, I²		*I.G.*, I²	
361	446/5	359	?	356	?
360	?	358	442/1	355, 355a	440/39

CHAPTER IV

THE RECORD OF EXPENSE FOR THE SAMIAN WAR

THE discovery that *I.G.*, I², 355 should be dated in 440/39 and that Δεμόστρατος Χσυπεταόν was secretary of the treasurers of Athena in that year raises an immediate question as to the restoration of *I.G.*, I², 293, which records the expenses of the Samian War. In this inscription it appears that the secretary of the treasurers of Athena in 440/39 was not Demostratos, but Phyromachos. However, this identification of Phyromachos as a secretary of the treasurers depends upon restoration. Since it will be necessary to examine this inscription in some detail, the text is repeated below as it is now given in the *Corpus:*

. . .⁵. .εκ –
. . . .εσε –
. . .σοσα –
. .ο Φρεα[ρριο –]
𐅋𐅉𐅉𐅈TTT –
'Αθεναῖοι ἀ[νέλοσαν ἐπὶ Μορυχίδο ἄρχοντος ἐς τὸν]
πρὸς Σαμίο[ς πόλεμον· ταμίαι hιερο͂ν χρεμάτον τε͂ς]
'Αθεναίας Γ[. . . . . . . .¹⁷. . . . . καὶ χσυνάρχοντε]
ς, hοῖς Φυρό[μαχος . . . . .¹⁹. . . . . ἐγραμμά]
τευε, ταμία[ι δὲ (?) . . . . .²⁷. . . . . ἐ]
χς Οἴο, Ναυσ[. . . . . .³¹. . . . .]
𐅋𐅋𐅋𐅊𐅉𐅈TTT [. . . . . . . .¹⁷. . . . . παραδεχσάμενοι]
παρὰ ταμιο͂[ν ἐπὶ Τιμοκλέος ἄρχοντος hοῖς 'Επιχαρ (?)]
ῖνος Περαι[εὺς ἐγραμμάτευε . . . . .¹⁷. . . . .]
ερον· hοι δὲ – – – – – – – – – – – – – – – – –
'Αφιδναῖος – – – – – – – – – – – – – – – – – –
𐅌𐅋𐅋𐅋𐅋𐅈TTT – – – – – – – – – – – – – – – –
χσύμπαντο[ς το͂ ἐς Σαμίος (?) ἀναλόματος κεφάλαιον]
𐅍𐅋[𐅋]𐅋𐅋 –

A photograph of the stone as now preserved in the Epigraphical Museum at Athens appears in Figure 4. One or two letters have been lost in the upper lines of the inscription since its first publication, but otherwise the stone has remained unharmed since its discovery. The final A given in line 3 of the *Corpus* is a clearly cut iota, and the O given as the third letter in line 4 is open to grave suspicion. Otherwise the present readings are correct. I suggest that in line 4 there were listed the members of a board of treasurers, all with names and demotics in the nominative case, as in lines 11 and 16. Line 4 should, consequently, be restored [. . .] Φρεά[ρριος – – – – – – – – – – – – – – –].

But more serious difficulties are encountered in the restored text. The board of treasurers is listed in lines 7-8 as ταμίαι ἡιερῶν χρεμάτον τῆς Ἀθεναίας, although this designation of the board is not otherwise found earlier than 434/3.[1] Another anomaly is that the chief treasurer of the board and his colleagues are mentioned in line 8, but not in line 12. We note also that the name of the secretary must be restored in line 9 with both patronymic and demotic, while the name of the secretary appeared in lines 13-14 without the patronymic. Such irregularity of record was usually avoided in the case of similar boards in a single inscription. But this argument cannot be pressed.

FIG. 4. Photograph of *I.G.*, I², 293

These are perhaps after all merely matters of style and should not be urged as proof that the present restoration is incorrect.

A more damaging objection to the present text is that ταμίαι in line 7 cannot be associated with any verb and consequently leaves an inexplicable grammatical difficulty. The verb παρέδοσαν

------

[1] The significance of this formula is pointed out by Ferguson, *The Treasurers of Athena*, p. 163, note 1.

must be supplied in line 8 after Ἀθεναίας in order that the inscription may be intelligible, but this leaves a space of only nine
letters for the name and demotic of the chief treasurer. In any
case the restoration cannot be made without doing extreme vio-
lence to the order of words in the sentence. Furthermore, it is
contrary to epigraphical practice to list the board twice, once as
ὁ δεῖνα καὶ χσυνάρχοντες and again as a group of ten men each
with name and demotic (lines 10–11). That the individual members of the board making the payment were listed at the conclusion of the record of that payment is clear from the words
ταμία[ι] in line 10 and ℎοι δὲ [ταμίαι], which must be restored
in line 15. The record is similar in this respect to the accounts
of the gold and ivory statue of approximately the same date.[1]
With a stoichedon line of forty letters it is impossible to allow
more than seventy letter spaces in lines 10 and 11 for the names
of the individual treasurers in this year. A conservative estimate of the average number of letters in a name and demotic is
fourteen. It thus appears that the length of line now used as the
basis for the restoration of *I.G.*, I², 293 allows only five members
in the board of treasurers for this year. Only sixty-five letters
are available in lines 15 and 16 for the board of treasurers in
441/0, so that we must assume, if the present restoration is correct, that this board consisted of four, perhaps at the most five,
members.

The necessity of listing with name and demotic the individual
treasurers of Athena gives, in fact, the best criterion for determining the length of line with which the inscription should be
restored. Assuming for the moment a board of ten members in
441/0, a quick calculation will show that the inscription must be
restored with a length of line more nearly approximating eighty
than forty letter spaces.

At present, the word παραδεχσάμενοι has been restored at the
end of line 12. It is impossible to justify this restoration.
Such formulae as παραδεχσάμενοι παρὰ τὸν προτέρον ταμιõν do
occur in the treasure records of the Pronaos, Hekatompedon,
and Parthenon, where sacred objects are handed down from one
board to another for safe keeping, but they have no place in a

---

[1] *I.G.*, I², 361, line 4; 360, line 5; 359, line 10; 358, lines 7–8 (for the restoration
cf. p. 38); 355, line 8.

record of war expenses. The 900 odd talents which the treasurers of 440/39 are supposed to have received from the treasurers of 441/0 must have been spent on the war. There is no question of this money passing from the custody of one board to that of its successors. The amounts of money listed here are expenses which must have been given to the generals in the field.

There is another historical difficulty also involved in the interpretation of these amounts of money. The war with Samos began in the spring of 440, after the collection of tribute in that year, and lasted through the greater part of 440/39. The editors of the *Corpus* assume that the amount in line 5 (128 talents) was expended in 441/0, and that the two amounts in lines 12 and 17 (368 talents and 908 talents) were expended in 440/39. If the treasurers of 441/0 had any responsibilities in connection with the payment of the 908 talents, then we must believe that more than three fourths of the expense of the war had been paid out from the treasury at a time when the war had hardly more than begun.

It is evident also from the study of this inscription that the amounts of money listed in lines 5, 12, and 17 may be added to give the total in line 19. From this it follows that no parts of these numerals can have appeared at the ends of the preceding lines. Whatever may have been the nature of the text, it either occupied completely the lines preceding the numerals, or else the ends of those lines were left uninscribed. A new introductory formula begins also in line 6, from which it may be inferred that line 5 was left uninscribed after the numeral. A similar observation may be made in the case of lines 17 and 18. There must have been an uninscribed space after the numeral in line 17. With this established practice of giving to each numeral a line by itself, irrespective of whether the figures completely occupied the space available on the line, it is evident that the end of line 12 must also be left blank and that the words παρὰ ταμιō[ν] in line 13 begin a new item of the entry. The possibility of restoring παραδεχσάμενοι, or any other word, at the end of the preceding line is excluded.

The sum total of money spent on the Samian War, according to the present restoration of lines 18 and 19, was approximately 1400 talents. Literary tradition gives the expense of the war as

1200 talents.[1] This discrepancy between the epigraphical and literary evidence can be in part obviated by assuming that only the amounts listed in *I.G.*, I², 293, lines 12 and 17, were spent against Samos. The total spent against Samos then appears as 1276 talents instead of 1404 talents. It must be assumed further that the amount listed in line 5, which is thus excluded from the Samian reckoning, was spent on some other undertaking at about the same time. I suggest that the 128 talents here recorded were spent against Byzantium, which revolted at the same time with Samos,[2] and further, that the total figure of 1404 talents in line 19 represents the grand total of expenses against both Samos and Byzantium. This interpretation of the inscription makes possible an easy explanation of the figures in lines 12 and 17 as the yearly totals of money spent against Samos in 441/0 and 440/39 respectively. The war lasted through only a small part of 441/0 and through the greater part of 440/39; we now are able to associate the greater sum expended with the year in which most of the fighting occurred.

The general principles by which a restoration should be planned are clear. The dates ought to be given for each payment by archon and by the first secretary of the Council. There should be no dates within the prytany because the sums listed in lines 12 and 17 are not individual payments made all on one day, but yearly totals. There were two payments only for Samos, and they were probably described as ἀνάλομα παρὰ ταμιõν or παρὰ ταμιõν ἀνάλομα. The second payment fell in 440/39, where the preserved letters in line 15 suggest the restoration [ἀνάλομα hέτ]ερον or [ἀνάλομα δεύτ]ερον. Furthermore, there should be some mention of the body of men who received the money, probably the generals in charge of operations against Samos. Line 8 should be restored not as [ταμίαι hιερõν χρεμάτον τês] 'Αθεναίας, because this designation of the board makes its first appearance in 434/3, but rather as [ἀπὸ τõν χρεμάτον τês] 'Αθεναίας Π[ολιάδος –], to indicate the source from which the treasurers drew the funds disbursed. They controlled the moneys of Athena Nike as well as of Athena Polias, and probably also the funds of Hermes as well.[3]

---

[1] Isocrates, XV, 111; Diodorus, XII, 28, 3; Nepos, *Timotheus*, I, 2.

[2] Thuc. I, 115.

[3] *I.G.*, I², 301, lines 12 and 69.

I have drawn up the following restoration, based upon a stoichedon line of ninety-three letters, in the attempt to present a more serviceable text of this important document.

```
 . . .⁵. .εκ[– – – – – – – – – – – – – – – – – – – – – – – –]
 . . . .εσε[– – – – – – – – – – – – – – – – – – – – – – – –]
 . . .σοσι[– – – – – – – – – – – – – – – – – – – – – – –]
 . . . Φρεά[ρριος – – – – – – – – – – – – – – – – – – – –]
5  ⊢ΔΔ⊓ΤΤΤ[– – – – – – – – – – – – – – – – – – – – – – –]
```

’Αθεναῖοι ἀ[νέλοσαν ἐν τοῖν δυοῖν ἐτοῖν τοῖν ἐπὶ Τιμοκλέος ἄρχοντος
   καὶ ἐπὶ Μορυχίδο ἄρχοντος ’Αθεναίοισι ἐς τὸν]
πρὸς Σαμίο[ς πόλεμον· τάδε παρέδοσαν ℎοι ταμίαι ἐκ πόλεος φσεφισαμένο τὸ δέμο τὲν ἄδειαν ἀπὸ τῶν ℎιερῶν χρεμάτον]
’Αθεναίας Π[ολιάδος· στρατεγοῖς τοῖς πρὸς Σαμίος Περικλεῖ Χολαργεῖ καὶ χσυνάρχοσι ἀνάλομα παρὰ ταμιῶν ἐκ πόλεο]
s ℎοῖς Φυρό[μαχος . . .±6. . . ἐγραμμάτευε ἐπὶ Τιμοκλέος ἄρχοντος
   καὶ ἐπὶ τὲς βολὲς ℎεῖ . . . . . .∓12. . . . . πρότος ἐγραμμά]
10 τευε· ταμία[ι – ℎέ]
   χs Οἶο Ναυσ[– –]
   ⊢⊢⊢⊢⊓ΔΔ⊓ΤΤΤ[– – – – – – – – – – – – – – – – – – –]
Παρὰ ταμιδ[ν ἐκ πόλεος ℎοῖς Δεμόστρατος Χσυπεταιὸν ἐγραμμάτευε
   ἐπὶ Μορυχίδο ἄρχοντος καὶ ἐπὶ τὲς βολὲς ℎεῖ ’Αρχ (?)]
ῖνος Περαι[εὺς πρότος ἐγραμμάτευε στρατεγοῖς τοῖς πρὸς Σαμίος
   Περικλεῖ Χολαργεῖ καὶ χσυνάρχοσι ἀνάλομα δεύτ]
15 ερον· ℎοι δὲ [ταμίαι ἐσαν – – – – – – – – – – – – – – – – –]
   ’Αφιδναῖος [– –]
   ⊓⊢⊢⊢⊢⊢⊓ΤΤΤ[– – – – – – – – – – – – – – – – – – –]
   χσύμπαντο[s κεφάλαιον τὸ ἐς Βυζαντίος καὶ Σαμίος ἀναλόματος]
   ✗⊢[⊢]⊢⊢[– –]

We do not know the demotic which should be restored in line 9 with the name Phyromachos, but the existence of the secretary cycle at this date enables us to assign Phyromachos to the eighth tribe, Hippothontis. The name and demotic of the secretary of the treasurers in the following year are known from *I.G.*, I², 355, and may be restored in line 13. It appears that [’Αρχ]ῖνος Περαι[εύς] was not the secretary of the treasurers of Athena, but rather the first secretary of the Council in this year. The treasurers of 440/39 are known from *I.G.*, I², 355, where a panel of seven names is preserved. Unfortunately, the names are given

there without demotics, although it is now known from line 16
of this inscription that one of the treasurers, probably Smokordos
or Pheideleides, belonged to the deme of Aphidnai, representing
the ninth tribe, Aiantis.

It may now be shown that *I.G.*, I², 358 is definitely excluded
from the last three years during which accounts of the overseers
of the gold and ivory statue were published. The inscription
cannot be dated in 439/8 because the secretary of the treasurers,
known from *I.G.*, I², 347 as [. . .⁵. . .] Λα[κ]ιάδες, is different from
the name and demotic which may be restored in *I.G.*, I², 358,
lines 9–11. The inscription cannot be dated in 440/39 because
I.G., I², 355 has already been assigned to this year, and because,
further, the treasurer from Aiantis appears with demotic 'Αφιδναῖος in *I.G.*, I², 293 and with demotic [Μα]ρα[θό]νιος in *I.G.*, I²,
358. The year 441/o is also impossible because the demotic of
the treasurer from Hippothontis in that year was [ἐ]χs Οἴο
(*I.G.*, I², 293), whereas the demotic of the treasurer from Hippothontis in *I.G.*, I², 358 was Κ[ο]ι[λεύs]. We have already shown
reason to believe that *I.G.*, I², 358 should be dated actually in
442/1.[1] This determination receives an added degree of probability with the elimination of the subsequent years as possible
dates for the document.

The discovery that ['Αρχ]ῖνος Περαι[εύs] (*I.G.*, I², 293, line 14)
was not a secretary of the treasurers of Athena does not in any
sense weaken the evidence for the secretary cycle from 443/2
to 434/3.[2] In fact, now that we know the date of *I.G.*, I², 293,
lines 13–17, to have been 440/39 instead of 441/o, it would have
been impossible to carry the cycle back as early as 440 if Archinos
had been a secretary of the treasurers. At the same time the
discovery that he was first secretary of the Council in 440/39
raises difficulties in the interpretation of a decree of this year
which has been preserved as *I.G.*, I², 50. It appears from the
last line of fragment *a* of this inscription that the first secretary
of the Council in 440/39 was from Rhamnus, and not from the
Peiraeus, as we have determined above.

The various fragments of *I.G.*, I², 50 were assigned to one
inscription by Wilhelm in 1898,[3] at which time he named four

[1] Cf. above, p. 39.   [2] Cf. above, p. 29.
[3] Wilhelm, "Altattische Schriftdenkmäler," *Ath. Mitt.*, XXIII (1898), 472.

pieces. He reserved a discussion of his reasons for grouping these pieces together until a later time. So far as I am aware the evidence which Wilhelm intended to present in favor of his grouping has not as yet been made public.[1] Only three of the four fragments mentioned by Wilhelm in 1898 were published in the *editio minor* of the *Corpus* in 1924. The fourth fragment is given by Hiller with the letter *d*, and the simple statement "*non vidi.*"

We are indebted to H. T. Wade-Gery for the recent publication of this important fragment, and for the proof that it must be, in fact, associated with the other fragments of *I.G.*, I², 50.[2] He was able to discover that it should be connected directly with fragment *a* of *I.G.*, I², 50, and that the two fragments together gave a very nearly complete board of Athenian generals. I am indebted to Wade-Gery for giving to me in advance of publication the results of his research upon these two fragments and for his restoration, which I accept as substantially correct and which I repeat here:

[στ]ρατεγ[οὶ ὄμνυον τὸν ḥόρκον: Σοκράτες ᾽Ερε]
χθείδος: Δεμ[οκλείδες Αἰγείδος: Φορμίον Πα]
νδιονίδος: Χ[. . . . .¹⁰. . . . . Λεοντίδος: Περικλ]
ês: Γλαύκον ᾽Α[καμαντίδος: Καλλ]ί[στρατος ḥοι]
νείδος: Χσε[νοφôν Κεκροπίδ]ος: Τλεμπ[όλεμος]
[Αἰαντίδος: . . . . ᾽Αντιοχίδο]s: βολὲ êρχε ḥό[τε]
[. . . . . . . .¹⁶. . . . . . . πρôτ]ος ἐγραμμάτευε ῾Ρα
[μνόσιος]

I give in Figure 5 and Figure 6 respectively photographs of fragments *d* and *a*, and in Figure 7 a facsimile of the restored document with restorations indicated in red. My own text differs significantly from that of Wade-Gery only in the last lines.

Luria's suggestion (*op. cit.*) that the older fragment should be dated in the time of Cleisthenes and that Tlempolemos, mentioned in line 5, was possibly the grandfather of the Tlempolemos who served as general in the Samian War can no longer be entertained. The names of the generals listed in this document show

[1] See also S. Luria, "Zur Geschichte der Präskripte in den voreuklidischen Volksbeschlüssen," *Hermes*, LXII (1927), 265–270.

[2] H. T. Wade-Gery, "Strategoi in the Samian War," *Cl. Phil.*, XXVI (1931), 309–313.

that it must be dated very close in point of time to the period of the Samian War.

The names of the generals for the year 441/0 are known. Eight of the ten members of the strategic board are listed by Androtion,[1] and the names of the other two were added by Wilamowitz from Marcianus.[2] The complete list is given by Beloch,[3] as follows:

Σωκράτης 'Αναγυράσιος	I
Σοφοκλῆς Σοφίλλου ἐκ Κολωνοῦ	II
'Ανδοκίδης Λεωγόρου Κυδαθηναιεύς	III
Κρέων Σκαμβωνίδης	IV
Περικλῆς Ξανθίππου Χολαργεύς	V
Γλαύκων Λεάγρου ἐκ Κεραμέων	V
Καλλίστρατος 'Αχαρνεύς	VI
Ξενοφῶν Εὐριπίδου Μελιτεύς	VII
Γλαυκέτης 'Αζηνιεύς	VIII
Κλειτοφῶν Θοραιεύς	X

In this list the ninth tribe Aiantis has no representative, while the fifth tribe is represented twice, by Pericles and Glaukon. In *I.G.*, I², 50 the eighth tribe Hippothontis has no representative, and the fifth tribe Akamantis again has the same double representation. The generals Socrates, Pericles, Glaukon, Kallistratos, and Xenophon appear in both lists. It is evident, however, that the two lists cannot both belong to the same year.

In his account of the Samian War, Thucydides (I, 117, 2) has given the names of six of the Athenian leaders who commanded the fleet. We know that Pericles was one of the generals. Mention is made of the others in such a way that we cannot be certain they all belonged to the board of *strategoi*. The reinforcements which came to Samos from Athens are referred to as αἱ μετὰ Θουκυδίδου καὶ "Αγνωνος καὶ Φορμίωνος νῆες and αἱ μετὰ Τληπολέμου καὶ 'Αντικλέους (νῆες). The men themselves are not named specifically as strategoi. But it is, nevertheless, commonly held that those names partly represent the board of generals of the

---

[1] *F.H.G.*, IV, 645 [Müller]; Aristeides, III, 485 [ed. Dindorf], and scholia.

[2] Ulrich von Wilamowitz-Moellendorff, *De Rhesi scholiis*, Progr. Greifswald, 1877, p. 13. The name Γλαυκέτης 'Αζηνιεύς appears in the manuscript of Marcianus as Κλαυκέτης 'Αθηναῖος.   [3] J. Beloch, *Gr. Gesch.*, II², 2, p. 261.

FIG. 5.   Fragment *d* of *I.G.*, I², 50

FIG. 6.   Fragment *a* of *I.G.*, I², 50

ΣΤΡΑΤΕΛΟΙΟΜΝΥΟΝΤΟΝΗΟΡΚΟΝ∶ΣΟΚΡΑΤΕΣΕΡΕ
ΧΘΕΙΔΟΣ∶ΔΕΜΟΚΛΕΙΔΕΣΑΙΛΕΙΔΟΣ∶ΦΟΡΜΙΟΝΓΑ
ΝΔΙΟΝΙΔΟΣ∶Χ   ΛΕΟΝΤΙΔΟΣ∶ΠΕΡΙΚΛ
ΕΣ∶ΛΑΥΚΟΝΑΚΑΜΑΝΤΙΔΟΣ∶ΚΑΛΛΙΣΤΡΑΤΟΣΗΟΙ
ΝΕΙΔΟΣ∶ΧΣΕΝΟΦΟΝΚΕΚΡΟΠΙΔΟΣ∶ΤΛΕΜΠΟΛΕΜΟΣ
ΑΙΑΝΤΙΔΟΣ∶   ΑΝΤΙΟΧΙΔΟΣ∶ΒΟΛΕΕΡΧΕΤΟΝΕ
ΝΙΑΥΤΟΝΗΟΤΕ   ΓΡΟΤΟΣΕΛΡΑΜΜΑΤΕΥΕΡΑ
ΜΝΟΣΙΟΣ

FIG. 7.   Drawing of fragments *d* + *a* of *I.G.*, I², 50, with restorations in red

[51]

year 440/39, and they are so quoted by Beloch (*op. cit.*). The list cannot be reconciled with that given by Androtion for the Samian War, and the universal assumption has been that the list given by Androtion belonged, therefore, to the year when the

FIG. 8.   Fragment *b* of *I.G.*, I², 50

war began (441/0), rather than to the year of the siege. This argument is sound, and may be applied with equal validity in determining the date of the list given in *I.G.*, I², 50.

If we hold that the commanders named by Thucydides were strategoi, then the college of generals named in *I.G.*, I², 50 cannot be assigned to either of the years 441/0 or 440/39, because of conflicts with both Androtion and Thucydides.

But we also know that *I.G.*, I², 50 cannot be assigned to 440/39 because the first secretary of the Council is given in fragment *a* of this inscription with the demotic 'Ρα[μνόσιος].[1] Our restoration of *I.G.*, I², 293 has shown that the first secretary of the Council in 440/39 was ['Αρχ]ῖνος Περαι[εύς].

We can only conclude that *I.G.*, I², 50 must be dated in the early part of the year 439/8, and that the ratification of the treaty of peace between Athens and Samos was consummated at an interval of some months after the conclusion of the war.

There is nothing surprising in this delay. The alliance between Perdikkas and Athens, which had its inception in the agreement between Perdikkas and the Athenian generals in the field in the autumn of 423 (Thuc. IV, 132), was not consummated

---

[1] Cf. Wade-Gery, "Strategoi in the Samian War," *Cl. Phil.*, XXVI (1931), 312. The letters PA have now been broken from the stone since its first discovery, but they have the authority of two competent epigraphists, Lolling (*I.G.*, I¹, Suppl. p. 125, no. 557) and Wilhelm.

by formal alliance until the spring of 422 (*I.G.*, I², 71 and commentary). Another instance of long deliberation before the ratification of a treaty is found in the negotiations between Argos and Athens, which extended from the summer of 417 to the spring of 416.[1] Even in the case of the alliance between Athens and Samos here under discussion the deliberations doubtless took

FIG. 9.   Fragment *c* of *I.G.*, I², 50

considerable time. I suggest as a probable date for the formalities of final ratification (*I.G.*, I², 50) the Panathenaic festival in Athens in the summer of 439.

The inscription records, therefore, not one of the boards of generals which participated in the fighting before Samos, but the board which entered upon its duties shortly after the conclusion of the war and which was in office at the time of ratification of the treaty of peace.

I give here photographs (Figures 8–9) of fragments *b* and *c* of *I. G.*, I², 50, which contain the terms of the peace and the oath of the Samians and Athenians. Some slight corrections must be made in the accepted text. In *I. G.*, I², 50, line 10, we must read

---

[1] Kolbe, "Das athenisch-argivische Bündnis von 416 v. Chr. G.," *Cl. Phil.*, XXV (1930), 105–116.

ΑΓΙ instead of ΑΝΙ, and at the end of line 22 the letters preserved seem to be ΟΥΤΕ∟[.]. Since fragments *a* and *d* have been restored with a length of line of thirty-five letters, we posit the same number of letters in each line of fragments *b* and *c* as well. Instead of the readings now given in the *Corpus* for fragment *c* we might suggest, for example, the following:

21 [— — — — — — — — — — — –κ]αὶ ἀ[γ]αθόν, [οὐδὲ ἀ]
    [ποστέσομαι ἀπὸ τὸ δέμο τὸ ᾿Α]θεναίον οὔτε λ[ό]
    [γοι οὔτε ἔργοι οὐδὲ ἀπὸ τὸν] χσυμμάχον τὸν ᾿Α
    [θεναίον, καὶ ἔσομαι πιστὸς τ]ôι δέμοι τôι ᾿Αθ
25 [εναίον. — — — — — —].

A complete restoration of the fragment seems difficult. We may note in passing that fragment *c* of *I.G.*, I², 50 is also published in the *Corpus* as *I.G.*, I², 102 under the erroneous date 412/1, where the readings at the end of line 22 have, however, been correctly given.

I am indebted to Homer Thompson for careful measurement of the thickness of the various fragments which make up this inscription. His observations show a regular increase in thickness of the marble toward the bottom of the stele, and enable us to say with some certainty that the first line of text in fragments *a* and *d* ([στ]ρατεγ[οὶ ὄμνυον τὸν hόρκον: Σοκράτες ᾿Ερε]) is in fact the sixteenth line below – – –κρατε. . . . . , now read as line 29 of fragment *c*.[1]

We have found that the date of our document must fall in the early part of the calendar year 439/8, and that the first secretary of the Council was from Rhamnus. This determination is in apparent conflict with the evidence of *I.G.*, I², 347, where the demotic of the first secretary of the Council has been restored as [Περγ]ασῆθεν in line 3. The conflict is only apparent, however, for the formula at the top of Col. V in *I.G.*, I², 347, which names the secretary of the ἀρχή and the first secretary of the Council, should be restored in lines 1 and 2 instead of in lines 2 and 3. The fact that fragment *U* of *I.G.*, I², 347 is uninscribed above the letters now preserved in line 2 merely indicates that the first

---

[1] Cf. also Wade-Gery, "Strategoi in the Samian War," *Cl. Phil.*, XXVI (1931), 311–312.

line of the date did not extend this distance to the right. Since
we now know that the first secretary of the Council in 439/8 was
from Rhamnus, we restore lines 1 and 2 of *I.G.*, I², 347 in such
a way that these final letters – – IOϟ form part of the demotic
['Ραμνόσ]ιος:

[ἐπὶ τῆς ἐνάτες ἀρχῆς h̔ει – – – – – – – – ἐγραμμάτευε] *vacat*

[– – – ^demotic ±8 – – – τει βολει – – ∓5 – – πρῶτος ἐγραμμάτευε 'Ραμνόσ]ιος

This is the disposition which appears in the initial lines of the
record of the following year, *I.G.*, I², 348. We are, unfortunately,
not able to make a certain determination of the length of the
name of the first secretary, though it is clear that the same name
must have appeared both here and in the next to the last line of
I.G., I², 50 (fragment *a*, line 4). Wade-Gery suggests that the
sixteen letter spaces available in *I.G.*, I², 50 were probably filled
by the name and the patronymic of the secretary. If this is true,
the name must have been given without patronymic in *I.G.*,
I², 347.

But it is difficult to be satisfied with this solution of the problem. In the first place, an unnatural order of words is required by
the restoration βολὲ ἐρχε h̔ό[τε . . . . ^nomen, nomen patris . . . . πρῶτ]ος
ἐγραμμάτευε 'Ρα|[μνόσιος]. The restoration is, of course, not
impossible, but a more normal order would have been achieved
by placing the demotic immediately after the patronymic.
Where there is an evident division of the name, as here, it is a
reasonable supposition that the name was recorded without
patronymic at all. But no single name can be supplied which will
occupy the available space of sixteen letters. Another objection
to the present rendering is the restoration h̔ό[τε – – –]. The
formula of date here employed cannot be paralleled exactly elsewhere. In *I.G.*, I², 5, where the text is usually cited in this connection, the reading is not the same: [ἔδοχσ]εν [:τει βολει]: καὶ
[τ]ôι δέμοι: h̔ό[τ]ε Παραιβάτε[ς ἐγραμμάτευε]. Nor is the same
construction found in the decree from 410 given by Andocides
(I, 96), which is also cited as a parallel case: ἄρχει χρόνος τοῦδε
τοῦ ψηφίσματος ἡ βουλὴ οἱ πεντακόσιοι ⟨οἱ⟩ λαχόντες τῷ κυάμῳ, ὅτε
Κλεογένης πρῶτος ἐγραμμάτευεν. Our only authority for the reading of the letters HO, which are now restored as part of the word
h̔ό[τε], comes from Lolling, for he alone saw the stone before

these letters were broken away. Lolling's transcript, however, does not give HO; in place of the H it has merely a single vertical stroke, broken away at the top, and so spaced laterally that it should be completed as T rather than as H (*I.G.*, I¹, Suppl., p. 125, no. 557). Kirchhoff's rendering in the first edition of the *Corpus* gives the restoration accordingly, as βουλὴ ἦρχε τοῦ *vel* τῶ[ν – –]. We may be confident that this reading is correct and that it should be retained. I suggest that the complete restoration should be βολὲ ἔρχε τὸ[ν ἐ|νιαυτὸν hότε . . .⁵ . . πρῶτ]ος ἐγραμμάτευε ῾Ρα|[μνόσιος]. We may now supply the same word of five letters for the name of the secretary both in *I.G.*, I², 50 and in *I.G.*, I², 347.

CHAPTER V

RECORDS OF EXPENSES OF STATE

THE character of the restoration suggested in the previous chapter for the inscription containing the accounts of the Samian War makes it seem advisable to give here a brief discussion of the history of these records. When money was borrowed by the Athenian state for the expenses of war there appears invariably the formula of introduction 'Αθεναῖοι ἀνέλοσαν – – –, with the date of the document given by both archon and first secretary of the Council.[1] The only exception to this type of introductory formula is found in *I.G.*, I², 298, which records expenses during the régime of the Four Hundred, when the regular Council had been disbanded. In this document, therefore, there is no mention of date by the first secretary of the Council. These inscriptions, from *I.G.*, I², 293 to *I.G.*, I², *309a*, inclusive, have all been given in the *editio minor* of the *Corpus* under the category *Tabulae Quaestorum Minervae*. This designation is only partly correct, for the documents with which we are dealing do not in any case give the complete record of the monetary transactions of the treasurers of the goddess in the same way that the records of treasure in the Pronaos, Hekatompedon, and Parthenon (*I.G.*, I², 232–292*b*) account for the stewardship of the sacred objects preserved in the temple.[2]

The expense accounts which have come down to us are invariably the expense accounts of the Athenian state; they do not list items other than those involving sums of money loaned by the treasurers to the state. That the items so recorded were actually loans, and not outright grants of money, is amply proved

[1] *I.G.*, I², 293 (cf. p. 47, above); *I.G.*, I², 295, 296, 297, 302, 304.

[2] I have already made reference (*The Athenian Calendar*, pp. 17 and 95–96) to this distinction, which should be generally recognized, between the records of money borrowed by the state from Athena's treasure and the records of the treasurers of Athena which covered their transactions during tenure of office, and on which they stood their audit. It is a question whether this latter type of record was ever published. No examples from the fifth century are known to us. Cf. Ferguson, *The Treasurers of Athena*, p. 16.

by the reckonings of the logistai preserved in *I.G.*, I², 324. We find that interest was carefully computed on each one of the payments made and that totals of principal and interest were drawn at the end of the fiscal year. At the end of each four-year period there was given a summary of amounts of principal and interest due from the state to the treasurers of Athena.[1] There is no record of how much money was received from the previous board and how large a balance was handed on to the succeeding board. The treasurers do not list the sums received within the year (ἐπέτεια), nor sums expended during the year, except the loans to the state. It is of no consequence in our present analysis that some of the inscriptions indicate whether money was loaned to the state out of income or out of reserve received from the foregoing board,[2] and that occasionally other indications are given as to the source from which expended funds were drawn.[3]

These records, therefore, are not primarily records of the treasurers of Athena at all, but records of money borrowed by the Athenian state from the treasurers of Athena. It is noteworthy that the records in the years from 418/7 to 416/5 (*I.G.* I², 302) are arranged as annual accounts, with the payments listed in chronological order within the year. This method of ordering the account differs from that of earlier records (e.g. *I.G.*, I², 296) in that the chronological sequence is observed throughout the document even though the money is expended for different purposes. In *I.G.*, I², 296 (432/1) the expenses for Macedonia and Potidaea are listed first (in chronological order within the rubric),[4] and then a separate category is added for expenses paid to the fleet. These later expenses are also listed

---

[1] The technical term used for a payment is δόσις (cf. *I.G.*, I², 324, and also 296, 300).

[2] *I.G.*, I², 304, line 3; *I.G.*, I², 301, *passim* (especially the phrases: ἐκ τὸ ἐπετείο hō αὐτοὶ χσυνελέχσαμεν, and, for example, ἀργυρίο hō παρελάβομεν παρὰ τὸν πρότερον ταμιõν).

[3] E.g. [ἐχς ’Οπισθ]οδόμο (*I.G.*, I², 324, line 20), ἐκ τοῦ ’Οπ[ισ]θοδόμο[υ] (*I.G.*, I², 305, line 13), [παρὰ Σα]μίον (*I.G.*, I², 297, line 16. Cf. p. 89), [παρὰ] Σαμ[ίον] (*I.G.*, I², 324, line 42, cf. p. 139), and distinctions between the treasure of Athena Polias and Athena Nike (e.g. *I.G.*, I², 298, lines 19 and 21). That distinctions were made in these records between moneys loaned by Athena Nike and Athena Polias is, in part, the justification for the restoration in *I.G.*, I², 293, line 8, proposed on p. 47, above.

[4] Cf. also Kolbe, *Thukydides im Lichte der Urkunden*, Stuttgart, 1930, pp. 19–22.

chronologically within the rubric. We do not know whether other categories of expense appeared in *I.G.*, I², 296, for the lower portion of the stone is now broken away, but it is certainly possible that the account was still further subdivided.[1] In the account of the year 433/2 (*I.G.*, I², 295) the record is distinctly topical. It is true that the two payments for the ships sent to Corcyra are the only ones recorded, but the introductory formula is significant: ['Αθεναῖοι ἀνέλ]οσαν ἐς Κόρκ[υραν τάδε - - -]. These two payments were made by different boards of treasurers of Athena, and belong, consequently, to different Panathenaic years.

This topical introductory formula of *I.G.*, I², 295 may be contrasted with the typically annual formula of *I.G.*, I², 302, line 24: Ἀθεναῖοι ἀνέλοσαν ἐ[πὶ Εὐφέμο ἄρ]χοντος καὶ [ἐπὶ τες βολες hει . . . . ⁹ . . . . πρ]ότος ἐγραμμάτευε.[2] Even where the annual formula was employed, there was at times a tendency to arrange the payments recorded during the year in topical rather than in strictly chronological order. This is evident from a study of *I.G.*, I², 302, lines 61-79.[3] The two payments for the soldiers at Melos were listed together, although in violation of strict chronological sequence, and the payments for Sicily were then listed together following them.

It is important to notice that in the earlier records the significant fact is not so much that the moneys were expended during a given year, but rather that there are grouped together those moneys spent for a given purpose. The record for Corcyra forms in this regard an intermediate link between the later annual records and the record for the campaign against Samos, as the text has been restored on p. 47, above. It has been thought heretofore that the words 'Αθεναῖοι ἀ[νέλοσαν - - - - -] in line 6 of *I.G.*, I², 293 implied the beginning of the expense account of a new year, different from that represented in lines 1-5.[4]

[1] Cf. Wade-Gery, "An Attic Inscription of the Archidamian War," *J.H.S.*, L (1930), 292.

[2] Meritt, "The Departure of Alcibiades for Sicily," *A.J.A.*, XXXIV (1930), Plate II, line 23. For the present numbering of the lines in the inscription cf. pp. 160 ff.

[3] For the text cf. Meritt, *op. cit.*, Plate II; also Plate XIII at the end of this volume, and pp. 160-163.

[4] *I.G.*, I², 293; cf. commentary in *Corpus*: "- - inde a v. 6 novi anni fieri initium manifestum est [Kirchh.]- -."

We now see that this interpretation is not at all necessary. In fact, it is more in harmony with the change in record from the topical to the purely chronological arrangement, traceable through *I.G.*, I², 295, 296, and 302, to assume that the words Ἀθεναῖοι ἀ[νέλοσαν - - - -] of *I.G.*, I², 293 indicate merely the new purpose for which the moneys then listed were spent. There is no reason for believing that items following line 6 were spent during any one year. We have found rather that the expenses which followed should be assigned to both years of the Samian War, each of the two figures being considered as a total for one year. Within the rubric [- - ἐς τὸν] | πρὸς Σαμίο[ς πόλεμον - - -] the correct chronological sequence was preserved, but outside the rubric, as in lines 1–5, there is no certainty, from this record alone, whether the expenses should be attributed to 441/0 or 440/39, or indeed to some year even earlier. It has been our conjecture that the moneys listed in lines 1–5 were spent against Byzantium and that these lines should therefore be assigned to one of the two years represented by the latter part of the document.

Between 441/0 and the end of the century there seems to have been a steady change in the character of the records following the introductory formula Ἀθεναῖοι ἀνέλοσαν - -. The early records were topical, covering one or more years (*I.G.*, I², 293); subsequent records were likewise topical, but confined to the expenses of one year only (*I.G.*, I², 295, 296). It appears from *I.G.*, I², 295 that this year was not the year of the Panathenaic interval, but rather the year of the archon or of the Council. This point cannot be decided from *I.G.*, I², 295 alone, but other evidence shows that the year involved was the year of the Council, the so-called senatorial or conciliar year.[1]

The next type of record is the annual account, such as *I.G.*, I², 302, with items listed in chronological order, in the main without reference to topical distribution.

In the records subsequent to 411, there is a tendency to include within the chronological framework of the year a subdivision indicating whether the expenses were drawn from reserves or from yearly income. Ferguson's studies of the treasur-

[1] Meritt, "Senatorial and Civil Years in Athens," *Cl. Phil.*, XXV (1930), 236–243.

ers of Athena have yielded the date 409/8 for the much-disputed inscription *I.G.*, I², 301.[1] We find in this inscription that every item is recorded either as ἐκ τὸ ἐπετείο hὸ αὐτοὶ χσυνελέχσαμεν ἀργύριον – – – or as hὸ παρελάβομεν παρὰ τὸν προτέρον ταμιὸν. There is, however, no separate section of the document devoted to expenses from the ἐπέτεια, with another separate section devoted to expenses from reserve. We note merely that the distinction is made and that items of both categories are interwoven into the chronological framework of the inscription.

Wade-Gery has proposed new and important restorations in this document, some of them principally by way of example.[2] I add the following new readings to those already proposed by him:[3]

Line 3: [– – – – ἐκ τὸ ἐπ]ετείο hὸ αὐτοὶ χ[συνε]

Line 8: [– – – – τ]ὸν ἐπετείον αὐτοὶ hὸν

Lines 13–15: [– – – – – – – –]Ͱ ἐκ τὸ Παρθενῶνος ἀρ[γυρ | ίο – – – – – – – ἐπετ]είο hὸ hοι χσύμμαχοι [ἀνο | μολογέσαντο – – – – – – – –]ͰΤΧΧΧΧ Ἀθεναίας Ν[ίκες]. Cf. Wade-Gery, *op. cit.*, p. 18, and *I.G.*, I², 304, line 34 (as given on p. 96, below).

Lines 18–20: [– – – – – Κε]φισ[ο]δότοι [᾽Αγκυλε]εῖ Πολυ^v | [– – – – – – – hὸν παρελάβομ]εν παρὰ τὸν προτέρον ταμιὸν | [– – – – – – – – – – – – – –]ΤΤΗΗΓͰ hέτερον τε͂ι αὐτε͂ι ἐ[^v]. There was a tendency in this part of the inscription to divide words at the ends of lines syllabically.

Line 23: [– – – – – – –]ε[ς π]ρυτανευόσες hελλενοτ[α^v].

Lines 25–27: [– – – – – – – –]ΗΗΓΔΔΔΔͰͰⅠⅠ hέτερο[ν^v | τε͂ι αὐτε͂ι ἐμέραι – – – – – – – – – – – χσυ]μ[πέρα]σμα σταθμὸν ΧΓ hέτ[ε^v]|ρον τε͂ι αὐτε͂ι ἐμέραι – – – – –] σταθμὸν ΓͰΗΗΗΓͰͰⅠⅠⅠⅠ^vv.

Line 32: The numeral is ͰΓΔΔ.

Lines 36–42: [– – – – –]σι παρέδομεν πέμπτε[ι | – – – – – – – –]ε

[1] Ferguson, *The Treasurers of Athena*, pp. 16–37. For an earlier dating cf. Wade-Gery, "An Attic Inscription of the Archidamian War," *J.H.S.*, L (1930), 293; *idem*, "The Ratio of Silver to Gold during the Peloponnesian War: *I.G.*, I², 301," *Num. Chron.*, X, Series V (1930), 17.

[2] Wade-Gery, "The Ratio of Silver to Gold during the Peloponnesian War: *I.G.*, I², 301," *Num. Chron.*, X, Series V (1930), 16–38 and 333–334.

[3] Through the courtesy of the British Museum I am able to give photographs of the preserved portion of this stone in Plates XIV–XVI. A facsimile also is given in Plate XVII.

[. .]\ι ἀργύριον ἐπίσεμο[ν. | ‒ ‒ ‒ ‒ ‒ ‒ ‒ ‒ ‒ κα]ὶ κ[ατ]ὰ γὲν καὶ κατὰ
θάλ[αττ^v|αν ‒ ‒ ‒ ‒ ‒ ‒ ‒ ‒ 'Επ]ι[κό]ροι Κοπρείοι ἀρ[γύριον | ‒ ‒ ‒
‒ ‒ ‒ ἐκ τὸ ἐπετείο hὸ αὐτοὶ χσυνελέχσα]μεν ꓷꓷꓷΤΤΤΧΧ[. .^{5}. . |
‒ ‒ ‒ ‒ ‒ ‒ ‒ ‒ Φ]λυεῖ ΤΤΤ ἐπὶ [τὲς . .^{5}. . | ‒ ‒ ‒ ‒ ‒ ‒ ‒ ‒ ‒ ‒
'Επικ]ό[ροι Κ]οπρείο[ι . . . . .^{11}. . . . .].

Lines 53–54: [‒ ‒ ‒ ‒ ‒ ‒ ‒] δεκαστά[σ]ιο[ν χρυ]σίο φθο[ῖδα^v|s
‒ ‒ ‒ ‒ ‒ σταθμὸν το]ύτον ΤΧΧΧΗΗΗꓑ.Δ. [ἀ]ργ[ύ]ριο[ν^v].

Lines 55–56: Read παρελ^v|[άβομεν ‒ ‒ ‒ ‒].

Line 59: The numeral is ꞪꞪꓩꓷꓷ.

Above the now recorded lines of the lateral face, at the very
top of the stone, are the clearly cut strokes of [.]ΙΟꙄ, which
have never been read before. After these letters the stone is
uninscribed down as far as line 64. These letters must be restored as part of a prescript giving the date of the summations
below. I suggest that the normal stoichedon line of twenty-one
letters was here employed and that the customary formula of
date should be supplied:

['Αθεναῖοι ἀνέλοσαν ἐπὶ Δι]   409/8 B.C.
[οκλέος ἄρχοντος καὶ ἐπὶ τ]
[ὲς βολὲς hὲι Νικοφάνες πρ]
[ὸτος ἐγραμμάτευε Μαραθό]
[ν]ιος
vacat 0.07 m.

Line 69: [. .]το hερμ[ὸ ‒ ‒ ‒ ‒ ‒].
Line 79: The numeral seems to be [.]ꓑΤꗘꓑΗΗ.
Lines 89–124: The readings have been given by Wade-Gery,
op. cit., pp. 37–38.

The inscription *I.G.*, I², 304 preserves on its obverse face the
accounts of the year 410/09, dated both by archon and by first
secretary of the Council. It is to be noted, however, that all the
expenses listed on the preserved portion of the stone are from
the yearly income. The preamble reads as follows:

'Αθεναῖοι ἀνέλοσαν ἐπὶ Γλαυκίππο ἄρχοντος καὶ ἐπὶ τὲς βολὲς ἑι
    Κλεγένες hαλαιεὺς πρὸτ[ος]
ἐγραμμάτευε· ταμίαι hιερὸγ χρεμάτον τὲς 'Αθεναίας Καλλίστρατος
    Μαραθόνιος καὶ χσυνάρχο[ν]
τες παρέδοσαν ἐκ τὸν ἐπετείον φσεφισαμένο τὸ δέμο· ‒ ‒ ‒ ‒ ‒ ‒

Since the last line of the document (line 40) is followed by an uninscribed space equivalent in height to one line of text, it is evident that whatever summation appears at the conclusion of the record must be restored at the end of line 40 and beginning of line 40 *bis*, where the stone is now broken away. This restoration must be somewhat as follows: κεφάλαιον ἀργυρίο σύμπαν ὃ Κ[αλλίστρατος Μαραθόνιος | καὶ συνάρχοντες παρέδοσαν - - - $\overset{c.\ 9}{- -}$ - - -] *vacat*. If we are to assume that the record of 410/09 was continued below this point, it would be necessary to limit the summation to expenses from income alone, leaving the rest of the record for expenses from reserve. But it is impossible to restore the concluding lines of the preserved inscription to conform to this interpretation. If it is assumed that lines 40 and 40 *bis* read: κεφάλαιον ἀργυρίο σύμπαν ὃ Κ[αλλίστρατος Μαραθόνιος | καὶ συνάρχοντες παρέδοσαν ἐκ τὸν ἐπετείον - - - $\overset{summa\ pecuniae}{- - - - - - - -}$ -], then the final letters of the word ἐπετείον and the entire figure for the sum total of money would fall on that part of the stone where the surface is at present preserved uninscribed. A facsimile of the record for 410/09 is given in Plate VI.

The conclusion seems inevitable that the loans to the state in 410/09 were all made from yearly income, and that there were no loans from reserve. We may question whether in this year there even existed such a reserve.[1] There is evidence in Thucydides VIII, 76, 6 that the treasurers of 410/09 inherited a treasury practically empty, and Ferguson has shown that the purpose of a decree passed in the third prytany of 410/09 (*I.G.*, I², 109) was the establishment of a reserve fund. That this reserve fund existed in 409/8 and was used to defray the expenses of the war along with income from current revenue is clear from the itemized account of expenses preserved in *I.G.*, I², 301.

Only a part of the obverse and the right lateral face of *I.G.*, I², 301 has been preserved. The obverse contained the record of current expenses of the year arranged in chronological order; the right lateral face contained the summary of silver and gold listed on the obverse. The record of the year 408/7 was probably inscribed on the reverse side of the stele which has come down to us as *I.G.*, I², 301. No fragments of this record are now

---

[1] Ferguson, *The Treasurers of Athena*, pp. 29–35.

preserved, except possibly *I.G.*, I², 307. We expect the record of expenses for 407/6 upon a separate stele, but find instead that it was cut on the reverse of *I.G.*, I², 304. Even so the beginning of the account for this year is lost, and we may assume that it appeared on the obverse, below the record of 410/09, where the stone is now broken away. The accounts for 406/5 (*I.G.*, I², 305) were again inscribed on a separate stele, as were also those of 405/4 (*I.G.*, II², 1686).¹ These last inscriptions record expenses from current income followed by a separate category for expenses from reserve (τάδε ἐκ τοῦ Ὀπ[ισ]θοδόμο[υ παρ]έδομε[ν] *I.G.*, I², 305).²

It is noticeable that the annual records of the earlier years (*I.G.*, I², 296) were inscribed separately upon one face of a marble stele, and not grouped in sequences of four years representing a Panathenaic quadrennium, as were the records of 418/7–415/4 (*I.G.*, I², 302). After the reëstablishment of complete democracy in 410, the longer records of the last years of the century were also separately inscribed (*I.G.*, I², 304, 305, *I.G.*, II², 1686), though with some confusion due to a strict necessity for economy in the use of stone. In the intervening years the evidence points to publication by Panathenaic intervals, as was the case with *I.G.*, I², 302.

Bannier's proof that *I.G.*, I², 297 must be assigned to the year 414/3 supports this interpretation.³ This inscription was cut on the reverse face of the stone which contains on its obverse the record of the year 432/1 (*I.G.*, I², 296). It commences at the top of the stone and continues for seventeen lines, after which there is an uninscribed space of approximately two lines. These seventeen lines contain, therefore, the complete record for the year. We may reasonably suppose that after a brief lacuna the records for the other years of the quadrennium were inscribed. The fourth year of this particular Panathenaic interval was disturbed by revolution and counter-revolution in Athens. The accounts of the treasurers who held office during the régime of the Four Hundred could not have been listed until after the

---

¹ For the date cf. Ferguson, *op. cit.*, pp. 18, 28, 77.

² Cf. Ferguson, *op. cit.*, p. 29.

³ Bannier, "Zu attischen Inschriften," *Berl. ph. Woch.*, 1915, p. 1613; Meritt, "The Departure of Alcibiades for Sicily," *A.J.A.*, XXXIV (1930), 144.

overthrow of the oligarchy. We find, in fact, that this record has been inscribed on the lateral face of the same stone, where it is now preserved as *I.G.*, I², 298. Below *I.G.*, I², 297 on the reverse, we may place the records of 413/2, 412/1, and of that part of 411/0 after the dissolution of the Four Hundred.[1]

The records of the logistai preserve for us the items for the years 426/5–423/2, another period of four years. These items listed by the logistai depend, of course, on the record of state expenses from moneys of Athena similar to *I.G.*, I², 302 and *I.G.*, I², 297, and we may postulate such a document, now lost, for the Panathenaic interval in question. Or it may be that the inscription giving the reckonings of the logistai was considered in itself a sufficient publication of these accounts. We shall be certain only when, if ever, some fragment of the record of borrowings from 426/5 to 423/2 is discovered in the course of archaeological exploration.

We have still to discover the stele containing the record of borrowings in the four years from 422/1 to 419/8. The record of borrowings in the four years from 430/29 to 427/6 is represented by one fragment only (*I.G.*, I², 300) which can be assigned with certainty, now incorrectly dated in 425/4 (?).

The text of *I.G.*, I², 300 is given here with the restorations recorded in the *Corpus*. The lines have been renumbered, and the new reading of line 11 depends upon a reëxamination by Kirchner of the manuscript of Mustoxydes. Kirchner informs me (by letter): "Ich habe an der Hand von Mustoxydes' Abschrift festgestellt, dass er in der Tat in Zeile 6 ein *vacat* hat. Im Übrigen hat Kirchhoff IG I 187 die Maiuskeln von Mustoxydes getreu wiedergegeben. Lediglich Z. 11 besteht eine Differenz. Hier hat Mustoxydes TOYTOTOXPONOY."

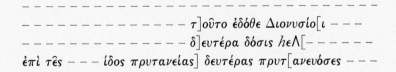

----

[1] There is no reason to believe with Bannier, "Weitere Bemerkungen zu den attischen Rechnungs- und Übergabeurkunden," *Rh. Mus.*, LXV (1910), 6, that the record on the reverse of this stele could hardly have covered a period of four years. Cf. also Ferguson, *The Treasurers of Athena*, p. 101, note.

<pre>
5 ─ ─ ─ ─ ─ ─ ─ ─ ─ ─ ─ ─ ─ ─ τὸ τοῖς [ἐ]κκα[ί]δ[εκα? ─ ─ ─
                             vacat
   ─ ─ ─ ─ ─ ─ ─ ─ ─ ─ ─ ─ πα]ρέδομέν α─ ─ ─ ─ ─ ─
   ─ ─ ─ ─ ─ ─ ─ ─ ─ ─ ─ ─ ─ ἐμέρα[ι λ]ο[ί]παὶ ἐσα[ν ─ ─ ─ ─
   ─ ─ ─ ─ ─ ─ ─ ─ ─ ─ ─ ─ ─ ΤΑΙΜΟΙΑΛΒΟΙΕΣΕ
10 ─ ─ ─ ─ ─ ─ ─ ─ ─ ─ ─ ─ ─ ΙΟΝΤΟΝΕΛΒΟΙΕΣΛ
   ─ ─ ─ ─ ─ ─ ─ ─ ─ ─ ─ ─ ─ τούτο τõ χρόνο(υ) ─ ─ ─ ─
   ─ ─ ─ ─ ─ ─ ─ ─ ─ ─ ─ ─ ─ ε τοῦτο ἐς τὰ ─ ─ ─ ─ ─ ─
   ─ ─ ─ ─ ─ ─ ─ ─ ─ ─ ─ ─ ─ ἐπὶ τῆς Παν[διονίδος πρυτανείας ─ ─
   ─ ─ ─ ─ ─ ─ ─ ─ ─ ─ ─ hελλεν]οταμίασ[ι ─ ─ ─ ─ ─ ─
</pre>

This inscription has the characteristic formulae of the records of the early part of the Archidamian War. In line 14 the form [hελλεν]οταμίασ[ι] appears in the dative case instead of the later [hελλεν]οταμίαι[s], as in *I.G.*, I², 324; days near the end of the prytany are reckoned from the last day with the formula ἐμέρα[ι λ]ο[ί]παὶ ἐσα[ν] (line 8) instead of from the first day of the prytany; and individual payments were described by the technical term δόσις, as in *I.G.*, I², 296 and 324. The words [δε]υτέρα δόσις hελ[λενοταμίασι] appear in line 3.

The inscription cannot be associated with *I.G.*, I², 296 and assigned to the year 432/1, since the campaigns about the Peloponnesus did not commence until the ninth prytany, while Pandionis is known to have held the third prytany of the year (*I.G.*, I², 296, line 10). Nor can the inscription be assigned to 431/0, to which year Wade-Gery's combination of *I.G.*, I², 294 + 299 + 308 probably belongs.[1]

From a study of the small fragment itself, known to us unfortunately only through copies, it is evident that the payment made during the prytany of Pandionis was at least as late as the fourth in the series, if we assume the entire document to belong to one year. The disposition of the first payment is indicated by the first line, from which it appears that Dionysios was a general, according to the universal interpretation of this formula, and not a hellenotamias, as suggested by Hiller (cf. *I.G.*, I², 300, note).

---

[1] Wade-Gery, "An Attic Inscription of the Archidamian War," *J.H.S.*, L (1930), 288–293. Cf. below, p. 86.

The second payment was listed in line 3. In line 8 appears the numeral signifying the date of the third payment. We are compelled to admit that the payment in the prytany of Pandionis (line 13) could not have been, therefore, either the first, second, or third. This conclusion rests on the assumption that the record belongs to a single year, but it is difficult to see how this assumption can be avoided. Since the stone itself is lost, it is impossible to verify the existence of an uninscribed space in line 6, which might be taken as an indication that the record of one year was brought to a close with line 5 and that the record of another year began in line 7. But if this were the case, the first line of the new record should contain the formula ['Αθεναῖοι ἀνέλοσαν ἐπὶ – – – ἄρχοντος καὶ ἐπὶ τὲς βολὲς ℎὲι – – – – – πρῶτος ἐγραμμάτευε· τάδε πα]ρέδομεν – – –. Such a restoration cannot be made without assuming an extraordinarily long line of approximately one hundred letters. If we concede that the restoration is possible, we must conclude that the payment in the prytany of Pandionis was the second (or perhaps the third) of the new year and that there were only two payments made in the previous year.

The record of this inscription may now be compared with the known list of borrowings from Athena's treasure recorded in *I.G.*, I², 324 for the years 426/5–423/2.

I.G., I², 300 cannot belong in its entirety to the year 423/2, because in this year the second loan from Athena was made during the prytany of Pandionis (*I.G.*, I², 324, line 40). There are still greater difficulties in the way of assigning only the last eight lines of *I.G.*, I², 300 to 423/2 and the first four lines to 424/3. Though we may now assume that the payment in Pandionis (line 13) was the second payment of the year, to conform with the known sequence in 423/2 (*I.G.*, I², 324, line 40), it appears that the first payment was made during one of the last days of a prytany (*I.G.*, I², 300, line 8), whereas in 423/2 we know that the first payment was actually made on the eleventh day (*I.G.*, I², 324, line 39). Furthermore, the record of 424/3, as preserved in *I.G.*, I², 300, lines 1–5, would contain only two payments, whereas we find in *I.G.*, I², 324, lines 25–36, that there were actually four payments in this year.

The date 424/3 is impossible for *I.G.*, I², 300 because no payment during this year was made in the prytany of Pandionis (*I.G.*, I², 324, lines 25–36).

The now suggested date 425/4 may also be shown to be impossible. If the entire inscription is to be assigned to this year, we are compelled to assume four payments in a year in which we know there were only two (*I.G.*, I², 324, lines 16–24); if only the last lines of *I.G.*, I², 300 are to be attributed to 425/4, then we find only two payments in the record of 426/5, where we know there were six (*I.G.*, I², 324, lines 2–16). The year 426/5 is also impossible because of the fact that the third payment was made in the prytany of Pandionis (*I.G.*, I², 324, line 7) and the fourth payment in the prytany of Akamantis (*I.G.*, I², 324, line 9), whereas in *I.G.*, I², 300 we must attribute either the fourth or some later payment to Pandionis.

There is left only the possibility of dating *I.G.*, I², 300 somewhere in the quadrennium from 430/29 to 427/6, unless the items which it contains can be attributed to special rubrics at the end of *I.G.*, I², 296 (432/1), where the stone is now lost, or — what is still more improbable — to special rubrics in the upper lines of *I.G.*, I², 294 + 299 + 308 (431/0),[1] or to a list now entirely lost from the year 433/2.[2]

A brilliant monograph by Walther Kolbe[3] on the events leading up to the outbreak of the Peloponnesian War has served to show that the thirty ships sent to Macedonia under the command of Archestratos (Thuc. I, 57, 6) probably left Athens in late April or early May of 432 (*op. cit.*, pp. 33–34) and that the departure of Kallias from Athens (Thuc. I, 61–64) must also be dated before the beginning of the Athenian year 432/1 (*op. cit.*, pp. 32–33). If money was borrowed from the treasury of Athena to finance these expeditions, we must posit a record of such expenses for the expeditions to Macedonia in the year 433/2. At present, the only preserved record for the expenses of this year is that for the two expeditions sent to Corcyra (*I.G.*, I², 295).

[1] For the date cf. Wade-Gery, "An Attic Inscription of the Archidamian War," *J.H.S.*, L (1930), 288–293. For the text cf. pp. 84–85, below.

[2] We know of no occasion for a payment in the second prytany of 433/2. Cf. *I.G.*, I², 300, line 4.

[3] Kolbe, *Thukydides im Lichte der Urkunden*, Stuttgart, 1930.

This document is complete and makes no mention of expenses for the campaigns in the north. The fact that the record for Macedonia in this year must have been inscribed upon a separate stele lends additional force to our argument that these early records were in fact topical — *ad hoc* rather than *ad annum*.

The record of expenses for the two expeditions to Corcyra has been the subject of a recent paper by Jotham Johnson (*A.J.A.*, XXXIII [1929], 398–400), in which he was able to show that without exception the lines of text in *I.G.*, I², 295 end in complete words or syllables. He has thus effected some improvements in the text as reconstructed before his study was undertaken. I give a photograph of the preserved portion of *I.G.*, I², 295 in Figure 10, with a facsimile drawing in Figure 11. The text of the inscription follows:

I.G., I², 295 (433/2 B.C.)

```
    ['Αθεναῖοι ἀνέλ]οσαν ἐς Κόρκυρα[ν τάδε· ἐπὶ 'Α]
    [φσεύδος ἄρχο]ντος καὶ ἐπὶ τῆς βολῆς ἧι Κρ[ι]
    [τιάδες Φαένο] Τειθράσιος πρότος ἐγραμμά
    [τευε, ταμίαι h]ιερὸν χρεμάτον τῆς 'Αθεναία[ς]
 5  [. . .⁶. . . ἐκ Κερ]αμέον καὶ χσυνάρχοντες hοῖς
    [Κράτες Ναύ]πονος Λαμπτρεὺς ἐγραμμάτευε
    [παρέδοσα]ν στρατεγοῖς ἐς Κόρκυραν τοῖς
    [πρότοις ἐκ]πλέοσι Λακεδαιμονίοι Λακιά
    [δει, Προτέαι] Αἰχσονεῖ, Διοτίμοι Εὐονυμεῖ
10  [ἐπὶ τῆς Αἰαν]τίδος πρυτανείας πρότες πρυ
    [τανευόσες τ]ρῆς καὶ δέκα ἐμέραι ἐσελελυ
    [θυῖαι ἐσαν ΔΔ]⊩Τ vacat
    [ἐπὶ 'Αφσεύδος] ἄρχοντος καὶ ἐπὶ τῆς βολῆς
    [ἧι Κριτιάδες] Φαένο Τειθράσιος πρότος ἐ
15  [γραμμάτευε τα]μίαι hιερὸν χρεμάτον τῆς 'Α
    [θεναίας . . .⁶. . .]ες 'Ερχιεὺς καὶ χσυνάρχον
    [τες hοῖς Εὐθίας Αἴ]σχρονος 'Αναφλύστιος
    [ἐγραμμάτευε παρέ]δοσαν στρατεγοῖς ἐς Κόρ
    [κυραν τοῖς δευτέρ]οις ἐκπλέοσι Γλαύκονι
20  [ἐκ Κεραμέον, Μεταγ]ένει Κοιλεῖ, Δρακοντί
    [δει Θοραιεῖ ἐπὶ τῆς] Αἰαντίδος πρυτανείας
    [πρότες πρυτανευόσε]ς τῆι τελευτ[αίαι ἐμέ]
    [ραι τῆς πρυτανείας ⊩] vacat
```

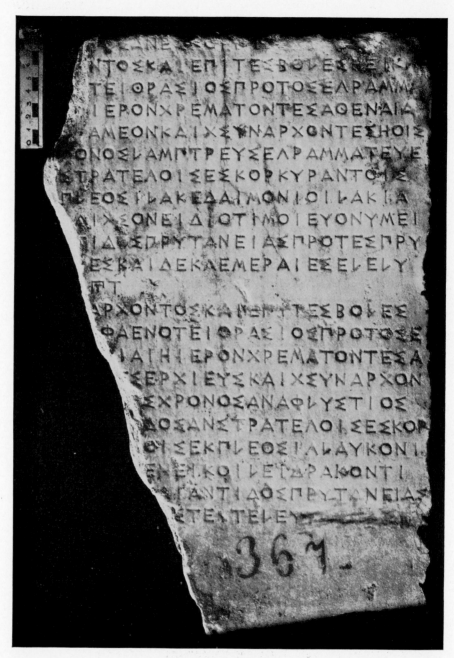

FIG. 10. Photograph of *I.G.*, I², 295

The latest discussion of the text of *I.G.*, I², 296 is that under-taken by Walther Kolbe in the monograph to which reference has already been made.[1] A transcript of the text itself has been

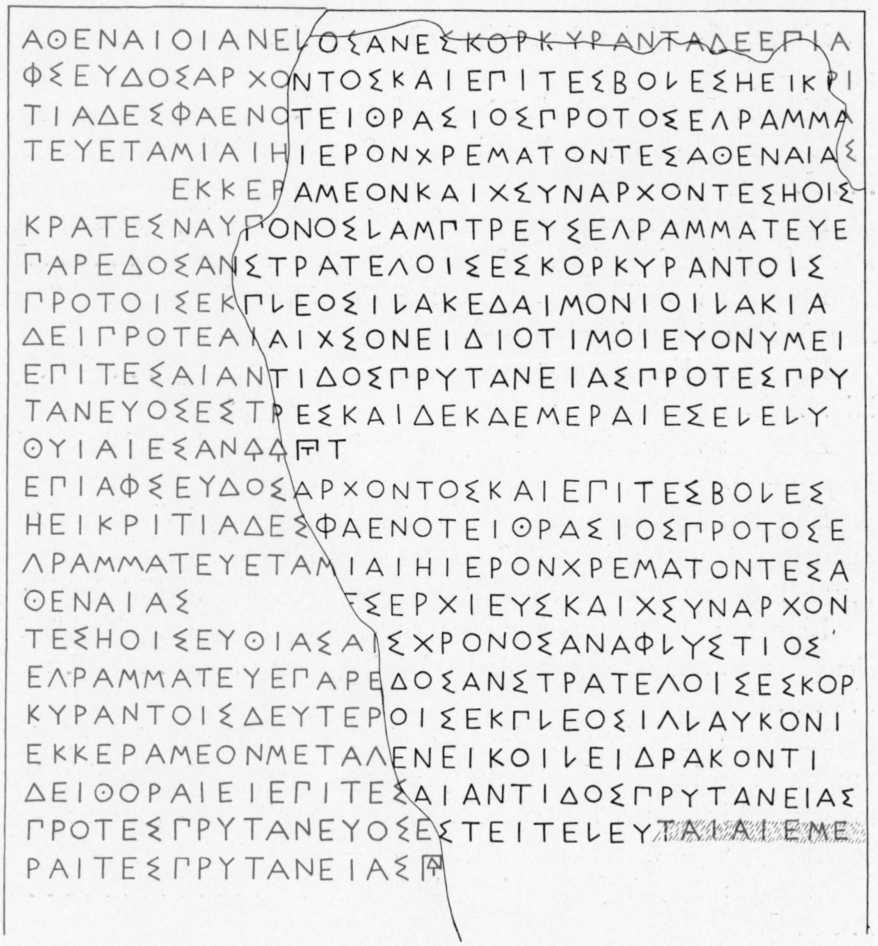

ΑΘΕΝΑΙΟΙΑΝΕΛΟΣΑΝΕΣΚΟΡΚΥΡΑΝΤΑΔΕΕΡΙΑ
ΦΣΕΥΔΟΣΑΡΧΟΝΤΟΣΚΑΙΕΓΙΤΕΣΒΟΛΕΣΗΕΙΚΡΙ
ΤΙΑΔΕΣΦΑΕΝΟΤΕΙΘΡΑΣΙΟΣΓΡΟΤΟΣΕΛΡΑΜΜΑ
ΤΕΥΕΤΑΜΙΑΙΗΙΕΡΟΝΧΡΕΜΑΤΟΝΤΕΣΑΘΕΝΑΙΑΣ
    ΕΚΚΕΡΑΜΕΟΝΚΑΙΧΣΥΝΑΡΧΟΝΤΕΣΗΟΙΣ
ΚΡΑΤΕΣΝΑΥΡΟΝΟΣΛΑΜΓΤΡΕΥΣΕΛΡΑΜΜΑΤΕΥΕ
ΓΑΡΕΔΟΣΑΝΣΤΡΑΤΕΛΟΙΣΕΣΚΟΡΚΥΡΑΝΤΟΙΣ
ΓΡΟΤΟΙΣΕΚΓΛΕΟΣΙΛΑΚΕΔΑΙΜΟΝΙΟΙΛΑΚΙΑ
ΔΕΙΓΡΟΤΕΑΧΑΙΧΣΟΝΕΙΔΙΟΤΙΜΟΙΕΥΟΝΥΜΕΙ
ΕΓΙΤΕΣΑΙΑΝΤΙΔΟΣΓΡΥΤΑΝΕΙΑΣΓΡΟΤΕΣΓΡΥ
ΤΑΝΕΥΟΣΕΣΤΡΕΣΚΑΙΔΕΚΑΕΜΕΡΑΙΕΣΕΛΕΛΥ
ΟΥΙΑΙΕΣΑΝΔΔΕΤ
ΕΓΙΑΦΣΕΥΔΟΣΑΡΧΟΝΤΟΣΚΑΙΕΓΙΤΕΣΒΟΛΕΣ
ΗΕΙΚΡΙΤΙΑΔΕΣΦΑΕΝΟΤΕΙΘΡΑΣΙΟΣΓΡΟΤΟΣΕ
ΛΡΑΜΜΑΤΕΥΕΤΑΜΙΑΙΗΙΕΡΟΝΧΡΕΜΑΤΟΝΤΕΣΑ
ΘΕΝΑΙΑΣ   ΣΕΡΧΙΕΥΣΚΑΙΧΣΥΝΑΡΧΟΝ
ΤΕΣΗΟΙΣΕΥΘΙΑΣΑΙΣΧΡΟΝΟΣΑΝΑΦΛΥΣΤΙΟΣ
ΕΛΡΑΜΜΑΤΕΥΕΓΑΡΕΔΟΣΑΝΣΤΡΑΤΕΛΟΙΣΕΣΚΟΡ
ΚΥΡΑΝΤΟΙΣΔΕΥΤΕΡΟΙΣΕΚΓΛΕΟΣΙΛΛΑΥΚΟΝΙ
ΕΚΚΕΡΑΜΕΟΝΜΕΤΑΛΕΝΕΙΚΟΙΛΕΙΔΡΑΚΟΝΤΙ
ΔΕΙΘΟΡΑΙΕΙΕΓΙΤΕΣΑΙΑΝΤΙΔΟΣΓΡΥΤΑΝΕΙΑΣ
ΓΡΟΤΕΣΓΡΥΤΑΝΕΥΟΣΕΣΤΕΙΤΕΛΕΥΤΑΙΑΙΕΜΕ
ΡΑΙΤΕΣΓΡΥΤΑΝΕΙΑΣ Ⱶ

FIG. 11. Drawing of *I.G.*, I², 295, with restorations in red

printed as an appendix to his work. Kolbe's studies have to a large extent confirmed the text as now given in the *Corpus*. I pass over some insignificant changes in restoration and note only the following variations:

Line 3: [Δ]ιότιμο[ς] Ἐγγυ[λ]ί[ονος .... πρῶτος ἐγραμμάτευε].
Line 5: The name of the prytanizing tribe must have con-

[1] Kolbe, *Thukydides im Lichte der Urkunden*, Stuttgart, 1930.

tained ten letters, since the only names available for the second prytany are Ἐρεχθείδος, Κεκροπίδος, and Ἀντιοχίδος. The number of letters in the demotic of the general Eukrates is thus also determined as eight.

Line 6: [- - ἐμέραι λοιποὶ ἐσαν τῆι πρυτανείαι . . . .[14] . . . . . . τάδε - - -].

Line 8: [- -ℎιε]ρονύμο[ι Εὔπυρ]ίδε[ι - - -].

Line 10: [- - ἐμέραι λοιποὶ ἐσαν τῆι πρυτανείαι . . . .[15] . . . .].

Line 12: Kolbe reads πρυτανεί[ας] for πρυτανεία[ς], and then restores [- -ἐμέραι λοιποὶ ἐσαν τῆι πρυτανείαι . . . .[19] . . . . . .].

Line 17: ⊢⋿⋔⟜⊣ [. . . .[8] . . . .: ταῦτα ἐδόθε τῆι στρατιᾶι τῆι ἐς Μακεδονίαν καὶ Ποτείδαιαν - - -].

Line 21: Kolbe reads the sum of money as [: . . .[s. . .8. . p.] . . .] ⊢⊢⋿⋔ΔΔ.

Line 23: τα[ῦτα ἐ]δόθε τῆι στρ[ατιᾶι τῆι ἐς Μακεδονίαν καὶ ἐς Ποτεί-δαιαν - - -].

Line 24: Kolbe reads πρυτ[ανείας] for πρυταν[είας], and then restores ἐμέραι λοιποὶ ἐσαν τῆι πρυτανείαι ἐννέα - -], which he continues into the next line with the numeral [⋔⋔]⋔⋔⋈⊓⋔ΔΔΔ⊓:

Line 25: Kolbe reads (after the numeral) τ[αῦτα] ἐγε τῆι ἐς Ποτε[ίδαιαν στρατιᾶι στρατεγὸς ἐς τὰ ἐπὶ Θράικες . . . .[21] . . . .].

Line 27: I follow Kolbe in omitting the restoration of the numeral and in referring the payment to Macedonian auxiliaries mentioned in Thuc. II, 29. Cf. Kolbe, *op. cit.*, p. 40, note 1.

Line 33: [- -ℎιερονύμοι Εὔπυρίδει - - -].

Line 36: Καρκίνο[ι Θορικίοι καὶ τõι παρέδροι . . . .[20] . . . .].

The new readings here proposed call for some comment, for it is impossible to accept them in their entirety. The text of line 3 has always been a puzzle, for no satisfactory restoration has ever been found for the letters which are there preserved on the stone. Certainly the suggestion made by Kolbe that we should read [Δ]ιότιμο[ς] Ἐγγυ[λ]ί[ονος . . . .] for the name of the secretary cannot be correct, for it involves a demotic in four letters, and an extraordinary patronymic which does not really satisfy the traces of letters on the stone. A close observation of

the photograph (Figure 12) will show that the letter phi is fairly
well preserved at the place on the stone where the final sigma of
[Δ]ιότιμο[s] is now universally restored. Following the phi is
a sigma or epsilon. In the photograph this letter resembles a
sigma more closely than any other letter, but on the squeeze the
strokes seem better interpreted as belonging to an epsilon. After
this letter there follow two letters, which may be either alphas, or
gammas, or deltas. Then comes an iota, to be followed in turn
by what looks to be the lower rounding of omicron or theta.
Such a letter seems hardly likely, however, for when completed it
does not lie high enough on the stone to agree with the other
letters in the same line. I interpret the marks here as the lower
part of epsilon or sigma, badly worn. The letters which appear
in this line may now be represented in sequence, as follows:

$$\text{I O T I M O} \, \Phi \, {\scriptstyle\Sigma \atop E} \, {\scriptstyle AA \atop \Lambda\Lambda \atop \Delta\Delta} \, \text{I} \, {\scriptstyle\Sigma \atop E}$$

It is evident that the name [Δ]ιοτίμο appears in the genitive
case and is itself the patronymic rather than the name proper.
The demotic which follows is Φεγαιε[ύs].

We have thus lost one name from our lists of secretaries of
the Council, but the addition to our knowledge of a new patronymic and demotic is more than equal recompense. The new
readings thus determined also affect materially the restorations of
lines 2 to 4 of this inscription. There must be some abbreviation
of the formula used in line 2 in order to make room for the name
of the secretary at the beginning of line 3. If we omit the phrase
καὶ ἐς Πελοπόννεσον we should have a name of seventeen letters,
which is impossible. We might omit the words καὶ Ποτείδαιαν
and thus obtain a name of thirteen letters, to give the reading
['Αθεναῖοι ἀνέλ]οσαν ἐς Μα[κεδονίαν καὶ ἐς Πελοπόννεσον ἐπὶ Πυθοδόρο
ἄρχοντος καὶ ἐπὶ τῆς βολῆς ἧι . . . | . . . [13] . . . . . . Δ]ιοτίμο Φεγαιε[ὺς
πρῶτος ἐγραμμάτευε – – – – – –]. But names of thirteen letters are
extremely rare, and we prefer if possible a name with the normal
number of eight to ten letters.

The observation has already been made that the record of
this year was primarily topical and only secondarily an annual
record. In accordance with this observation we must restore

in line 2 the type of formula which appears in the opening lines of *I.G.*, I², 295, a record which is also topical in character, rather than annual. The addition of the word τάδε brings the number of letters in the name of the scribe down to nine, and we so restore it. The lacuna of seven letter spaces created between lines 3 and 4 by our new readings is given over to the patronymic of the chief treasurer of Athena. We now read these lines in full:

['Αθεναῖοι ἀνέλ]οσαν ἐς Μα[κεδονίαν καὶ ἐς Πελοπόννεσον τάδε· ἐπὶ
  Πυθοδόρο ἄρχοντος καὶ ἐπὶ τῆς βολῆς ἧε]

[ι . . . . .⁹. . . . . Δ]ιοτίμο Φεγαιε[ὺς πρῶτος ἐγραμμάτευε· ταμίαι
  ℎιερῶν χρεμάτον τῆς 'Αθεναίας Εὐρέκτες . . .]

[. . . . . 'Ατενεὺ]ς καὶ χσυνάρχοντ[ες, ℎοῖς – – – – – – – – – – –].

I refer to the photograph (Figure 12) and to the facsimile in black and red (Plate I) for the disposition of the letters in the stoichedon arrangement of the line. Incidentally, the absence of any mention of Potidaea in the introductory formula confirms Kolbe's thesis (*op. cit.*, p. 23) that no loans were made for campaigning at Potidaea earlier than the third prytany of 432/1 (*I.G.*, I², 296, lines 6–11).

In lines 6, 10, and 12 I can see no advantage in the restoration ἐμέραι λοιποὶ ἦσαν τῆι πρυτανείαι over the traditional ἐμέραι ἐσελελυθυῖαι ἦσαν. I prefer to keep the older reading, which allows dates during the first two thirds of the prytany, approximately, rather than during the last one third. There is, so far as I know, no way of determining the exact dates. In lines 8 and 33 I also prefer not to restore the demotic [Εὐπυρ]ίδε[ι], with Kolbe. There are several other possibilities, such as [Αἰθαλ]ίδε[ι], [Παιον]ίδε[ι], and [Χολλε]ίδε[ι].

In line 9 the name of the secretary of the hellenotamiai may be restored from *I.G.*, I², 213, lines 3–5 (*S.E.G.*, V, 23). We read [ℎοῖς . . μοχάρες Μυρρινόσιος ἐγραμμάτευε].

In line 17 Kolbe's restoration of the numeral as ⊢⊓⊓△⊓ [. . . .⁸. . . .] is incorrect, for there is still preserved on the stone (Figure 12) a mark of punctuation after the figure ⊓, as well as before the figure ⊢⊢. The numeral as preserved is complete, with no figures lost through the fracturing of the stone. Including the marks of punctuation before and after, the four figures occupy a space of six letters only, and so invalidate also Kolbe's resto-

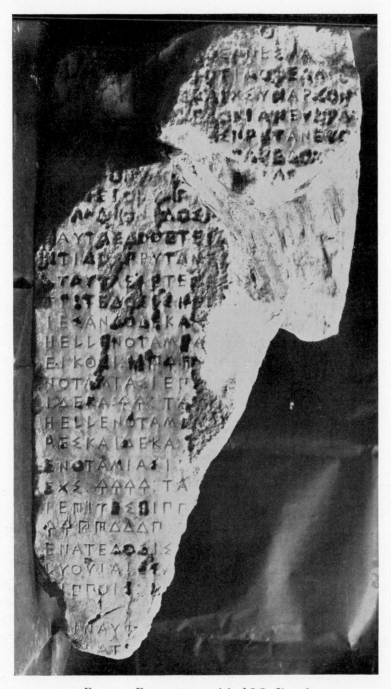

Fig. 12. Fragments *a* and *b* of *I.G.*, I², 296

ration for the rest of the line. I suggest the supplement [ταῦτα ἔγε τῆι ἐς Μακεδονίαν καὶ Ποτείδαιαν στρατιᾶι . . . . . .¹² . . . . .].

In line 19 we may restore, on the analogy of line 17, ταῦτα [ἔγε τῆι στρατιᾶι τῆι ἐς Μακεδονίαν καὶ Ποτείδαιαν . . . . . .¹⁸ . . . .].

In line 21 the first letter of the numeral is preserved in the weathered portion of the stone as Τ. The complete numeral must be restored, including marks of punctuation before and after, to occupy fourteen letter spaces. The reading is: Τ[. .⁵ . .] ΗΗ⊏ΔΔ[.:].

In view of the necessary restorations in lines 17 and 19 the traditional text is to be preferred in line 23 to Kolbe's suggested emendation.

In line 24 the reading of the *Corpus*, πρυταν[είας – –], is correct.

There can be no certainty about the figures lost, if any, from the beginning of the numeral in line 25, and no restoration can be made. The numeral is not here inscribed in perfect stoichedon order (Figure 13), though it is so represented in Kolbe's text. I call attention to the fact that the name of the general with demotic can occupy only a space of twenty letters, if restored according to the suggestion made by Kolbe, which seems to me somewhat better than the formula indicated in the *Corpus*.

In line 28 the reading is κ[εφ]άλαιον instead of κεφάλαιον.

In line 30 I restore [τῆ]ι ναυφ[άρκτ]οι στρατιᾶι τ[ῆ]ι περὶ [Πελοπόννεσον ταμίαι ἐπὶ Πυθοδόρο ἄρχοντος παρέδομεν στρατεγοῖς].

In the latter part of the inscription, which deals with the payments made to the generals in command of the fleet about the Peloponnesus, certain changes in the text are necessitated by the discovery that the small fragment *I.G.*, I², *309a* (E.M. 6703) belongs to this part of the record. The connection was first pointed out to me by H. T. Wade-Gery in the Epigraphical Museum at Athens, and subsequently Wilhelm's note to the same effect appeared in *S.E.G.*, III, p. 9. I give a photograph of the fragment in question in Figure 14, and call attention to the facsimile (Plate I) for the restorations which it necessitates.

One of the important consequences of the identification of this new fragment is the certain assurance it gives that the ninth tribe in prytany was Hippothontis, as has been in fact generally recognized. The other very useful bit of information gained from this fragment is the knowledge that the generals who received

Fig. 13. Fragment *c* of *I.G.*, I², 296

the money for expeditions about the Peloponnesus were listed individually with their colleagues, and not with a paredros.[1] We read in line 36: ταῦτα ἐδόθε Καρκίνο[ι Θορικίοι καὶ χσυν]άρχοσ[ι – – – – –], with an interval before the next item δευτέρα δόσις just

––––––
[1] Cf. Kolbe's restoration (*op. cit.*) of lines 36, 38, 39.

sufficient for the words τêι ναυφάρκτοι στρατιâι, which I supply. In line 38 we must also restore the word χσυνάρχοσι instead of παρέδροι. Compensation is possible by reducing from eight to six

the number of letter spaces devoted to the numeral. In line 39 we again restore χσυνάρχοσι in place of παρέδροι, with the possibility of compensation by reading in line 40 [--êσαν ἐσελε]λυθυîαι ἑ[μέραι - - -] instead of [ἑμέραι ἐσελε]λυθυîαι ê[σαν - - -].

FIG. 14. Small fragment of *I.G.*, I², 296, previously published as *I.G.*, I², 309*a* (E.M. 6703)

The normal order of words in this formula seems to have been ἑμέραι ἐσελελυθυîαι êσαν (*I.G.*, I², 295, lines 11–12; *I.G.*, I², 296, lines 14–15, 26–27) with the numeral giving the number of days either before or after. In *I.G.*, I², 324 there occurs one example of a different order in the phrase τέτταρες ἑμέραι êσαν ἐσελελυθυîαι (line 4). But even so the suggested possible restoration of line 40 as [- - êσαν ἐσελε]λυθυîαι ἑ[μέραι- -] seems hardly satisfactory.

An examination of the readings at present accepted for this part of the inscription shows that they depend largely on restoration. If the restorations prove to be incompatible with the phrase καὶ χσυνάρχοσι in lines 38 and 39, which we know to have appeared in line 36, then the restorations must be changed. I suggest the following for lines 38–40:

[ταῦτα ἐδόθε Καρ]κίνοι Θορικίοι κ[αὶ χσυνάρχοσι· τρίτε δόσις hελλενοταμίασι στρατεγοîς τοîς περὶ Πελ]

[οπόννεσον Σοκράτ]ει hαλαιεî κα[ὶ χσυνάρχοσι ἐπὶ τês Ἀκαμαντίδος
πρυτανείας δεκάτες πρυτανευόσες τ]

[έτταρες ἑμέραι ἐσελε]λυθυîαι ê[σαν - - - - - - - - - - -].

The order of words in the formula of date τέτταρες ἑμέραι ἐσελελυθυîαι êσαν has the authority of *I.G.*, I², 295, lines 11–12; the other lines of *I.G.*, I², 296 are too badly broken to prove that the same order did not appear in other places in this same inscription. With the restoration here proposed it is impossible to keep Λεοντίς as the name of the tenth tribe in prytany, for then there would be no possibility of restoring the date within the prytany with a word of ten letters. We have chosen Akamantis in preference to Pandionis, because this latter tribe is known to have held the third prytany (line 10), but in restoring Akamantis as the tenth tribe we necessitate the substitution of Λεοντίδος in place of 'Ακαμαντίδος in lines 11-12.

This substitution is desirable in any case, for it eliminates the exceptional final nu-movable at the end of the word heλ-λενοταμίασι in line 11. The nu-movable is never used in this inscription, although there are many instances where the combination heλλενοταμίασι ἐπὶ actually appears on the stone (lines 18, 20, 22, 24, 26). The difficulty of restoring the word 'Ακαμαντίδος in lines 11-12 without resorting to the nu-movable indicates that the correct tribal name for this passage is Λεοντίδος, the only other possible restoration. Lines 11-12 may now be read:

[τ]αῦτα ἐδόθε τêι [στρατιᾶι τêι ἐς Μακεδονίαν καὶ Ποτείδαιαν·
    δευτέρα δόσις heλλενοταμίασι ἐπὶ τês Λεο]
ντίδος πρυτανεία[ς τετάρτες πρυτανευόσες ἐμέραι ἐσελελυθυῖαι – –].

One further change, in line 26, is necessitated by the new readings of lines 38-40. The dittography can no longer be read ἐπὶ τ[ês Λε[[τês Λε]]οντίδος – – –]. We must supply rather ἐπὶ τ[ês [[τês]] 'Ακαμαντίδος πρυτανείας – – – –]. I believe that the simple duplication of a single word gives a more satisfactory explanation of the dittography and that it lends further support to the validity of our interpretation.

The order of prytanies in 432/1 may now be outlined as follows:

  I 'Ερεχθείς, Κεκροπίς, or 'Αντιοχίς (by elimination)
  II 'Ερεχθείς, Κεκροπίς, or 'Αντιοχίς (by elimination, line 5)
 III Πανδιονίς (line 10)
 IV Λεοντίς (lines 11-12)
  V Αἰγείς or Οἰνείς (line 14)
 VI Αἰγείς or Οἰνείς (line 16)
 VII 'Ερεχθείς, Κεκροπίς, or 'Αντιοχίς (by elimination, line 18)
VIII Αἰαντίς (line 20)
 IX hιπποθοντίς (lines 22, 24, 31, 35, 37)
  X 'Ακαμαντίς (lines 26, 39)

I record here also the new text of *I.G.*, I², 296:

Θ [ε ο ί]
['Αθεναῖοι ἀνέλ]οσαν ἐς Μα[κεδονίαν καὶ ἐς Πελοπόννεσον τάδε· ἐπὶ
    Πυθοδόρο ἄρχοντος καὶ ἐπὶ τês βολês ʰê]
[ι . . . .⁹. . . . Δ]ιοτίμο Φεγαιε[ὺς πρῶτος ἐγραμμάτευε ταμίαι
    ʰιερῶν χρεμάτον τês 'Αθεναίας Εὐρέκτες . . .]
[. . . . 'Ατενεὺ]s καὶ χσυνάρχοντ[ες ʰοῖς 'Απολλόδορος Κριτίο
    'Αφιδναῖος ἐγραμμάτευε παρέδοσαν στρατεγο]
5 [ῖς τοῖς ἐς Μακ]εδονίαν Εὐκράτ[ει . . . .⁸. . . . καὶ χσυνάρχοσι
    φσεφισαμένο τῶ δέμο ἐπὶ τês . . .⁶. . . . ίδος πρυτ]
[ανείας δευτέρ]ας πρυτανευό[σες ἐμέραι ἐσελελυθυῖαι ἦσαν . . . .
    . . . . .²¹. . . . . τάδε ἐς Μακεδονία]
[ν καὶ Ποτείδαιαν] παρέδομ[εν ʰελλενοταμίασι . . . . .¹⁶. . . . . .
    . . . Φιλεταίροι 'Ικαριεῖ Φιλοχσένοι . . . .]
[. ʰιε]ρονύμο[ι . . .⁵. .]ίδε[ι . . . . .³⁹. . . . .
    . . . . Χαρίαι Δαιδαλίδει . . . .⁹. . . . .]
[. . .]ιει 'Ολυμπ[ιοδόροι . . . . .²⁶. . . . .
    ʰοῖς . .μοχάρες Μυρρινόσιος ἐγραμμάτευε ἐπὶ τê]
10 [s Π]ανδιονίδος π[ρυτανείας τρίτες πρυτανευόσες ἐμέραι ἐσελελυθυῖαι
    ἦσαν . . . . .²². . . . .]
[τ]αῦτα ἐδόθε τêι [στρατιᾶι τêι ἐς Μακεδονίαν καὶ Ποτείδαιαν·
    δευτέρα δόσις ʰελλενοταμίασι ἐπὶ τês Λεο]
ντίδος πρυτανεία[ς τετάρτες πρυτανευόσες ἐμέραι ἐσελελυθυῖαι
    ἦσαν . . . . .²⁶. . . . .]
[.] ταῦτα ἔγε τêι ἐς [Ποτείδαιαν καὶ Μακεδονίαν στρατιᾶι στρατεγὸς
    ἐς τὰ ἐπὶ Θράικες Φορμίον Παιανιεύς]
τρίτε δόσις ʰελλ[ενοταμίασι ἐπὶ τês .ι.ίδος πρυτανείας πέμπτες
    πρυτανευόσες ἐμέραι ἐσελελυθυῖα]
15 ι ἦσαν δόδεκα: 𐅄[. . . . .⁹. . . . . : ταῦτα ἐδόθε τêι στρατιᾶι τêι ἐς
    Μακεδονίαν καὶ Ποτείδαιαν· τετάρτε δόσις]
ʰελλενοταμία[σι ἐπὶ τês .ι.ίδος πρυτανείας ʰέκτες πρυτανευόσες
    ἐμέραι ἐσελελυθυῖαι ἦσαν δύο καὶ]
εἴκοσι: 𐅅𐅅𐅄𐅅 : [ταῦτα ἔγε τêι ἐς Μακεδονίαν καὶ Ποτείδαιαν
    στρατιᾶι . . . . .¹². . . . . πέμπτε δόσις ʰελλε]
νοταμίασι ἐπ[ὶ τês . . .⁶. . . .ίδος πρυτανείας ʰεβδόμες πρυτανευόσες
    ἐμέραι ἐσελελυθυῖαι ἦσαν . . .⁵. . . κα]
ὶ δέκα: 𐅄𐅄 : ταῦτα [ἔγε τêι στρατιᾶι τêι ἐς Μακεδονίαν καὶ
    Ποτείδαιαν . . . . .¹⁸. . . . . ʰέκτε δόσις]

20 *h*ελλενοταμίασι [ἐπὶ τ**ε͡**]s Αἰ[αντίδος πρυτανείας ὀγδόες πρυτανευόσες ἐμέραι ἐσελελυθυῖαι ἔσαν τέττα]
ρες καὶ δέκα: Τ[. . .⁵. .]ΗΗ⊞ΔΔ [.: ταῦτα ἐδόθε μισθὸς *h*ιππεῦσι
Μακεδόσι . .⁵. .κοσίοις· *h*εβδόμε δόσις *h*ελλ]
ενοταμίασι ἐ[πὶ τ**ε͡**s] *h*ιπποθον[τίδος πρυτανείας ἐνάτες πρυτανευόσες ἐμέραι ἐσελελυθυῖαι ἔσαν δέκα *h*]
έχς: ⋔⋔⋔⋔: ταῦ[τα ἐ]δόθε τ**ε͡**ι στρ[ατιᾶι τ**ε͡**ι ἐς Ποτείδαιαν Φορ-
μίονι Παιανιε**ῖ**· ὀγδόε δόσις *h*ελλενοταμίασ]
ι ἐπὶ τ**ε͡**s *h*ιππ[οθον]τίδος πρυταν[είας ἐνάτες πρυτανευόσες ἐμέραι
λοιποὶ ἔσαν τ**ε͡**ι πρυτανείαι . . .⁷. . .]

25 ⋔⋔⊠⊓ΔΔΔⲦ: τ[αῦτα] ἔγε τ**ε͡**ι ἐς Ποτε[ίδαιαν στρατιᾶι στρα-
τεγὸs ἐς τὰ ἐπὶ Θράικες . . . . .²⁰. . . . .]
ἐνάτε δόσις [*h*ελλ]ενοταμίασι ἐπὶ τ[**ε͡**s [[τ**ε͡**s]] Ἀκαμαντίδος πρυτανείας δεκάτες πρυτανευόσες ἐμέραι ἐσελε]
λυθυῖαι ἔσα[ν *h*ε]πτὰ καὶ δέκ[α]: ⋔Ⲧ̄ΤΤ [. . . : ταῦτα ἐδόθε
μισθὸς *h*ιππεῦσι Μακεδόσι . .⁵. .κοσίοις καὶ σῖτος]
[*h*]ίπποις: Κ[εφ]άλαιον τ**ο͡** ἐς Μα[κεδονίαν καὶ
Ποτείδαιαν ἀναλόματος — — —]
vacat　　　*vacat*　　　*vacat*

30 [τ**ε͡**]ι ναυφ[άρκτ]οι στρατιᾶι τ[**ε͡**]ι περὶ [Πελοπόννεσον ταμίαι ἐπὶ
Πυθοδόρο ἄρχοντος παρέδομεν στρατεγοῖς]
[Σοκ]ράτε[ι *h*αλ]αιεῖ Προτέαι Αἰχσον[εῖ Καρκίνοι Θορικίοι ἐπὶ τ**ε͡**s
*h*ιπποθοντίδος πρυτανείας ἐνάτες πρυ]
[τανευόσες ἐ]μέραι λοιποὶ ἔσαν ὀκτ[ὸ τ**ε͡**ι πρυτανείαι . . . . .¹¹. . . . .
τάδε *h*ελλενοταμίασι . . . . .¹³. . . . .]
[. . . Φιλεταί]ροι Ἰκαριεῖ Φιλοχσέν[οι . .⁵. . *h*ιερονύμοι . .⁵. . .
ίδει . . . . .³⁰. . . . .]
[. . . . . . .⁹. . . . . Χ]αρίαι Δαιδαλίδει Ἐπ[. . . . . .¹⁶. . . . .
Ὀ]λυμπ[ιοδόροι . . . . .²³. . . . . παρέδο]

35 [μεν ἐπὶ τ**ε͡**s *h*]ιπποθοντίδος πρυτα[νείας ἐνάτες πρυτα]νευόσ[ες
ἐμέραι λοιποὶ ἔσαν . . .⁵. . . τ**ε͡**ι πρυτανείαι]
[. . . . .¹⁰. . . . .] ταῦτα ἐδόθε Καρκίνο[ι Θορικίοι καὶ χσυν]άρχοσ[ι
τ**ε͡**ι ναυφάρκτοι στρατιᾶι· δευτέρα δόσις ἐπ]
[ὶ τ**ε͡**s *h*ιπποθο]ντίδος πρυτανείας [ἐνάτες πρυτανευόσ]ε[s ἐμέραι
λοιποὶ ἔσαν . . . . τ**ε͡**ι πρυτανείαι . . .⁶. . .]
[ταῦτα ἐδόθε Καρ]κίνοι Θορικίοι κ[αὶ χσυνάρχοσι· τρίτε δόσις
*h*ελλενοταμίασι στρατεγοῖς τοῖς περὶ Πελ]
[οπόννεσον Σοκράτ]ει *h*αλαιεῖ κα[ὶ χσυνάρχοσι ἐπὶ τ**ε͡**s Ἀκαμαντίδος
πρυτανείας δεκάτες πρυτανευόσες τ]

FIG. 15. Photograph of *I.G.*, I², 294 + 308

40   [ἔτταρες ἐμέραι ἐσελε]λυθυῖαι ἔ[σαν – – – – – – – – – – – – – –]
      [. . . . . .²³. . . . .] ι – – – – – – – – – – – – –

Since Wade-Gery's rediscovery of fragment *a* of *I.G.*, I², 294,
confirming the relative positions for fragments *a* and *b* (E.M.
5173 and 6707) as determined by Bannier,[1] and his further observation that *I.G.*, I², 299 (E.M. 6706) and 308 (E.M. 6748)[2]

FIG. 16.   Photograph of *I.G.*, I², 299

also belong to the same inscription, it has been possible to reconstruct a portion of still another of these records of state expense
from the early years of the Archidamian War.[3] I give photographs of the preserved fragments in Figures 15 and 16. A comparison of these photographs with those of *I.G.*, I², 296 shows
such striking similarity in letter forms and in the spacing of the

[1] Wade-Gery, "An Attic Inscription of the Archidamian War," *J.H.S.*, L (1930),
288–293; Bannier, "Zu den attischen Rechnungsurkunden des fünften Jahrhunderts,"
Rh. Mus., LXI (1906), 210.

[2] The inventory number is incorrectly given as E.M. 6478 in the *Corpus*. E.M.
6748 is correct.

[3] Wade-Gery gives photographs of the preserved fragments of this inscription
in *J.H.S.*, L (1930), 288–289.

letters on the stone, that one is inclined, on this ground alone, to assign the document to the early years of the war.

My own interpretation of the document is in essential agreement with that of Wade-Gery. The first seven lines record the payments made in some one year to the hellenotamiai, followed by a summation giving the total amount of these payments in line 9. Lines 11–15 record a different class of payments made in the same year to the τριεροποιοί, together with a summation. The last line of the inscription contains the grand sum total of moneys borrowed from Athena during the year.

The date tentatively suggested by Wade-Gery is 431/0.[1] Arguments in favor of this date are the close similarity in form between this inscription and *I.G.*, I², 296 and the fact that the reduced expenses of 430/29–427/6 (except 428/7) probably allowed the Athenians to begin in 430 the practice of inscribing the records of a complete four-year period instead of merely the record of one year on one stone. I assume, therefore, that the practice of grouping the records of one Panathenaic quadrennium together began in 430. We know that it continued until 410.

My restorations follow closely those proposed by Wade-Gery in his first edition of the composite document, and I agree with him in positing a line of eighty-six letters.[2]

[- - - - - - - - - - - - - - - - - - - -]πολι (or υ) [- - - -]
[- - - - δόσις hελλενοταμίασι ἐπὶ τês Παν]διονίδο[s πρυτανείας . .]
[- - - πρυτανευόσες - - - - ἐμέραι ἐσελελυθυîαι êσαν - - - - - -
το]ûτο ἐδόθ[ε . . . . . .¹² . . . . .]
[- - - - - - - - - - - - - - - - - - -]τιδας κα[. . . . . .¹³ . . . . . .]
5 [. . . . . . . .¹⁶ . . . . hεβδ]ό[με δόσις hελλενοταμίασι ἐπὶ τês
- ⁻ ⁻ -ίδος πρυτανεί]ας ὀγδόε[s πρυτανευόσε]
[s hένδεκα ἐμέραι ἐσελελ]υ[θυîαι êσαν . . . .⁹ . . . . τοûτο ἐδόθε
στρατεγοîσι Ἀριστοτ]έλει Θορα[ιεî καὶ χσυνά]
[ρχοσι - - - - - - - - - - - - - - -]   *vacat*
                    vacat
[ἀναλόματος κ]εφ[άλαιον] ἐπὶ τ[ês Ἀντιμέδος ἀρχês καὶ χσυναρχόντον hελλενοταμίασι] ✕ΗΗΗ⊩ΔΓΤΤ [- - - -]

¹ Wade-Gery, *op. cit.*, 291, note 11.
² Wade-Gery, *op. cit.*, 291. Cf. also *I.G.*, I², 293 (p. 47, above), 296, 301, 302.

10

vacat

[τάδε ναυπεγο]ῖσ[ι παρέ]δομεν τα[μίαι ἐπὶ Εὐθυδέμο ἄρχοντος καὶ
τριεροποιοῖσι . . . ⁷ . . .]ι[. . . . ⁸ . . . . καὶ τοῖ]

[s χσυνάρχοσι τ]ρ[ιάκον]τα ὄσιν ἐπὶ [τες – – ^{c. 10} – –ίδος πρυτανείας
– – – ^{c. 6} – –πρυτανευόσες – – ^{c. 5} – – ἐμέραι ἐσελελυ]

[θυῖαι ἐσαν 𐅅 ^{vv}]ᵛ τ[ριερ]οποιοῖσι π[αρέδομεν ἐπὶ τες . . . .ίδος
πρυτανείας . . .⁶. . . πρυτανευόσες . . . .⁹. . . .]

[. . .⁷. . . καὶ τοῖ]s χ[συν]άρχοσι δέκ[α ἐμέραι τες πρυτανείας
ἐσελελυθυῖαι ἐσαν τει ἐς Μακεδονίαν καὶ Ποτεί]

15 [δαιαν στρατι]αι 𐅅ᵛ[ᵛᵛ]ᵛ κεφάλαιον [ἀναλόματος ἐπὶ τες Ἀντιμέδος ἀρχες καὶ χσυναρχόντον τριεροποιοῖσι Η]

[χσύμπαντος] ἀναλό[μ]ατος κεφά[λαιον – – – – – – – – – – – – – –]

A considerable proportion of the restoration above is hypothetical and is given merely by way of example. The last payment to the hellenotamiai (line 5) was made in the eighth prytany, and the absence of payments in the last two prytanies of
the year may possibly be considered as evidence that the document belongs in the year of the revolt of Lesbos rather than in
431/0. But we do not know with what regularity or at what
times the payments in 431/0 were made. Aristotle (line 6) may
have been general in any one of the early years of the war,[1] and
the appearance of his name does not enable us to decide between
431/0 and 428/7.

In line 11 there is an introductory formula which resembles
that of *I.G.*, I², 296, line 30.[2] I suggest that τα[μίαι ἐπὶ Εὐθυδέμο
ἄρχοντος] be restored as the subject of the verb [παρέ]δομεν. The
restorations here proposed by Wade-Gery show a slight irregularity, in that the word [τριεροποιο]ῖσ[ι] can be restored at the
beginning of the line only by assuming an initial uninscribed
letter space. I propose for the beginning of the line [τάδε ναυπε-
γο]ῖσ[ι] and then suggest that, after the verb and subject of the
sentence, we write [καὶ τριεροποιοῖσι . . .⁷ . . .] ι[. . . .⁸. . . . καὶ
τοῖς χσυνάρχοσι], thus bringing the last words of this phrase close
to the enigmatic letters ρ. . .⁵. .τα ὄσιν in line 12. A probable
restoration here seems to be [τ]ρ[ιάκον]τα ὄσιν, which gives a continuous reading for these two lines.

---

[1] Wade-Gery, *op. cit.*, 292.

[2] See p. 81, above.

In line 14 the date by both civil month and prytany would be so extraordinary that a restoration of this type must be rejected.[1] I have no very satisfactory restoration to propose to fill the long lacuna in this line, but suggest as possible δέκ[α ἐμέραι τêς πρυτανείας ἐσεληλυθυîαι êσαν τêι ἐς Μακεδονίαν καὶ Ποτεί| δαιαν στρατι]âι.

The large sum of money recorded in lines 9 and 15 (well over 1300 talents) points either to 431/0 (Potidaea) or to 428/7 (Lesbos) as a necessary date for the document. For purely epigraphical reasons the former date seems slightly more probable. This probability has now been raised almost to certainty as the result of a recent study by Professor West, in which he uses *I.G.*, I², 299 as evidence for the cost of major operations early in the Archidamian War.[2] By comparing the amounts of loans made to the state from Athena's treasure from 433/2 to 427/6 and the amounts of interest accrued on those loans (*I.G.*, I², 324) West has found that the large sums recorded in *I.G.*, I², 299 must have been borrowed earlier than 428/7.

We have already observed that the inscription recording loans to the state from the treasury of Athena in 414/3 was cut on the reverse face of the stele containing the record for 432/1.[3] Since we know that the lines on the obverse face of the stone each contained the equivalent of eighty-four letters, it is possible to calculate very closely the original width of the stele. By actual measurement on the preserved portions of *I.G.*, I², 296 we find that twenty-one letters occupy a horizontal distance of 0.238 m. The complete line of eighty-four letters must have occupied, therefore, a distance of 4 × 0.238 = 0.952 m. If we may assume the same width of uninscribed margin both before and after the text proper, a further 0.016 m. must be added to determine the entire width of the stone as 0.968 m.

The stone is quadrangular in cross-section, and must have had a width of 0.968 m. across the reverse face as well. This observation is important in that it makes possible the determination of the original length of line in *I.G.*, I², 297. Here the uninscribed margin to the right of the text was greater than on the

---

[1] Wade-Gery, *op. cit.*, 291, note 11.

[2] West, "Cleon's Assessment and the Athenian Budget," *Trans. Am. Phil. Assoc.*, LXI (1930), 217–239.　　　　[3] Cf. p. 64, above.

Fig. 17.   Photograph of *I.G.*, I², 297

obverse, measuring 0.016 m. If we assume a similar margin along the left-hand edge, there remains for the text proper a total width of 0.968 − 0.032 = 0.936 m. The letters on the preserved portion are regularly spaced and measure 0.191 m. for each sixteen letter spaces. A line of eighty letters would thus occupy a width of 0.955 m., or 0.019 m. more than the calculated space available. We must reduce the length of line, therefore, to seventy-eight letters, which is, I am convinced, the correct determination.[1] With this length of line it is possible to build up an eminently satisfactory restoration of the inscription, the text of which I give here. A photograph of the preserved portion is reproduced in Figure 17, and the facsimile in black and red, showing also the relation of *I.G.*, I², 297 to *I.G.*, I², 296 and 298, is given in Plate I.

['Αθεναῖοι ἀνέλοσαν ἐπὶ Τεισάνδρο ἄρχοντος καὶ ἐπὶ τῆς βολῆς ἧει
........¹¹...... πρῶτος] ἐγρα[μμάτ]

[ενε· ταμίαι ἱιερὸν χρεμάτον τῆς 'Αθεναίας Τεισαμενὸς ..⁵..
Παιανιεὺς καὶ συνάρχον]τες ἱο[ῖς Πο]

[λυμέδες 'Ατενεὺς ἐγραμμάτευε παρέδομεν στρατεγοῖς ἐς τὰ ἐπὶ
Θράικες Εὑετίονι Μελ]εσ[ά]νδρ[ο . .]

[....⁸.... καὶ συνάρχοσι καὶ ἱελλενοταμίαις καὶ παρέδροις
............¹⁷........ Κεφ]αλῆθε[ν καὶ]

5   [συνάρχοσι φσεφισαμένο τὸ δέμο ἐπὶ τῆς ἱπποθοντίδος δευτέρας
πρυτανευόσες καὶ] ἑμέραι [. . .]

[... καὶ .....¹⁰.....τῆς πρυτανείας ..⁵...ἐπὶ τῆς ...⁶...ίδος
πέμπτες πρυτανευόσ]ης εἰκοστῆ[ι τ]

[ἐς πρυτανείας παρέδομεν τοῖς στρατεγοῖς Νικίαι Κυδαντίδει καὶ
συνάρχοσι] καὶ ἱελλενοταμ[ία]

[ις καὶ παρέδροις ....¹⁷........ Κεφαλῆθεν καὶ συνάρχοσιν ⊦ΔΔ· ἐς τὰς ν]αῦς τὰς κομιζόσας [τ]

[ὰ χρέματα τὰς μετὰ Εὐρυμέδοντος πρότας ἐκπλεόσας ἐπὶ τῆς
...⁶... ίδος πέμπ]τες πρυτανευόσες [.]

10 [..... καὶ εἰκοστεῖ τῆς πρυτανείας παρέδομεν φσεφισαμένο τὸ δέμο
...⁶... ἡ]αῦται δὲ ἐς Σικελία

---

[1] A letter from Homer Thompson, at the American School of Classical Studies at Athens, gives independent measurements substantially the same as those I have offered here. Thompson concludes that his "mathematical calculations would seem to indicate that there were 78 letters to the line in *I.G.*, I², 297."

[ν ἐγον τὰ χρέματα τοῖς στρατεγοῖς Νικίαι Κυδαντίδει καὶ συνάρ-
    χοσιν· ἐπὶ τες Ἐ]ρεχθείδος heβδό
[μες πρυτανευόσες ....⁸.... τες πρυτανείας παρέδομεν στρατεγοῖς
    ἐς Σικελίαν Δεμ]οσ[θ]ένει Ἀφι
[δναίοι ...⁶... ·ἐπὶ τες ...⁶... ίδος ...⁶... πρυτανευόσες
    ...⁸.... τες πρυτανείας παρ]έδομε[ν ..]
[- -] καὶ heλλε
15 [νοταμίαις - - - - -· ἐπὶ τες - - -ίδος - - -πρυτανευόσε]s heικοστ
[ει τες πρυτανείας - - - - - - - - - - - - - - παρὰ Σα]μίον παρέ
[δομεν -Κ]υδαθεν[α]
[ιεῖ -] vacat

Attention may be called to some of the general considerations which have been observed in reconstructing the foregoing
text. The record of each payment contains the verb παρέδομεν, as
is evident from the preserved portions of lines 13 and 16. The
participles συνάρχοντες and συνάρχοσι are written without initial
chi, after the usual fashion of the later (*I.G.*, I², 304) as distinct
from the earlier (*I.G.*, I², 296, 324, 302) documents. I have restored συνάρχοσιν at the end of a sentence and before vowels
(lines 8 and 11). The word heμέραι does not occur in the formula
of date within the prytany, except in line 5, where the formula
employed is unique in this inscription. It finds its parallel in
I.G., I², 302, lines 5 and 27.[1] So far as the content of the inscription is concerned, the text must be compared with that part of
the seventh book of Thucydides which records the events of
414/3.

In only minor points do my readings from the stone differ
from those given in the *Corpus*. In line 1 part of the first alpha
in ἐγρα[μμάτευε] is preserved. Near the end of line 3 there is an
upright stroke which I interpret as part of the letter rho. In
line 6 the reading εἰκοστῆ[ι] is reasonably clear. In line 7, where
the word [ἐσ]αν is now restored in the *Corpus*, the letters καὶ may
be distinguished. The restoration [ἐμέραι ἐσελελυθυῖαι ἐσ]αν is
probably a relic from the time when editors believed the date
of the document to be 427/6; it has no place in the restoration
of an inscription from 414/3. A control of these variant readings is given by the photograph in Figure 17.

    [1] For the text of *I.G.*, I², 302, cf. pp. 160–163.

The introductory formula of *I.G.*, I², 297 is similar to those preserved in *I.G.*, I², 302, where the name of the first secretary of the Council was given with neither patronymic nor demotic. In this case the name is not known, but it must have contained eleven letters in the nominative case. The chief treasurer of Athena and the secretary of the treasurers of Athena are known from *I.G.*, I², 248, though our inscription gives the additional information that the patronymic of the chief treasurer contained five letters in the genitive case. This is more probable than a genitive in four letters and offers an additional reason for restoring [συνάρχον]τες in line 2 without the initial chi.

I assume that the first payment of the year was made to the generals in Thrace, concerning whose operations at the close of summer we are informed by Thucydides (VII, 9). This seems the more probable because the name of the general given by Thucydides is exactly suited to the lacuna available in the inscription and the date is easily restored to agree with the known time of his campaign. If the restoration is correct, it appears that Euetion was the son of Melesander, and it is natural to identify the father with the Athenian general who lost his life in Lycia in 430/29 (Thuc. II, 69). In line 4, the demotic Κεφαλέθεν belongs to the chief hellenotamias of 414/3, concerning whom we are otherwise uninformed. In earlier years, in which these records mention moneys paid to the hellenotamiai for the generals, or to the hellenotamiai and the generals, the practice had been to list the board of hellenotamiai first (*I.G.*, I², 324, lines 2–3; *I.G.*, I², 302, lines 31–32, 77–79; for the text cf. pp. 160–163). That this order was not invariably followed is shown, however, by the record of the first payment in 415/4, where the restoration must be στρ[ατ]εγοῖς Τελεφόν[οι . . .⁵. . . καὶ χσυνάρχοσι καὶ hελλενοταμίαι καὶ] παρέδροι Φερεκλείδει Περαιεῖ.¹ In *I.G.*, I², 297 the hellenotamiai were certainly listed after the generals, for the words καὶ hελλενοταμίαις appear in both line 7 and line 14. We do not hesitate, therefore, to consider Melesander (line 3) the patronymic of the general and Κεφαλέθεν (line 4) the demotic of the hellenotamias. The name and patronymic of the hellenota-

¹ For the sequence hελλενοταμίαι καὶ παρέδροι, with name and demotic, reference may also be made to *I.G.*, I², 302, lines 77–79 (cf. p. 163, below).

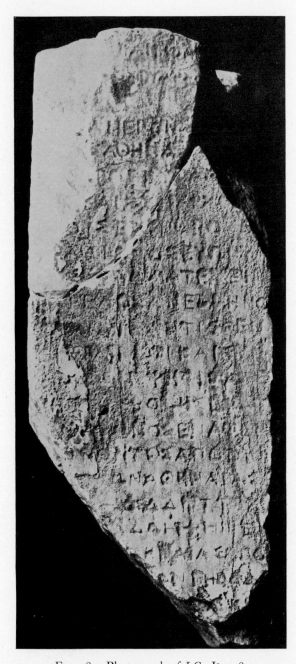

FIG. 18.   Photograph of *I.G.*, I², 298

mias occupied, I assume, seventeen letter spaces, being the same in both lines 4 and 8. In line 5 the restoration seems to me certain. If this is true, it appears that Hippothontis held the second prytany of the year. The date within the prytany is not certain, though the formula to be employed in the restoration is evidently the same as that which appears in *I.G.*, I², 302, lines 5–6 (cf. p. 160, below).

The record of the second payment begins in line 6. This payment must have been made in the fifth prytany, for the day Prytany V, 20 falls very near the time of the winter solstice, and Thucydides (VII, 16) tells us that the money was voted and carried to the army in Sicily by Eurymedon at about this time. The name of the prytany is not known, though it must have been the same for both the second and third payments. The sum of money was probably 120 talents, and I have so restored it (Thuc. VII, 16).

In line 8 begins the record of the third payment, which was made for the ships which sailed to Sicily with Eurymedon. This grant was doubtless made soon after the twentieth day of the prytany. The restoration of line 9 may be compared with *I.G.*, I², 295, lines 7–8, and the entire entry should be read in the light of Thucydides (VII, 16).

The fourth payment, of which a record appears in line 11, was made to Demosthenes, who sailed for Sicily in the early spring of 413.[1] The formula στρατεγοῖς ἐς Σικελίαν Δεμοσθένει ᾿Αφιδναίοι can be paralleled by that of *I.G.*, I², 324, line 18: στρατεγοῖς περὶ Πελοπόννεσον Δεμοσθένει ᾿Αλκισθένος ᾿Αφιδναίοι, both examples being without the usual καὶ (χ)συνάρχοσι after the general's name.

From line 13 to line 18 the inscription is too fragmentary to permit of even tentative restoration, although it seems clear from the repetition of the verb παρέδομεν that the record of the fifth payment was inscribed in lines 13–15, and the record of the sixth payment in lines 15–18. The stone is uninscribed at the end of line 18 and for a short distance below this point. Evidently the sixth payment was the last of the year. After the brief uninscribed surface the accounts of the year 413/2 must

---

[1] Thuc. VII, 20. Cf. also *I.G.*, I², 328 for the correspondence between Prytany VII and the civil month Gamelion.

have been recorded, although no part of this document that can be assigned with certainty has been preserved.

We have already noted that below the record of 413/2 were probably inscribed also the records of 412/1 and of 411/0, except that the account of moneys borrowed by the Four Hundred were cut on the edge of the stone where they are now preserved in part as *I.G.*, I², 298 (Figure 18). Some changes must be made in the text of *I.G.*, I², 298 as it is now given in the *Corpus*, and I present a revised transcript based on the facsimile copy in Plate I:

['Αθηναῖ]οι ἀνήλω[σαν ἐπὶ]
[Μνασιλ]όχου ἄρχο[ντος]
　　　　vacat
[ταμί]αι ἱερῶν χ[ρημάτ]
5　[ων τῆ]s 'Αθηναία[s 'Ασω]
[πόδω]ρος Κυδαθ[ηνα]
[ιεὺs] καὶ συνάρχο[ντ]
[εs] οἷς Εὔανδρος 'Ε[ρ]
[ι]θαλίωνος Εὐωνυμ
10　[ε]ὺς ἐ[γρ]αμμάτευεν
παρέδοσαν ἑλληνο
ταμίαις 'Αντισθέν

ει 'Ερμείωι καὶ συν
ἀρχοσιν ψηφισαμέ
15　νης τῆς βολῆς 'Εκατ
[ο]μβαιῶνος ἐνάτει
[φθί]νοντος ἀπὸ τῶν
[χρημάτ]ων 'Αθηναίας
[Πολιά]δος: ΔΔΓΤΤΧΧ
20　[- - - - -] ΓΔΔΗΗΗΙΙΙΙ τῆ
[s Νίκης 'Α]θηναίας ἀπὸ
[τῶν χρημάτ]ων ΓΗΔΔΔ[.]

CHAPTER VI

BORROWINGS FROM ATHENA IN 410/09 B.C.

The restoration of the last two lines of the inscription which preserves the record of borrowings from Athena in 410/09 (*I.G.*, I², 304, lines 40, 40 *bis*) has already been discussed. The document of the year was complete in the forty-one lines, now largely preserved, and all expenses, it seems, were made in this year from current income.[1] Through the courtesy of Les Archives Photographiques I am able to reproduce in Plates II–V photographs which show the text of this inscription as it is now preserved in the Louvre. Along the right-hand margin of the lower portion of the inscription it seems to me — from the photographs — that letters read by earlier editors have been in part obscured by the plaster now used to support the stone, but Professor Michon assures me (by letter) that such is not the case. I give in the facsimile (Plate VI), therefore, the present contour of the surface, indicating also in black the letters not now visible which were read by those who first copied the inscription. The text of the document, as determined by the photographs and in the facsimile plate, follows here:

I.G., I², 304 A (410/09 B.C.)

᾽Αθεναῖοι ἀνέλοσαν ἐπὶ Γλαυκίππο ἄρχοντος καὶ ἐπὶ τῆς βολῆς εῖ
    Κλεγένες hαλαιεὺς πρôτ[os]

ἐγραμμάτευε· ταμίαι hιερôγ χρεμάτον τῆς ᾽Αθεναίας Καλλίστρατος
    Μαραθόνιος καὶ χσυνάρχο[ν]

τες παρέδοσαν ἐκ τôν ἐπετείον φσεφισαμένο τô δέμο·ἐπὶ τῆς Αἰαντίδος
    πρότες πρυτανευόσες hε[λλ]

[ε]νοταμίαις παρεδόθε: Καλλιμάχοι hαγνοσίοι: Φρασιτελίδει ᾽Ικα-
    ριεῖ: hίπποις σῖτος ἐδόθε: ᾽Αθεναίας Πολ[ιά]

5 [δ]os: ΤΤΤΧΧΧΗΗΔΔΔΓΗ⊢C: Νίκες: ⊡ΔΔΔΔⲎⲒⲒⲒⳆ: ἐπὶ
    τῆς Αἰγείδος δευτέρας πρυτανευόσες: ἀθλοθέταις παρεδ[ό]

θε ἐς Παναθέναια τὰ μεγάλα: Φίλονι Κυδαθεναιεῖ καὶ συνάρχοσιν
    ᾽Αθεναίας Πολιάδος: ⊓Χ: hιεροποιοῖς κατ' [έ]

---

[1] Cf. p. 63, above; Ferguson, *The Treasurers of Athena*, pp. 33–35.

νιαυτὸν: Διύλλοι.ηερχιεῖ καὶ συνάρχοσιν ἐς τὲν ἑκατόμβεν: ⟦X⟧HΔ-

ⱵⱵⱵ: ἐπὶ τῆς Οἰνείδος τρίτες πρυταν[ε]

νόσες: ηελλενοταμίαις παρεδόθε: Περικλεῖ Χολαργεῖ καὶ συνάρχο-

σιν: hίπποις σῖτος ἐδόθε: ΤΤ⟦X⟧ΗΗΗΗΔ[∶]

ἕτερον τοῖς αὐτοῖς ηελλενοταμίαις hίπποις σῖτος ἐδόθε: ΤΤ⟦X⟧ΗΗ-

ΗΗ: ἕτερον τοῖς αὐτοῖς ηελλενοταμία[ις]

10 hέρμονι ἐδόθε ἄρχοντι ἐς Πύλον: Ⱶ̄Τ: ἕτερον: τοῖς αὐτοῖς ἑλ-

λενοταμίαις ἐς τὲν διοβελίαν: ΤΤ: ἐπὶ τῆς Ἀκ

αμαντίδος τετάρτες πρυτανευόσες: ηελλενοταμίαις παρεδόθε: Περι-

κλεῖ Χολαργεῖ καὶ συνάρχοσιν: σ[ῖ]

τος (hί)πποις ἐδόθε: ΤΤΤ: ἕτερον τοῖς αὐτοῖς ηελλενοταμίαις ἐς

τὲν διοβελίαν ἐδόθε: Ⱶ̄ΤΤΤΧΗΗΗ⟦⟧Ⱶ̄Ⱶ: ἐπὶ τ[ε]

5 Κεκροπίδος πέμπτες πρυτανευόσες: ηελλενοταμίαις παρεδόθε:

Περικλεῖ Χολαργεῖ καὶ συνάρχοσιν ἐ[ς]

τὲν διοβελίαν: ΤΤΤΤΧΧΗΗ: ἐπὶ τῆς Λεοντίδος hέκτες πρυτα-

νευόσες: τρίτει ἑμέραι τῆς πρυτανείας

15 ἑλλενοταμίαις παρεδόθε: Διονυσίοι Κυδαθεναιεῖ καὶ συνάρχοσιν

∶ΧΗΗ⟦⟧ΔΔΔⱵⱵⱵ: ἐνάτει τῆς πρυτανε[ί]

ας ηελλενοταμίαις Θράσονι Βουτάδει καὶ συνάρχοσιν: ΤΤΤΧⱵ̄-

ΔΔΔ̄ⱵⱵⱵⱵⱵ∶ hενδεκάτει τῆς πρυτανείας hε

λλενοταμίαις παρεδόθε Προχσένοι Ἀφιδναίοι καὶ συνάρχοσιν στρα-

τεγοῖ ἐχς Ἐρετρίας: Εὐκλείδει ἀνομολόγ

εμα: ΧΧΧ⟦Ⱶ̄⟧ΗΗΔΔΔΔⱵⱵ: τρίτει καὶ δεκάτει τῆς πρυτανείας

ηελλενοταμίαις Περικλεῖ Χολαργεῖ καὶ συνάρχοσιν: [.]

ΧΧΧΧ⟦Ⱶ̄⟧ΗΗΗΗⱵⱵ̄Ⱶ: ὀγδόει καὶ εἰκοστεῖ τῆς πρυτανείας: ηελ-

λενοταμίαις: Σπουδίαι Φλυεῖ καὶ συνάρχοσιν: ΤΤΧΧ[.]

20 Η: τριακοστεῖ τῆς πρυτανείας τὰ ἐχ Σάμο ἀνομολογέθε: ηελλενο-

ταμίαι ∶ Ἀναίτιοι Σφεττίοι καὶ πάρεδροι [Π]

ολυαράτοι Χολαργεῖ: ⟦Ⱶ̄⟧Ⱶ̄ΤΤΧ: ἐπὶ τῆς Ἀντιοχίδος ἑβδόμες

πρυτανευόσες: πέμπτει τῆς πρυτανείας παρεδ[ό]

θε Διονυσίοι Κυδαθεναιεῖ καὶ συνάρχοσιν ἐς τὲν διοβελίαν∶Τ:

ἑβδόμει τῆς πρυτανείας ηελλενοταμίαις Θρ[ά]

σονι Βουτάδει καὶ συνάρχοσιν ἐς τὲν διοβελίαν: ΤΧΗΗΔΔΔ̄Ⱶ̄Ⱶ-

ⱵⱵⱵ∶ τῆι αὐτῆι ἑμέραι ηελλενοταμίαις Φαλάνθοι [Ἀ]

λοπεκέθεν καὶ συνάρχοσιν σῖτον hίπποις: ΤΤΤΤ: hέκτει καὶ δεκά-

τει τῆς πρυτανείας ηελλενοταμίαις Προ[χσέ]

25 νοι Ἀφιδναίοι καὶ συνάρχοσιν: Χ⟦Ⱶ̄⟧ΔΔΔ̄Ⱶ̄ⱵⱵⱵ: τετάρτει καὶ

εἰκοστεῖ τῆς πρυτανείας ηελλενοταμίαις Εὐπόλι[δι Ἀ]

φιδναῖοι καὶ συνάρχοσιν: ⋈ΗΗΗΗ: ἑβδόμει καὶ εἰκοστεῖ τε̂s
πρυτανείας ʰελλενοταμίαις Καλλίαι Εὐονυμ[εῖ κ]

αἱ συνάρχοσιν: ΤΧΧ⊟⊟ΔΓΙΙΙⅭ: ἐπὶ τε̂s ʰιπποθοντίδος ὀγδόες
πρυτανευόσες δοδεκάτει τε̂s πρυτανείας: ʰελ[λενο]

ταμίαις παρεδόθε Προχσένοι ᾿Αφιδναῖοι καὶ συνάρχοσιν: ΤΤΤ⊟Η-
ΔΔΔΙⰘⰘΙΙΙΙ: τετάρτει καὶ εἰκοστεῖ τε̂s πρ[υτα]

νείας ʰελλενοταμίαις ἐδόθε Διονυσίοι Κυδαθεναιεῖ καὶ συνάρχοσιν
:ΤΤΤΧΧΧΧΗΗΗΔΓⰘⰘΙⅭ: ʰέκτει καὶ τριακοσ[τεῖ]

30 τε̂s πρυτανείας ʰελλενοταμίαις ἐδόθε Θράσονι Βουτάδει καὶ συνάρχοσιν: ΤΧΧΧΗΗΗΔΔΓⰘⰘⰘΙΙΙ: ἐπὶ τε̂s ᾿Ερεχθείδ[ος]

ἐνάτες πρυτανευόσες δοδεκάτει τε̂s πρυτανείας: ʰελλενοταμίαις
ἐδόθε Προχσένοι ᾿Αφιδναῖοι καὶ συνάρχοσιν [:.]

ΧΧΗ⊟ΔΔΔΓⰘⰘⰘ: τρίτει καὶ εἰκοστεῖ τε̂s πρυτανείας :ʰελ-
λενοταμίαις ἐδόθε Διονυσίοι Κυδαθεναιεῖ καὶ συνάρχοσ[ιν]

[:]ΤΤΤ⊟ΗΗ⊟ΔΔΔΙⰘⰘΙΙΙ: ʰέκτει καὶ τριακοστεῖ τε̂s πρυτανείας: ʰελλενοταμίαις ἐδόθε Θράσονι Βουτάδει καὶ σ[υν]

[ά]ρχοσιν: ΤΤΧΧΧ⊟ΗΗΗ⊟ΙⅭ: ἔκτει καὶ τριακοστεῖ τε̂s πρυτανείας τὰ ἐχ Σάμο ἀνομολογέσα[ντο ʰοι σύ]μμαχ[οι]

35 [:το]ῖς στρατεγοῖς ἐς Σάμοι Δεχσικράτει Αἰγιλιεῖ :ⴹⴹΤΧ: Πασι-
φόντι Φρεαρρίοι: ⊟Τ: ᾿Αριστοκρά[τει . . . .⁸. . . .]ι: ⊟: Ε[. . .]

[. . . .] Εὐονυμεῖ: ⊟ΧΧΧ⊟ΗΗΗ⊟ΔΔΔΓⰘ: Νικεράτοι Κυδαντίδει τριεράρχοι :ΧΧΧ: ᾿Αριστοφάνει ᾿Ανα[φλυστίοι τριε]-
ράρ[χοι]

[. . . .⁷. . . .] ἐπ[ὶ] τε̂s Πανδιονίδος δεκάτες πρυτανευόσες ἐνδεκάτει
τε̂s πρυτανείας ελλενο[ταμίαις ἐδόθε] Προ[χσ]

[ένοι ᾿Αφιδναῖοι] καὶ συνάρχοσιν: ⊟ΗΗΗΗΔΔΔΔΙⰘΙΙΙΙ: τρίτει
καὶ εἰκοστεῖ τε̂s πρυτανείας ʰελλεν[οταμίαις ἐδόθε . . . .]

[- - - -ᶜ·¹⁴- - - -καὶ συνάρχοσι]ν: ΤΤ⋈⊟ΔΔΔΔΙΙΙ: ἔκτει καὶ
τριακοστεῖ τε̂s πρυτανείας ʰελ[λενοταμίαις ἐδόθε . . .]

40 [- - - - - -ᶜ·¹⁹- - - - - - καὶ συνάρχ]οσιν: ⊟ΧΧΧΧ⊟ΗⰘ⊟ΓⰘΙΙΙΙ:ᵛᵛ κεφάλαιον ἀργυρίο σύμπαν ὃ Κ[αλλίστρατος Μαραθόνιος]

40 ᵇⁱˢ [καὶ συνάρχοντες παρέδοσαν - - - -]   vacat

Attention should be called to some of the changes which have
been made from the restorations now published in the *Corpus*.
Toward the end of line 34 the letters MAX are distinctly visible
upon the stone and are so transcribed in *I.G.*, I, 188. The photograph shows also part of another M, broken away at the left
and at the bottom. The initial letters preserved at the beginning

of line 35 are ΙΣΣΤΡΑΤΕΛΟΙΣ. It is no longer possible to restore here the demotic Μα[ραθόνι]ος. I suggest in its place the reading ἀνομολογέσα[ντο hοι σύ]μμαχ[οι | ⁚ το]ῖς στρατεγοῖς ἐς Σάμοι, which fulfills also the necessary requirements of the available space upon the stone (cf. Plate VI). It may be observed further from the facsimile plate that the demotic Ἀνα[καιεῖ] does not occupy the required space on the stone at the end of line 36. A word of eleven letters should be restored here, and I have supplied Ἀνα[φλυστίοι].

Restorations are uncertain at the beginning and end of the last few lines of the inscription, though in each case the disposition of the letters on the facsimile plate allows an approximate estimate of the number of letters to be restored. The estimates given above differ somewhat from those recorded in the *Corpus*.

This document is of extraordinary interest, because it bears directly on difficult questions of civic and financial administration, and because it affords evidence for the nature of the Athenian calendar in one of the critical years concerned with this study. We learn, first of all, the order in which the various tribes held the prytany throughout the year, and, in the latter part of the inscription, the exact dates on which payments were made from Athena's treasury. There is also, throughout the inscription, a partially separate listing of members of the boards of hellenotamiai and others who received the moneys borrowed. And finally there are given the names of eleven of the hellenotamiai who held office during the conciliar year 410/09.

One of the important pieces of evidence for calendar determination is the fact that a payment to the *athlothetai* for the Panathenaic festival is listed in *I.G.*, I², 304, lines 5–6, as being made in the second prytany of the year. In this volume and elsewhere [1] I have given my reasons for believing that the payments for the Panathenaia of which we have record (three) were made before the festival. If this interpretation is correct, then we have in *I.G.*, I², 304 evidence to show that some part of the second prytany of 410/09 must have fallen before the Panathenaic festival of that year. It does not matter that the payment is listed as

[1] P. 108; Meritt, *The Athenian Calendar*, pp. 93–95; *idem*, "The Departure of Alcibiades for Sicily," *A.J.A.*, XXXIV (1930), 143; *idem*, "Senatorial and Civil Years in Athens," *Cl. Phil.*, XXV (1930), 242.

though made by the treasurers who entered office at the time of the festival. This was merely a matter of clumsy bookkeeping, which finds its excuse in the fact that the conciliar year, on the basis of which these records were kept, down to 409 at least, was not coincident with the Panathenaic year.[1]

The fact that this anomaly of record existed in 410/09 can be proved, quite independently of the payment for the Panathenaia, by evidence which I have not before brought to bear upon the problem and which I outline here. We are concerned first with the composition of the hellenotamiac board in 410/09.

It happens that in *I.G.*, I², 304, lines 3–5, there is preserved a record of payment during the first prytany of certain moneys to be spent for the cavalry. The money was handed over by the treasurers of Athena to the hellenotamiai, Kallimachos and Phrasitelides. It is fortunate that the demotics have also been given with the names of these two hellenotamiai, for we are able to show that they cannot have belonged to the same board with the other hellenotamiai mentioned in the same inscription. Since we know that the boards of hellenotamiai changed office at the time of the Panathenaic festival,[2] we are thus able to determine that the two hellenotamiai, Kallimachos and Phrasitelides, belonged to the retiring board and that the other hellenotamiai mentioned in the following lines belonged to the board of 410/09. We prove, therefore, that some part, at least, of the first prytany must be dated before the Panathenaic festival, because the hellenotamiai who received the money for the cavalry during the first prytany must have retired from office at the time of the festival.

There are recorded in *I.G.*, I², 304, lines 1–40, the names of eleven hellenotamiai, as follows:

Καλλιμάχοι ʰαγνοσίοι	(line 4)
Φρασιτελίδει Ἰκαριεῖ	(line 4)
Περικλεῖ Χολαργεῖ	(lines 8, 11, 13, 18)
Διονυσίοι Κυδαθεναιεῖ	(lines 15, 22, 29, 32)
Θράσονι Βουτάδει	(lines 16, 22–23, 30, 33)
Προχσένοι Ἀφιδναίοι	(lines 17, 24–25, 28, 31, 37–38)

---

[1] Meritt, "Senatorial and Civil Years in Athens," *Cl. Phil.*, XXV (1930), 239–243; Ferguson, *The Treasurers of Athena*, p. 146, note.

[2] Cf. p. 126, below.

Σπουδίαι Φλυεῖ   (line 19)
'Αναιτίοι Σφεττίοι   (line 20)
Φαλάνθοι 'Αλοπεκῆθεν   (lines 23–24)
Εὐπόλιδι 'Αφιδναίοι   (lines 25–26)
Καλλίαι Εὐονυμεῖ   (line 26)

Of these, Kallias belonged to the tribe Erechtheis (I), Phrasitelides to Aigeis (II), Dionysios to Pandionis (III), Pericles, Anaitios, and Kallimachos to Akamantis (V), Thrason to Oineis (VI), Spoudias to Kekropis (VII), Proxenos and Eupolis to Aiantis (IX), and Phalanthos to Antiochis (X).

Various explanations have been given to account for the fact that eleven hellenotamiai, instead of the usual ten, are recorded in this inscription. There have also been attempts to explain the apparent lack of uniformity in the way the official tribes were represented on the hellenotamiac board. Gilbert suggested that Phrasitelides was in fact a paredros, though our inscription states explicitly that he was hellenotamias (ℎελλενοταμίαις Καλλιμάχοι ℎαγνοσίοι Φρασιτελίδει 'Ικαριεῖ) and though the only known paredros of this year, Polyaratos (lines 20–21), is carefully designated as such.[1] Gilbert's view has been followed by Swoboda in his article on the hellenotamiai in Pauly-Wissowa-Kroll (s.v. Hellenotamiai, p. 178, line 25). It is at best a desperate remedy and has no evidence in its favor; Gilbert was unable to account in any other way for the eleven hellenotamiai in the record of expenses for this year.

Boeckh long ago proposed to reduce the number of the hellenotamiai to ten, which he believed to be the size of the normal board, by assuming that Kallimachos and Phrasitelides, whose names are given in connection with the payment in the first prytany, belonged to the board of the previous year, 411/0, while the other nine hellenotamiai in the rest of the inscription belonged to the board of the year 410/09.[2] This solution of an apparent difficulty was possible so long as one could assume that the payment made in the first prytany preceded in point of time the Panathenaic festival. Boeckh made this assumption and has

---

[1] G. Gilbert, *Handbuch der griechischen Staatsalterthümer*, Leipzig, 1881, p. 236.

[2] Boeckh, *Staatshaushaltung der Athener*, I³, 219; I², 244. Cf. also Bannier, "Zu attischen Inschriften," *Berl. ph. Woch.*, 1915, p. 1613.

been adversely criticized for it. Swoboda says (*op. cit.*): "Böckh hat diese Dinge nicht besonders glücklich behandelt." We have discovered above, however, that there can be no valid objection to Boeckh's proposition that the first payment preceded the date of the festival. I maintain that Boeckh's solution of the problem was in this respect essentially correct, though he would probably have been the first to claim (as others have done since his time) that no payment could have been credited to the treasurers Kallistratos and his fellows that had been made before the festival date on which they entered office. And, as we shall see, the necessity for assigning Kallimachos and Phrasitelides to the previous year does not exist because there is any difficulty in explaining a board of more than ten members, as Boeckh and others have thought, but because we cannot concede that *three* members of any one board belonged to the same tribe. If Kallimachos belonged to the board of the year 411/0, then we find that in no case are there more than two hellenotamiai from any one tribe in the board of the year 410/09.

Those who hold that all the hellenotamiai mentioned in *I.G.*, I², 304, lines 1–40, belonged to the board of one year only, have difficulty in explaining the irregular division of the members among the tribes. Akamantis is represented, for example, by three (Gilbert) or two (Boeckh) hellenotamiai; Aiantis had two members; and other tribes had one representative, or no representative at all. Swoboda (Pauly-Wissowa-Kroll, *s.v.* Hellenotamiai, p. 178, line 45) postulates "eine gewisse Berücksichtigung der Phylen," though he claims that the hellenotamiai might be chosen rather *for* than *from* the tribes represented, in such a way that one tribe might be represented twice while some other tribe was not represented at all.

To my mind, this interpretation is certainly incorrect, and I suggest instead that the two hellenotamiai (Boeckh) from Akamantis and the two hellenotamiai from Aiantis indicate that the board in this year was composed of twenty members, chosen regularly two from each tribe. It is purely a fortuitous circumstance that, if we reckon Kallimachos and Phrasitelides as belonging to the previous Panathenaic year, the names of only nine members of this board of twenty have been preserved in *I.G.*, I², 304.

4413

I wish to call attention here to the evidence which bears on this point given in Aristotle's *Constitution of Athens* (30, 2). Among the provisions of the constitution drawn up in 411 we find the following lines: ταμίας τῶν ἱερῶν χρημάτων τῇ θεῷ καὶ τοῖς ἄλλοις θεοῖς δέκα, καὶ ἑλληνοταμίας καὶ τῶν ἄλλων ὁσίων χρημάτων ἁπάντων εἴκοσι οἳ διαχειριοῦσιν, καὶ ἱεροποιοὺς καὶ ἐπιμελητὰς δέκα ἑκατέρους. Now we know that throughout this period the boards of treasurers of the goddess and of the Other Gods remained separate (*I.G.*, I², 298, 253) and consisted of ten members each. Whatever may be the exact significance of the words καὶ τῶν ἄλλων χρημάτων ἁπάντων – – – οἳ διαχειριοῦσιν, it is equally clear that Aristotle is recording the constitutional provision for a board of hellenotamiai consisting of twenty members. Furthermore, this constitution was actually put into effect after the fall of the Four Hundred.[1] Since the functions of the kolakretai, which were transferred to the hellenotamiai in 411, continued to be exercised by the hellenotamiai down to the end of the Peloponnesian War,[2] there is no reason to assume that the board of twenty hellenotamiai, organized at the time of the transfer, was ever replaced again by the older board of ten.

When we find in *I.G.*, I², 304 that two of the tribes were represented by two members each on the board in 410/09, we have confirmation not only that the board of twenty was in existence at that time, but also that this board was made up of two members from each tribe, just as the previous board of ten had been made up with one representative from each tribe.[3]

In order to fix clearly in mind the fact that these treasurers were chosen in such a way as to give equal representation to all tribes, we may note that in the period when the board consisted of only ten members the evidence indicates that there was never more than one member from each tribe. This scrupulous regard for tribal equality was observed also in the choice of the treasurers of the goddess (*I.G.*, I², 358, 359, 255). On this point our epigraphical evidence is supported by the testimony of Aristotle

---

[1] Ferguson, "The Constitution of Theramenes," *Cl. Phil.*, XXI (1926), 72–75; *idem*, *Cambridge Ancient History*, V, 339; *idem*, *The Treasurers of Athena*, p. 3.

[2] E. Meyer, *Forschungen*, II, 137; *idem*, *Gesch. d. Altertums*, IV, 590; Ferguson, *Cambridge Ancient History*, V, 343, note 1.

[3] *I.G.*, I², 296, lines 7–9, 32–34; *I.G.*, I², 216; *I.G.*, I², 218; *I.G.*, I², 220.

('Aθ. Πολ., 47, 1). The full complement of ten treasurers was
not in every year selected (*I.G.*, I², 355 and 358), but in no case
was there more than one treasurer from any one tribe. The
same fundamental principle of selection was applied also to the
treasurers of the Other Gods. From the provisions of the well-
known decree of Kallias (*I.G.*, I², 91) we learn that these treasurers were to be selected in the same manner as were the treasurers
of the goddess (lines 13–15: ταμίας δὲ ἀποκναμένε[ν το]ύτον τὸν
χρεμάτον ηόταμπερ τὰς ἄλλας ἀρχάς, καθάπερ τὸς τὸν ηι[ερὸ]ν τὸν τὲς
'Αθεναίας). We find in the case of this board also that the full
complement of ten was not always obtained,[1] though our epigraphical evidence for the fifth century indicates that only one
treasurer was ever chosen from a single tribe. I find, in this connection, that Kolbe has listed the treasurers of the Other Gods
for the year 420/19 (*I.G.*, I², 370) as belonging to their various
tribes in this order: VII, I, II, V, VI, III, X, (VII or II), IX.[2]
This arrangement of the tribes rests, however, upon an erroneous
interpretation of the demotics given with the names of the
treasurers in *I.G.*, I², 370. The demotic ηαλαιεύς which is given
with the name of the treasurer last but one in our list represents
in this case a tribal affiliation with Aigeis (II). The demotic of
the third treasurer is given as [Κο]λονêθεν, and the deme Kolonos
also has been assigned to the tribe Aigeis by Kolbe. This attribution cannot here be supported. A glance at the table in Pauly-
Wissowa (*s.v.* Δῆμοι) will show that subsequent to the fifth
century there was a deme Kolonos, so far as the original ten
tribes were concerned, in each of the tribes Aigeis (II), Leontis
(IV), and Antiochis (X). I suspect a typographical error in the
index of the *Corpus* (*editio minor*, Vol. I, p. 325), where Kolonos
is assigned to either Aigeis, or Oineis, or Antiochis (II?, VI?, X?).
There is nowhere any evidence that Kolonos may have belonged
to Oineis. Since one of the demes Kolonos is amply attested as
belonging to Leontis (IV) in subsequent years, and since treasurers from Aigeis (II) and Antiochis (X) already appear in *I.G.*, I²,

---

[1] *I.G.*, I², 310, lines 91–94; *I.G.*, I², 370, lines 10–12. Cf. also Kolbe, "Zur atheni-
schen Schatzverwaltung im IV. Jahrhundert," *Philologus*, LXXXIV [N. F. XXXVIII],
(1925), 261–267, especially 262.

[2] Kolbe, "Das Kalliasdekret," *Sitzb. Ak. Berlin*, 1927, p. 324, note 1. Professor
Kolbe notes: "Es fehlen Phyle IV und VIII; dafür ist II oder VII zweimal vertreten."

370, line 12 ('Αλοπεκε̂θεν X and ηαλαιεύς II), I suggest that in this inscription the demotic Κολονε̂θεν must have belonged to the tribe Leontis (IV). I give the sequence of tribes, represented by the treasurers of the Other Gods with their demotics in 420/19 (*I.G.*, I², 370, lines 11–12), as follows: VII, I, IV, V, VI, III, X, II, IX. There was no treasurer during this year from the tribe of Hippothontis, but we may also note that no single tribe was represented by more than one member on the board.

Inasmuch as we find that the boards of treasurers of Athena and of the Other Gods (each consisting of ten members) were chosen with one representative from each tribe and since the same principle held true for the selection of the hellenotamiai when the number of members of their board was also ten, it is legitimate to conclude that the same respect for uniform representation on the board was still observed when the number of hellenotamiai was increased from ten to twenty in 411. Subsequent to this date we shall expect to find two representatives from each tribe as members of the hellenotamiac board. It is not permissible, however, to assume that there were three.[1]

The consequence of this observation is that Kallimachos and Phrasitelides, whose names appear in line 4 of *I.G.*, I², 304, must have belonged to the board of hellenotamiai of 411/0, and that the other nine hellenotamiai mentioned in the inscription must have belonged to the board of the following year, 410/09. Since the hellenotamiai changed office at the time of the Panathenaic festival,[2] some part at least of the first prytany of the conciliar year 410/09, including the day when money was given by the treasurers of the goddess to Kallimachos and Phrasitelides, must have fallen before the date of the festival itself. It is, of course, an inaccuracy of record that the treasurers of the goddess who entered office at the time of the festival are represented as making the payment, though for this inaccuracy we have found parallel cases and ample explanation.

For purposes of reference in our subsequent discussion I give below a portion of the table of correspondences between the

---

[1] In 407/6 the hellenotamiai Lysitheos Thymaitades and (. . . . . . .)on Kopreios both belonged to Hippothontis. See discussion of *I.G.*, I², 304, lines 41 ff., and text on pp. 119–122, 125–127, below.

[2] Cf. p. 126, below.

Julian calendar and the Athenian senatorial (conciliar) and civil calendars taken from my earlier study.[1] The years involved are the first seven years of the second Metonic cycle.

Years of Metonic cycle	Date of Attic year	Julian interca- lation	Senatorial year	Civil year	Attic interca- lation	Correspondences between Julian, senatorial, and civil calendars
1	413/2	O	365	354	O	July 5 — Pryt. I, 1 — Thar. 22 (414/3)
2	412/1	O	365	354	O	July 5 — Pryt. I, 1 — Skir. 3 (413/2)
3	411/0	O	[366]	384	I	July 5 — [Pryt. I, 1] — Skir. 14 (412/1)
4	410/09	I	366	354	O	July 6 — Pryt. I, 1 — Thar. 26 (411/0)
5	409/8	O	366	355	O	July 6 — Pryt. I, 1 — Skir. 9 (410/09)
6	408/7	O	365	354	O	July 7 — Pryt. I, 1 — Skir. 20 (409/8)
7	407/6	O	365	355	O	July 7 — Pryt. I, 1 — Hek. 1

The correspondences down to 411/0 are dependent on the equation given by Aristotle ('Aθ. Πολ., 32, 1) and the equation which is implicit in *I.G.*, I², 328,[2] but after the year 411 the table must now be considerably revised. We no longer carry the separate conciliar year down to the last years of the war, but we know that it had been abandoned before 407/6.[3] It may have been abandoned a year or two earlier; at any rate, the theoretical date given by Aristotle for the year 411/0 and the date implicit in *I.G.*, I², 304 for 407/6 cannot now be used to build up the correspondences in the intervening years, because there is no longer any assurance of a continuous sequence of conciliar years covering the whole period. Since this is true, we must also take full cognizance of the confusion which affected the conciliar year in 411.

So long as we believed that the time sequence of the conciliar year was unbroken by the events of 411, it was necessary to postulate for 411/0 a civil year of thirteen months, if the payment

[1] Meritt, *The Athenian Calendar*, p. 118.

[2] Cf. Meritt, *The Athenian Calendar*, pp. 93–94; *idem*, "The Spartan Gymnopaidia," *Cl. Phil.*, XXVI (1931), 71–72.

[3] Meritt, "Senatorial and Civil Years in Athens," *Cl. Phil.*, XXV (1930), 236–243.

for the Panathenaia in 410 (*I.G.*, I², 304, lines 5–6) was to be dated before the Panathenaia.[1] The evidence of Aristotle here had to be discounted, for he gives only twelve months to 411/0 ('Aθ. Πολ., 33).[2] In any case either 411/0 or 410/09 had to be considered an intercalary year in order to allow the proclamation of honors to Thrasyboulos, the assassin of Phrynichos, to take place at the Dionysia and in the eighth prytany of 410/09 (*I.G.*, I², 110).[3]

These items of evidence now come before us in a different light, and the problem of finding the sequence of ordinary and intercalary years in the civil calendar from 411/0 to 407/6 must be considered afresh. Is it possible to find a solution, in itself reasonable, which takes full account of the irregularities of 411, of the evidence of Aristotle on the character of 411/0, and of the epigraphical evidence for the period from 411 to 407? I believe that such a solution is possible and that the key to its discovery lies in an understanding of the significance which the transfer of government from the Five Thousand to the complete democracy in 410 had for the conciliar year.

Naturally, the year of ten prytanies, in which the official ten tribes of Athens held the prytany in turn, could exist only when the democratic Council of the Five Hundred was in power. On the twenty-second of Thargelion in 411 the regular succession of prytanies in the conciliar year was interrupted by the usurpation of power by the Four Hundred. They remained in control for four months, and the government they represented was replaced (in late summer) by the moderate democracy of the Five Thousand. Under the Five Thousand the administrative unit of time was again called a prytany, though it had no tribal significance and could not, in consequence, be designated in the old-fashioned way by a tribal name.[4] These quasi-prytanies continued during

[1] Meritt, *The Athenian Calendar*, pp. 94–96.

[2] Meritt, *op. cit.*, p. 96; Dinsmoor, *The Archons of Athens*, p. 344, note 4.

[3] Meritt, *op. cit.*, p. 98, note 1. The suggestion of Dinsmoor that we should restore in lines 12–13 of *I.G.*, I², 110 καὶ [ἀνειπεῖν Παναθεναίον τõι γυμνικõι] ἀγõνι seems to me inadmissible in view of the fact that the Panathenaia were more than four months away. Cf. Dinsmoor, *The Archons of Athens*, p. 346, note 6.

[4] Ferguson, *Cambridge Ancient History*, V, 338–339. Cf. the decree quoted by (Plut.), *Vit. dec. or.*, 833–834, given in *I.G.*, I², pp. 297–298; Ferguson, "The Constitution of Theramenes," *Cl. Phil.*, XXI (1926), 74.

the rule of the Five Thousand and must have been replaced by the normal tribal prytanies only after the reëstablishment of complete democracy and the Council of the Five Hundred in the spring or early summer of 410.

If, with Ferguson, we date the battle of Cyzicus in late April of 410, the Attic equivalent will be the month of Munichion if 411/0 was an ordinary year, as Aristotle implies (ʼAθ. Πολ., 33).[1] At some time during the months of Thargelion and Skirophorion the Spartan offer of peace was rejected by Athens (while Theopompos was still archon) and the Council of the Five Hundred restored.[2] We know that the Council of the Five Hundred was again functioning for the conciliar year 410/09 when Glaukippos was archon, and that Aiantis held the first prytany of that year (*I.G.*, I², 304).

The question arises how the administrative divisions of time were arranged in the interval between the restoration of the Council of the Five Hundred and the beginning of the year when Glaukippos was archon. Certainly the ten official tribes represented in the restored Council could not each preside for the normal prytany length of thirty-six or thirty-seven days, for the interim was at most only two months — perhaps one month, or even less. They may have divided the time left toward the end of the year 411/0 into short prytanies of from three to six days each, so that each tribe might have an equal privilege of presiding before the new year began. But there is no need to assume that the civil and conciliar years began simultaneously in 410. I suggest as the simplest of all explanations that there was no interval such as we have here assumed, but that *the year of the Council for which Kleigenes was first secretary began immediately upon the restoration of the full democracy and the Council of the Five Hundred.* Aiantis (*I.G.*, I², 304) was thus the first tribe to hold the prytany under the new order, and the regular succession of prytanies continued as in olden times throughout the year 410/09. The date of Prytany I, 1 may have been somewhere near the middle of Skirophorion, two months, or perhaps less, after the battle of Cyzicus. A glance at the table on page 176 will show that there

---

[1] Ferguson, *Cambridge Ancient History*, V, 485; Meritt, *The Athenian Calendar*, pp. 118–119.

[2] Ferguson, *op. cit.*, p. 485.

were many instances of earlier prytany years which began equally far in advance of the corresponding civil years. We know too little of the exact sequence of events after the battle of Cyzicus to be able to date Prytany I, 1 more definitely. Such a conciliar year as I have outlined is properly described (*I.G.*, I², 304) as the year ἐπὶ Γλαυκίππο ἄρχοντος καὶ ἐπὶ τῆς βολῆς ἑι Κλεγένες πρῶτος ἐγραμμάτευε.

I wish to discuss in this connection the earliest known decree of this year, given by Andocides (I, 96–8) and quoted in *I.G.*, I², p. 298. The decree was passed in the prytany of Aiantis, the first prytany of the year, and provides that all Athenians shall take an oath to maintain the newly recovered democratic form of government. The important part of the document for our purposes, however, is the provision that the decree shall be valid from the beginning of the year of the Council when Kleigenes was first secretary — ἄρχει χρόνος τοῦδε τοῦ ψηφίσματος ἡ βουλὴ οἱ πεντακόσιοι ⟨οἱ⟩ λαχόντες τῷ κυάμῳ ὅτε Κλεογένης πρῶτος ἐγραμμάτευεν. Ferguson has rightly called our attention to the fact that these lines prove that the previous Council was not that of the Five Hundred and that it was not elected by lot.[1] The decree must have been valid, therefore, from the first day of entrance into office of the reinstated Council of the Five Hundred, which we thus learn to have been Prytany I, 1 of the conciliar year 410/09, when Aiantis held the first prytany.[2]

Our contention that there was no interim between the quasi-prytanies of the Five Thousand and the regular prytanies of 410/09 finds complete justification in the provisions of this document recorded by Andocides.

We return for a moment to the question of the payment for the Panathenaia in the second prytany of 410/09. If we equate Prytany I, 1 tentatively with Skirophorion 15, then any date after Hekatombaion 21 will fall in the second prytany of the year. Since we have already observed (p. 98) that the records of payments for this year were based on the conciliar year as distinct from the civil year, such a time relationship is entirely

---

[1] Ferguson, "The Constitution of Theramenes," *Cl. Phil.*, XXI (1926), 75; Beloch, *Gr. Gesch.*, II², 2, 314.

[2] Wilhelm, "Fünf Beschlüsse der Athener," *Jahresh. d. öst. arch. Inst.*, XXI–XXII (1924), 144, fails to recognize this.

possible. In view of the other evidence in favor of payments before the festival (especially *I.G.*, I², 305) I suggest that such was the case here also. It is certainly no longer possible to prove the contrary.

Dinsmoor has argued that the conciliar and civil years were equated after the breakdown of the conciliar year in 411.[1] I am quite prepared to agree with him that the decision to equate the two years was reached at this time, but I cannot believe that the restored democracy would wait patiently for such a theoretical advantage to the calendar in order to install the new Council of the Five Hundred on Hekatombaion 1. The installation of the new Council was a matter not of calendar convenience but of political reform, backed by vigorous democratic action. Since the equation of civil and conciliar years could be effected at some early convenient time, I suggest that the length of prytanies was so determined in 410/09 that Prytany I, 1 of 409/8 should fall on Hekatombaion 1 of the same year. If we construe 410/09 as an ordinary year in the civil calendar and assume that the new Council entered office, as suggested, on Skirophorion 15 of 411/0, then the conciliar year 410/09 contained $354 + 16 = 370$ days and the separate prytanies numbered approximately thirty-seven days each. We find that the old separate conciliar year loses its identity at this time, and that our calendar scheme must be constructed for subsequent years with Prytany I, 1 regularly equated with Hekatombaion 1.

The disappearance of the conciliar year as such was accompanied by a change in the fiscal year, in which the Panathenaic interval was made the basis for recording the moneys borrowed by the state from Athena. We know already that this change took place between 410/09 and 407/6.[2]

The corresponding dates Prytany I, 1 (410/09) = Skirophorion 15 (411/0), which we have used in the foregoing argument, are entirely hypothetical. If we wish to bring the reëstablishment of complete democracy back closer in point of time to the battle of Cyzicus, we may give to Prytany I, 1 in 410/09 an earlier date in the civil calendar and increase the length of the

---

[1] Dinsmoor, *The Archons of Athens*, p. 348.

[2] Meritt, "Senatorial and Civil Years in Athens," *Cl. Phil.*, XXV (1930), 236–243.

conciliar year 410/09. This will also bring a greater part of Prytany II before the Panathenaic festival. The possibility of prytanies numbering thirty-nine days each is not to be excluded, for according to the new plan they were soon to become normal during every intercalary civil year. At the same time the regular payments at approximate twelve-day intervals during the last prytanies of 410/09 (I.G., I², 304) suggest that the length of prytany was more nearly thirty-six or thirty-seven days than thirty-nine.

Instead of the old sequence of ordinary and intercalary years in the civil calendar from 413/2 to 407/6, which I had proposed in my first study of the calendar as O O I O O O O, we now have determined the sequence O O O O I O O. The succession of four ordinary years at the beginning of the second Metonic cycle is the remedy for the irregularity introduced into the calendar by an extra intercalary year at the end of the first cycle, and it soon brought the first day of the civil year to its normal position at the first new moon after the summer solstice. Our argument is supported by this additional astronomical advantage. The revised table of correspondences between the Julian and the Athenian calendars is given on page 176.

In spite of the evidence from the decree quoted by Andocides, it has been generally assumed for the past decade that the Council of the Five Hundred was reinstated some little time before the beginning of the conciliar year 410/09. This assumption is based upon Wilhelm's attribution of I.G., I², 105 to the archonship of Theopompos,[1] and is necessary, if this date for the inscription is correct. The preamble and introductory formulae of I.G., I², 105 are characteristic of the period of complete democracy, but quite different from those used by the Five Thousand.[2] The tribe in prytany is named as Akamantis, while under the Five Thousand the official tribal names were not employed. Mention is also made of the Demos, together with the Boule, in the formula of decree; the Boule alone was named under the Five Thousand (I.G., I², p. 298). Akamantis is known to have held the fourth

---

[1] Wilhelm, "Fünf Beschlüsse der Athener," *Jahresh. d. öst. arch. Inst.*, XXI–XXII (1924), 123–147.

[2] Wilhelm, *op. cit.*, p. 144; Ferguson, "The Constitution of Theramenes," *Cl. Phil.*, XXI (1926), 75.

prytany of 410/09 (*I.G.*, I², 304, line 11), but a date so late in the year falls under the archonship of Glaukippos, and the name Glaukippos cannot be restored in line 3 of *I.G.*, I², 105. If this inscription is to be dated in 410, the name of the archon must be Theopompos, and the tribe Akamantis must have been holding the prytany under the restored democracy at some time earlier than the prytany of Aiantis, which we know to have held the first prytany of the conciliar year 410/09 (*I.G.*, I², 304, line 3).

We have found that this interpretation is impossible, for the restoration of complete democracy — and the end of the rule of the Five Thousand — dates from Prytany I, 1 (Aiantis) of 410/09. We must reëxamine, rather, the evidence for dating *I.G.*, I², 105 in 410. So far as the physical requirements of the stone are concerned, the name of the archon might be supplied as Ἀντιγένες, with the date of the decree then determined as 407/6.

The decree embodies a public vote of gratitude to the Macedonian king Archelaos for his services past and present to the Athenian people. We may accept, with Wilhelm, the restoration of lines 25–31, which gives us a reference to the campaign against Pydna in 411/0 and to the specific kind of help — the furnishing of shipbuilding materials — for which the Athenians were indebted to Archelaos. Theramenes gave aid with his fleet to the Macedonian army before Pydna in 411/0 (Diodorus, XIII, 49, 1; Xenophon, *Hell.* I, 1, 12), and doubtless received assistance from Archelaos in return for this service. The Athenians in the previous year also had been given material for ships by Archelaos, for Andocides tells of the importation of such supplies to Samos during the time of the Four Hundred (Andocides, II, 11). It is evident from line 4 of this decree that help is again expected from Archelaos in the building of ships ([ἐς τ]ὲν πο[ίε]σιν τὸν [νεόν]). These references, however, do not serve to date the inscription in 411/0, for the gratitude expressed by the Athenian people was for benefactions past and present. The decree may have been passed as well in 407/6 as in 411/0.

When we refer to the present restoration of the text we find that the Council is charged with bringing back the Athenian army from Macedonia, with remanning the ships, and with sending the army to Ionia as quickly as possible to patrol the district. The text reads as follows:

$$[- - - - - - τ ε̂ς δ ὲ] κομιδε̂ς τ ο̂ν νε[ο̂]$$
$$15 \quad [ν α ἰ οἰκαδ' ἀχσοσι τ ὲν ἐ]γ Μακεδονίας σ[τ]$$
$$[ρατιὰν τ ὲν βολὲν ἐπιμ]ελ[ε]θε̂ναι h όπος$$
$$[ἀν σταλο̂σιν hος τάχισ]τα 'Αθέναζε καὶ π$$
$$[λεροθο̂σιν καὶ ἐς 'Ιονί]αν κομίζεται hε$$
$$[στρατιὰ φυλάχσοσα φυ]λακὲν τ ὲν ἀρίστ$$
$$20 \quad [εν - - - - - - - - -]$$

Since we know of Athenian military operations in Macedonia in 411/0 and do not know of any operations there in 407/6, the inscription seems to fit rather better into the sequence of events in the earlier year. Without considering the possibility of a date in 407/6 this has been Wilhelm's interpretation.[1] I call attention, however, to the fact that these lines give evidence for an army in Macedonia only by virtue of a restoration, and that the present text is not without difficulties of interpretation for the epigraphist as well as the historian. If the presence of an army was desired in Ionia, why was not the Macedonian squadron transferred directly to the new theatre of operations? We are asked to believe that ships brought back one army from Macedonia to Athens and then carried another army to Ionia. The Athenians seem to have been interested more in getting ships as quickly as possible from Macedonia to Athens than in recalling their army, which is mentioned in only an incidental way. One wonders whether the restoration $[τ ὲν ἐ]γ$ Μακεδονίας $σ[τρατιάν]$ may not be entirely wrong. If we examine the first part of the document and avoid the implications of restoration, we find that it is concerned with the making of ships, and the bringing back of ships (— from Macedonia), so that an army (?) may be taken to some strategic point (Ionia?) for guard duty. We obtain a better interpretation of the inscription, in my estimation, if we assume that the ships were to be made where the timber was available, and then brought back to Athens as quickly as possible for the transportation of troops. All reference to the army from Macedonia, which confuses the issue, should be eliminated.

From the point of view of epigraphical usage in restoration we should attempt also to preserve where possible the aspirate

[1] Wilhelm, "Fünf Beschlüsse der Athener," *Jahresh. d. öst arch. Inst.*, XXI–XXII (1924), 141; cf. also Ferguson, *Cambridge Ancient History*, V, 343, 485.

at the beginning of words which regularly show the aspirate in those parts of the document where the inscription is preserved. Objection should be made to the line [αἰ οἴκαδ' ἄχσοσι τὲν ἐ]γ Μακεδονίας σ[τρατιάν] for this additional reason, namely, that it is epigraphically improbable. If the present sense is to be retained, some different wording, at least, should be devised. But I propose to abandon this reading altogether, on the ground that we have to deal only with the building of ships and getting them to Athens for use as soon as possible.

Since the ships were to be constructed in Macedonia we can understand why the generals, who were in control of easy communication between Athens and the north, were charged with the transfer of funds to the ναυπηγοί. Naturally, they provided passage also for those who were to work on the ships. I read in lines 9–11:

[– – – – τὸς δὲ τεταγ]μένος πλὲν ἐπὶ τ
[ἐν ἐκπόεσιν τὸν νεὸν h]ος τάχιστα αποσ
[τελάντον hοι στρατεγ]οί – – – – – – –

The Council was to provide for the bringing to Athens of completed ships, so that they might be manned as quickly as possible and sent to Ionia. I propose for lines 14–20 the following restoration:

[– – – – – – – τῆς δὲ] κομιδῆς τὸν νε[ὸ]
15 [ν hὰς ἂν hοι ναυπεγοὶ ἐ]γ Μακεδονίας σ[τ]
[έλλοσι τὲν βολὲν ἐπιμ]ελ[ε]θῆναι, hόπος
[ἂν σταλῶσιν hος τάχισ]τα Ἀθέναζε καὶ π
[λεροθῶσι καὶ ἐπὶ Ἰονί]αν κομίζεται hε
[στρατιὰ φυλάχσοσα φυ]λακὲν τὲν ἀρίστ
20 [εν· – – – – – – – – – – – – – – – – –]

A reward was offered for the first man to finish and bring his ship to Athens. The provision for the reward is contained in lines 22–24, where I change the construction slightly because of the present irregularity in writing ὁ δῆμος instead of the normal (for this inscription) hο δῆμος.

[– – – – τοῖ δὲ πρότοι ἐλθ]όντι καὶ κομ[ι]
[σαμένοι ναῦν δôναι δορεὰν κ]αθά[περ ἔδ]
[οχσεν τôι δέμοι· ἐπειδὲ δὲ Ἀρχέλας καὶ]
[νῦν καὶ ἐν τôι πρόσθεν χρ]ό[ν]οι ἐσ[τὶν – –]

We have already noted that the name of the archon Ἀντιγένες should be supplied in line 3. Our analysis of the text of the inscription shows that the connection with events in 411/0 is found only in the second part of the decree, where Archelaos is being praised for past as well as present benefactions. There can be no objection so far to a date for the document in 407/6. The closest link with 411/0 was the apparent mention of an Athenian army in Macedonia. This was entirely a matter of restoration, and introduced, in fact, a disturbing element into the otherwise straightforward provisions of the first part of the decree.

The decree really provides for new ships to do guard duty in Ionia, and the tenor of the document is evidence that there is some haste about pressing them into service. In the early summer of 410, which is the date that Wilhelm gives to the decree, the combined Athenian fleets in the Hellespont had just won the battle of Cyzicus and reëstablished an undisputed supremacy on the sea.[1] The need for haste in providing a patrol squadron for Ionia is not easily explained at just this time. On the other hand, if we date *I.G.*, I², 105 in 407/6, we find that Ionia is very much in need of all the protection that Athens can give. Not only was a strong Spartan fleet concentrated at Ephesus, but a vigorous and capable admiral (Lysander) was in command, adding further difficulties for the Athenians by his close coöperation with Persia.[2]

We return once more to the text of *I.G.*, I², 105. The name of one of the generals is given in line 5 — or rather, we have the initial letter Π, which belongs to such a name. The younger Pericles, who had been hellenotamias in 410/09, was promoted to the generalship in 409/8 (*I.G.*, I², 301, line 22);[3] we may supply his name here also if the date 407/6 is accepted for the inscription. Lines 4–7 may be restored as follows:

$$[- - - - - - - ἐς \ τ]ὲν \ πο[ίε]σιν \ τὸν \ [νε]$$
$$[ὸν \ δανεῖσαι \ τὸς \ στρα]τεγὸς \ τ[ὸ]ς \ μετὰ \ Π[ε]$$
$$[ρικλέος \ ἀργύριον \ παρ]ὰ \ τὸν \ ν[ῦ]ν \ ὄντον \ ἀ$$
$$[ποδεκτὸν \ τοῖς \ ναυπεγ]οῖς· \ - - - - - - -$$

[1] Ferguson, *Cambridge Ancient History*, V, 343.

[2] Ferguson, *op. cit.*, V, 352–353.

[3] Ferguson, *The Treasurers of Athena*, p. 43, note 1.

At the same time it must be admitted that some other restoration might have been possible if the date were 410, for we do not have an exhaustive list of generals for 411/0. The suggested restoration for these lines is, therefore, more in the nature of a possible prosopographical identification than an argument for date.

The conclusive argument that *I.G.*, I², 105 cannot belong in 410 is found, in my opinion, in the decree given by Andocides (I, 96). Before the prytany of Aiantis in 410/09 there could have been no prytany (as in *I.G.*, I², 105) bearing the name Akamantis. We find that epigraphically 407/6 is just as satisfactory a date as 410, while the analysis of the provisions of the decree shows that it can be reconciled with the events of 407/6 known from other sources as well as with the events of 410.[1]

The entire text of the document is given here:

[ἔδοχσεν τε̑ι βολε̑ι καὶ το̑]ι δέμοι, Ἀκα[μα]
[ντὶς ἐπρυτάνευε, Φελ]λεὺς [ἐγρ]αμ[μ]άτ[ευ]
[ε, Ἀντιγένες ἐρχε, Σιβ]ύρτιο[s ἐ]πεστά[τε],
[. . . . . .¹⁰. . . . εἶπε· ἐς τ]ὲν πο[ίε]σιν τὸν [νε]
5 [ὸν δανεῖσαι τὸς στρα]τεγὸς τ[ὸ]s μετὰ Π[ε]
[ρικλέος ἀργύριον παρ]ὰ τὸν ν[ῦ]ν ὄντον ἀ
[ποδεκτὸν τοῖς ναυπεγ]οῖς· ἡὸ δ' ἂν δανεί
[σοσιν, ἀποδόντον αὐτο]ῖς πάλιν ἡοι τρι
[εροποιοί. τὸς δὲ τεταγ]μένος πλὲν ἐπὶ τ
10 [ὲν ἐκπόεσιν τὸν νεὸν h]ος τάχιστα ἀποσ
[τελάντον ἡοι στρατεγ]οί· εἰ δὲ μέ, ἐσαγό
[σθον προδοσίας ἐς τὸ δ]ικαστέριον· hο[ι]
[δὲ hελιασταὶ περὶ τὸ μ]ὲ ἐθέλοντος ἀπι
[έναι κρινόντον. τε̑ς δὲ] κομιδε̑ς τὸν νε[ο̑]
15 [ν, hὰς ἂν hοι ναυπεγοὶ ἐ]γ Μακεδονίας σ[τ]
[έλλοσι, τὲν βολὲν ἐπιμ]ελ[ε]θε̑ναι, hόπος
[ἂν σταλο̑σιν hος τάχισ]τα Ἀθέναζε καὶ π
[λεροθο̑σι καὶ ἐπὶ Ἰονί]αν κομίζεται hε
[στρατιὰ φυλάχσοσα φυ]λακὲν τὲν ἀρίστ
20 [εν. ἐὰν δέ τις μὲ ποέσει] κατὰ ταῦτα, ὀφέλ
[εν μυρίας δραχμὰς αὐτὸ]ν hιερὰς τε̑ι Ἀθ
[εναίαι. το̑ι δὲ πρότοι ἐλθ]όντι καὶ κομ[ι]

[1] Ferguson, *op. cit.*, p. 42, note 1.

[σαμένοι ναῦν δõναι δορεὰν κ]αθά[περ ἔδ]

[οχσεν τõι δέμοι. ἐπειδὲ δὲ ᾿Αρχέλας καὶ]

25 [νῦν καὶ ἐν τõι πρόσθεν χρ]ό[ν]οι ἐσ[τὶν ἀν]

[ὲρ ἀγαθὸς περὶ ᾿Αθεναί]ος τός τε ἐκπ[λεύ]

[σαντας ᾿Αθεναίον ἀνέλ]αβεν καὶ ἐς τὸ [ἐπ]

[ὶ Πύδνει στρατόπεδον] ἀπέπεμφσεν κα[ὶ]

[εὖ ἐπόεσεν ᾿Αθεναίον τ]ὸ στρατόπεδον κ

30 [αὶ ἔδοκεν αὐτοῖς χσύλ]α καὶ κοπέας καὶ

[ἄλλα hόσον ἐδέοντο παρ'] αὐτõ ἀγαθά, ἐπα

[ινέσαι ᾿Αρχέλαι hos ὄν]τι ἀνδρὶ ἀγαθõι

[καὶ προθύμοι ποιὲν hό,]τι δύναται ἀγαθ

[ὸν καὶ ἀνθ' ὃν εὐεργέτε]κεν τέν τε πόλιν

35 [καὶ τὸν δêμον τὸν ᾿Αθεναί]ον ἀναγράφσα

[ι αὐτὸν καὶ ἐκγόνος προξένο]s καὶ ε[ὐερ]

[γέτας ἐμ πόλει ἐστέλεν λιθίνεν] κ[αὶ ἐπι]

[μέλεσθαι αὐτὸν – – – – – – – – – – – – –]

CHAPTER VII

BORROWINGS FROM ATHENA IN 407/6 B.C.

FERGUSON has recently shown that the inscription published in the *Corpus* as *I.G.*, I², 304 B should, in fact, be assigned to the year 407/6. This attribution of date has been generally accepted for many years, but only since the publication of Ferguson's study has there been definite assurance that the traditional date is correct.[1] The records of the years 409/8 (*I.G.*, I², 301) and 408/7 (lost) were too long to be inscribed on the obverse face of the stele which carried the record for 410/09 (*I.G.*, I², 304 A), and were recorded on a separate block of stone, part of which is now preserved in London. We may assume with some probability that the record of borrowings from Athena in 408/7 was inscribed on the reverse (and left lateral face) of the stele which preserved on its obverse and right lateral face the accounts for 409/8. The treasurers of 407/6 were therefore faced with the necessity of erecting a new stele or of utilizing the still uninscribed lower portion of the obverse of *I.G.*, I², 304 A. In this case their accounts could, of course, be continued on the reverse of the same stone. The upper portion of this stone is at present preserved, and the inscription on the reverse (*I.G.*, I², 304 B) is proof that this latter method of publication was, in fact, employed.[2]

As preserved in the Louvre, the stone is 1.16 m. in height. The principal face is inscribed with the record of borrowings from Athena in 410/09 (*I.G.*, I², 304 A). The text of this document occupies 0.49 m. and commences at a point 0.03 m. below a cymatium (0.06 m. high) which separates the inscribed surface from the anaglyph which surmounts the stele. The width of the stone across the inscribed surface is 0.77 m.; across the anaglyph, 0.62 m. The cymatium is carried across both lateral faces of the stele, though not across the reverse. It would thus

[1] Ferguson, *The Treasurers of Athena*, pp. 28–32.

[2] There were probably other reasons why the record for 409/8 was not cut on the same stone with *I.G.*, I², 304 A. Cf. Ferguson, *op. cit.*, pp. 32–33.

appear that the reverse face was not intended originally to be used for epigraphical record. The anaglyph is 0.57 m. in height and, together with the cymatium, occupies more than half the present height of the stele. Below the inscription on the obverse is an uninscribed surface of approximately 0.01 m. Below this the stele seems to have been cut across horizontally in post-classical times.

On the reverse the record of the accounts for 407/6 commences with a payment for the diobelia made on Metageitnion 21, at a point 0.29 m. above the post-classical bottom of the stone. Approximately 0.02 m. more of the surface than on the obverse face was here lost when the original stone was cut in two. The twenty-five lines which have been preserved represent the payments made by the treasurers of Athena from Metageitnion 21 to Boedromion 14 inclusive.

The record must have been continued on the original stele below the post-classical cutting, but even so there was not sufficient room to list all the payments. When the bottom of the stone was reached the stone-cutter returned to the upper portion of the reverse face and continued the inscription from a point directly behind the cymatium. The perfectly smooth surface behind the anaglyph, so far as I have been able to judge, was never inscribed. This upper continuation of the document begins with payments made during the early days of Munichion.

We must postulate, therefore, the loss of a sufficient amount of stone to accommodate the records from Boedromion 15 through Elaphebolion — a period of six and one-half months.[1] It would thus seem possible to estimate approximately the extent of that portion of the stele which has been lost. Unfortunately, the record of a month from the middle of Metageitnion to the middle of Boedromion must have occupied about twenty-eight lines, while the record for Munichion occupied only twelve lines (66–77). Each line requires about 0.01 m. on the stone (slightly more), and it is only possible to suggest that the minimum amount of stone lost from the original stele was 0.78 m. and that the maximum amount of stone lost may have been as much as 1.82 m. Even these figures are hardly reliable, for the

---

[1] The year 407/6 was an ordinary year. Cf. Meritt, "Senatorial and Civil Years in Athens," *Cl. Phil.*, XXV (1930), 239.

record of Thargelion seems to have contained only one payment, which was inscribed in three lines (78–80).

It has already been observed that these records of borrowings by the state from Athena's treasure in 407/6 were based upon the Panathenaic year.[1] It is evident, therefore, that the portion of the record for 407/6 which was inscribed on the lower part of the obverse face of the stele included only those loans which were made between Hekatombaion 28 and Metageitnion 20. If we may make any deductions from the length of the record in Metageitnion and Boedromion which appears on the reverse, it is possible to estimate the amount of space occupied by the text on the obverse (and belonging to 407/6) as approximately 0.25 m. Even if it be granted that the amount of stone lost from the original stele was the suggested minimum of 0.78 m., this conclusion necessitates the assumption that an uninscribed surface of more than 0.50 m. was left between the end of the accounts of 410/09 and the beginning of the accounts of 407/6. It is evident, I believe, that the extended form of the record employed during Metageitnion must have given place relatively early in the year to the more concise form of record found in Munichion and Thargelion. In this way the assumed total height of the stele may be reduced and the extent of the uninscribed surface on the obverse face of the stone diminished.

The end of the record for 407/6 breaks off in line 92 with an incomplete entry, although there was still available on the stone at this point an uninscribed surface of 0.035 m.[2]

The determination of the text of this inscription is extremely difficult because of the badly weathered condition of the surface of the marble, but I have given in the facsimile copy (Plate XI) those letters or traces of letters which I have been able to read from the stone. Through the courtesy of Les Archives Photographiques, I am also able to reproduce in Plates VII–X photographs of the reverse face of the stele, which may be used to some extent as a control in studying the facsimile plate. Many of the readings, however, were obtained after patient study of the stone itself under different conditions of light and shadow, and with

[1] Meritt, "Senatorial and Civil Years in Athens," *Cl. Phil.*, XXV (1930), 242–243. Cf. p. 108, above.

[2] Cf. Ferguson, *The Treasurers of Athena*, p. 32.

the help of squeezes, charcoal wash, and plastic impressions. A
definitive control in doubtful cases can be given only by careful
inspection of the stone as now preserved in Paris.

The following text is based upon the readings in Plate XI:

I.G., I², 304 B (407/6)
Lower part

41   ἐπὶ τῆς Ἐρεχθείδος δευτέρας πρ[υτανευόσες ἑλλενοταμίαις παρέδομεν
  Λυσιθέοι Θυμ]αιτά

42   δει καὶ συνάρχοσι τρίτ[ει] καὶ δεκάτε[ι τῆς πρ]υτα[νείας δεκάτει
  φθίνοντος Μεταγειτ]νιῶνος

43   ἐς τὲν διοβελίαν Ἀθενα[ία]ι Νίκει Γ[...⁵...] ἑλλε[ν]ο[ταμίαις καὶ
  παρέδροις] Θ[ρ]α[συλ]όχοι Θορικ

44   ίοι καὶ συνάρχοσι ἑβδό[μ]ει καὶ δεκάτει [τῆς πρ]υτ[ανείας ἕκτει
  φθίνοντος] Μεταγειτνιῶνο[ς]

45   ἐς τὲν διοβελίαν ΗΔΗΗ [ἑ]λλενοταμίαις [καὶ παρέδροις Λυσιθέοι
  Θυμαιτ]άδει καὶ συνάρχοσ[ι]

46   ἑβδόμει καὶ δεκάτει τε͂[ς] πρυτανείας ἕ[κτει φθίνοντος Μεταγειτνιῶνος
  ἐς] τὲν διοβελίαν Ἀ

47   θεναίαι Νίκει ΓΗΗΗΗ[.]Δ[ΔΔ]ΓΗ ἑλλενοταμίαι[ς καὶ παρέδροις Προτάρχοι] Προβαλισίοι καὶ σ

48   υνάρχοσι ὀ[γδ]όει καὶ δεκάτει [τῆς πρυτανείας πέμπτει φθίνοντος
  Μεταγ]ειτνιῶνος ἐς τὲ

49   ν διοβελία[ν] ΔΗΗ ἑλλενοταμίαις καὶ παρέδροις [Προτάρχοι Προ-
  βαλισίοι] καὶ συνάρχοσι ἐνά

50   τει καὶ δεκ[άτ]ει τῆς πρυτανείας τε[τ]ράδι φθί[ν]οντος Μετα[γε]ιτ-
  νιῶνος ἐς τὲν διοβελίαν ΗΗΓ

51   ἑλλενοταμίαις καὶ παρέδροις Λυσιθέοι Θυμαιτάδει καὶ συνά[ρχο]σι
  δευτέραι καὶ εἰκοστ[ε͂ι]

52   τῆς πρυτανείας ἕνει καὶ [ν]έαι Μεταγειτνιῶνος ἐς τὲν διοβελίαν
  ΔΓΙΙΙΙ ἑλλενοταμίαις [καὶ]

53   παρέδροις Θρασυλόχοι Θ[ο]ρικίοι καὶ συνάρχοσι τρίτει καὶ εἰκοστε͂ι
  τῆς πρυτανείας [ν]ο[με]

54   νίαι Βοεδρομιῶνος ἐς τὲν διοβελίαν ΗΓΔΗΙΙ ἑλλενοταμίαις καὶ
  παρέδροις Λυσιθέοι Θυ[μαι]

55   τάδει καὶ συνάρχοσι τετάρτει καὶ εἰκοστε͂ι τῆς πρυτανείας δευτέραι
  Βοεδρομιῶνος ἐς [τὲν]

56 διοβελίαν ΓΗΙΙΙC ἐλλενοταμίαις καὶ παρέδροις [Λ]υσιθέοι Θυμαιτάδει καὶ συνάρχοσι ἔκτει

57 καὶ εἰκοστῆι τῆς πρυτανείας τετράδι ἰσταμένο Βοεδρομιῶνος ἐς τὲν
διοβελίαν ⊡ΔΔΔΓ[.]Ι ἐλ

58 λενοταμίαις καὶ παρέδροις Λυσιθέοι Θ[υμ]αιτάδει καὶ συνάρχοσι
τριακοστῆι τῆς πρυταν[εί]

59 ας ὀγδόει ἰσταμένο Βοεδρομιῶνος ἐς τὲν διοβελίαν Ἀθεναίαι [Ν]ίκει
⊡ΓΗ ἐλλενοταμία[ις κα]

60 ὶ παρέδροις Λυσιθέοι Θυμαιτάδει καὶ συνάρχοσι τριακοστῆι τῆς
πρυτανείας ὀγδόει ἰστ[αμέ]

61 νο Βοεδρομιῶνος ἐς τὲν διοβελίαν ⊡ΔΔΔΗ ἐλλενοταμίαις καὶ
παρέδροις Προτάρχοι [[Προτάρ]]

62 [[χοι]] Προβαλισίοι καὶ συνάρχοσι ἔκτει καὶ τριακοστῆι τῆς πρυτανείας τετράδι ἐπὶ δέκα [Βοε]

63 [δ]ρομιῶνος [ἐς τὲν δ]ιοβελίαν ΔΔΓΗΗΗΤ ἐλλενοταμίαις καὶ παρέδροις Λυσιθέοι Θυμαιτάδ[ει]

64 [κα]ὶ συνάρχ[οσι ἔκτει καὶ τριακ]οστῆι τῆς πρυτανεία[ς τε]τράδι ἐπὶ
δέκα Βοεδρομιῶνος [ἐς τὲν]

65 [διοβελίαν] . . . . 43 . . . .
. . . . . . ιτ –

I.G., I², 304 B (407/6)

Upper part

66 [. . . . λ]ογισταῖ[ς . . . . 23 . . . .] ΙΥΡΝ[. .]
ΤΟΝΚΑΙΓ . . . Α 20

67 [. . . .]ι Νομενίο Μαραθονίο[ι . . . .]Δ . . . 7 . . . Ο . . . . . 12 . . . . .
Ο . . . . 9 . . . . Ο[. . Πα]ιονίδει [. . . .]

68 [. . .]θεν Φαινίπποι Παιονίδε[ι] τρίτ[ει κα]ὶ εἰκοσ[τῆι τῆς πρυ]τα-
[νεία]ς τρίτ[ει] Μονιχιῶνο[ς] ἱ[στ]

69 [αμ]ένο ᵛ ΤΧΧΓΗ[ΗΗ]ΙΙ[ΙΙ]ᵛ [ἐλ]λενοταμίαι[ς καὶ] παρέ[δροις
καὶ στρατεγοῖ τῆς ἐν Σάμοι στρατ[ιᾶς Κ]

70 [όν]ονι ἔκτει καὶ εἰκοστῆι τῆς πρυτανείας ἔ[κ]τε[ι Μ]ον[ιχι]ô[νος
ἰσταμέν]ο [ᵛ . . . 7 . . .]ΤΤᵛ ἐπὶ [τê]

71 [ς . . .ε]ίδο[ς] ἐλλενοταμίαις [καὶ π]αρέδρο[ι]ς Λυσιθέο[ι Θυμαιτ]ά-
δ[ει καὶ συνά]ρχοσιν δευτέραι

72 [τὲ]s πρυτανείας ἐβδόμε[ι] ἐπ[ὶ] δέ[κ]α Μονι[χι]ὸ[νος . . .]Δ. .Ι. . .
  [ἑ]λλενο[ταμίαις] κ[αὶ] παρέδροις Ἀ

73 [θε]νοδόροι Μελιτεῖ [κ]αὶ συν[άρ]χοσιν τε[τ]άρ[τ]ε[ι τὲς πρυτανείας
  ἐνάτει ⟨ἐπὶ δέκα⟩ Μονιχιὸν]ο[s] ἐ[s] τ[ὲν] δ[ὶ]

74 [οβ]ελίαν ᵛ ΤΤ[.]ᵛ λογισταῖ[s] Ἀ[ρ]χεδέμοι [Μ]αρ[αθονίοι καὶ
  συνάρχοσιν καὶ ἑλλενοταμί]α[ι . . .⁵. .]

75 [. .]ονι Κοπρείοι ἐβδόμει τὲ[s] πρυτανείας ἐνά[τ]ε[ι Μονιχιὸνος
  φθίν]ο[ντος . . . .]Ο. . . .¹⁰. . . .

76 ι λογισταῖς [Ἀρ]χεδέ[μοι] Μαρ[α]θον[ί]οι . . . . .³⁵. . . . .
  . . . . .Ο.Ο. . .⁶. . .

77 πέμπτηι καὶ δεκάτηι [τ]ῆ[s πρυ]τ[ανείας ἔνει καὶ νέαι Μονιχιὸνος
  – – – – – – – –ᶜ·³⁶– – – – – – – – –]

78 βονος λογισταὶ Ε̣.ΤΟΝΟ.ΟΛΟ̣ṆX̣ΗΗ𐅄. .[λ]ο[γ]ισταὶ[– – – –
  – – – – – – – – – – – δευτέραι καὶ εἰκοστῆι]

79 τῆς πρυτανείας ἐβδό[μηι] Θαργηλιῶνος [ἱσταμένο ἐς Θ]ορικό[ν – – –
  – – – – – – – – – – – –]

80 μοι Παιονίδηι καὶ συνάρχοσιν [– – – – – – – – – – – – – – – –
  – – – – – δοδεκάτηι τῆς πρυτανείας πέμ]

81 πτηι ἱσταμένο Σκιροφοριῶνος ΙΟ. .Ο.ΝΟ – – – – – – – – – – –
  –

82 τοι Φαληρεῖ καὶ συνάρχοσιν δοδεκάτηι [τῆς] πρ[υταν]εί[ας πέμπτηι
  ἱσταμένο Σκι]ρο[φοριῶνος – – – – – – ἑλληνοτα]

83 μίαις καὶ παρέδρ Λυ[σ]ιθέοι Θυμαιτάδηι κ[αὶ συνάρχοσιν – – – – –
  – – – – – – – – – – – – – – ἑλληνοτα]

84 μίαις καὶ παρέδροις Προτάρχοι Προβα[λισίοι] καὶ συνάρχο[σιν – –
  – – – – – – – – – – – – – – – – φθίνον]

85 τος Σκιροφοριῶνος [ἐ]s Θορι[κ]όνᵛΤᵛλογισταῖ[s Ἀρχ]εδήμο[ι Μαραθονίοι καὶ συνάρχοσιν καὶ ἑλληνοταμίαις καὶ παρέδροις . . .⁷. . .
  ο]

86 νι Κοπρείοι καὶ συνάρχοσιν τρ[ίτηι] καὶ [εἰκ]ο[στ]ῆι τῆς [πρυτα-
  νείας ἕκτηι ἐπὶ δέκα Σκιροφοριῶνος – – – – – – –]

87 ιαι Εὐαγγέλοι ΜΙΛΜΟΙ . . . . Ο𐅝ΕΚΤΟΝΔ . . . .⁸. . . . 𐅝Υ – –
  – – – – – – –

88 καὶ συνάρχοσιν τρίτηι καὶ τριακο[σ]τῆι [τῆς πρυτ]ανείας [πέμπτηι
  φθίνοντος Σκιροφοριῶνος – –ᶜ·⁶– – ἐπὶ τῆς Ἐρεχθηίδος πρότης]

89 πρυτανευόσης [ἑ]λληνοταμίαις [κ]αὶ πα[ρ]έδ[ρ]οις Λ[υ]σι[ι]θ[έ]ο[ι

Θυμαιτάδηι καὶ συν]άρ[χ]ο[σιν – – –_c._9_ – – – τῆς πρυτανείας – –
_c._9_ – – –]

90 τὸ μηνὸς Ἑκατομβαιῶνος [ἐς τὴ]ν διοβελί[αν – – – – – – – – – – –
– – – – – – – – – – – – – – εἰκοστῆι τῆς πρυτανεί]

91 ας εἰκοστῆι τὸ μηνὸς Ἑκατομβαιῶνος [– – – – – – – – – – – – ἐ]

92 πὶ τῆς Ἐρεχθηίδος πρότης πρ[υ]τα[νε]υό[σης – – – – – – – – –]
       vacat

It is not necessary to give here all the variant readings of
these lines, nor to indicate in detail the many points in which this
text differs from those previously published. But attention may
be called to significant passages where previous editors have
given readings which may still be of service in the reconstruction
of the document and with which the facsimile plate here given
should be compared.[1]

Line 50: Hiller, following earlier editors, reads HℙΔ.

Line 59: Hiller reads ℙΓHΙ. I agree with earlier editors in
reading ℙΓHΙ.

Line 66: Waddington (cf. *I.G.*, I, 189) reads . . . . . OΓΙϹΤΑΙϹᵛ
. . . . ΓΡΛ.ΛΙ – – – – OΙΥΡΓ . . ΤΟΛΚΛΙΕΚΤΡ.

Line 67: Waddington (cf. *I.G.*, I, 189) reads ΜΑΡΑΘΟΝΙΟΙ . . .
ΕΔΕΙ.

Line 71: Clarac (cf. *I.G.*, I, 189) reads . . . . . ΛΟϹΕΛΛΕΝΟΤΑ
ΜΙΑΙϹΚΑΙΓΑΡΕΔΡΟΙϹ. Toward the end of the line Waddington (*I.G.*, I, 189) gives . . . . . ΛΔΕΙ.ΛΙϹΥ – – –.

Line 74: Waddington (cf. *I.G.*, I, 189) reads the numeral as ΤΤΙ.

Line 76: Waddington (cf. *I.G.*, I, 189) reads ⌐ΟΛΙϹΤΑΙϟΑ.ΧΕ
ΜΙΜΟΙΜΑΡΛΘΟΝΙΟΙΚ. The restoration is evidently λογισταῖς Ἀ[ρ]χεδέμοι Μαραθονίοι κ[αὶ συνάρχοσιν – – –]. Cf. also
line 74.

Line 78: Mueller (cf. *I.G.*, I, 189) reads . . . . . . OϹΙϹΤΑ.Ε.

Line 79: Mueller (cf. *I.G.*, I, 189), toward the end of the line,
reads – – – OΡΙ – – – ΝΤΙΟ – –.

Line 82: On the right side of the stone Mueller (cf. *I.G.*, I, 189)
reads ΡΟΦΟΡ.Ο – – – – ΤΟ.ΟΙΟΜ.

---

[1] Variants are given by Kirchhoff, in his text and notes on *I.G.*, I, 189. No
variants are recorded by Hiller (*I.G.*, I², 304).

Line 87: Waddington (cf. *I.G.*, I, 189) reads ΚΑΙΕΥ.ΙΙΕΛΟΙΛΛΛ
ΜΟΙ . . . ΟϞΕΚΤΟΝ.   Mueller (cf. *I.G.*, I, 189) reads ΚΑΙΕ
. . Γ.Ι.ΕΑΟΕΟΙΑΛΟΙ . . . ΟϞΕΚΤΟΝ.

Line 89: Mueller (cf. *I.G.*, I, 189) reads, near the center of the
stone, ΑΡΧΟϞΙ.

This inscription is particularly helpful in the study of the
Athenian calendar in the fifth century, for the dates on which
payments of money were made from the treasury of Athena are
given by both the day of the prytany and the day of the month.
A comparative table best illustrates the extent of this evidence.[1]

Pryt. II, 13	Metageitnion 21	Line 42
Pryt. II, 17	Metageitnion 25	Lines 44, 46
Pryt. II, 18	Metageitnion 26	Line 48
Pryt. II, 19	Metageitnion 27	Line 50
Pryt. II, 22	Metageitnion 30 (last day)	Lines 51–52
Pryt. II, 23	Boedromion 1	Line 53
Pryt. II, 24	Boedromion 2	Line 55
Pryt. II, 26	Boedromion 4	Line 57
Pryt. II, 30	Boedromion 8	Lines 58–59, 60
Pryt. II, 36	Boedromion 14	Lines 62–64
. . . .		
Pryt. VIII, 23	Munichion 3	Line 68
Pryt. VIII, 26	Munichion 6	Line 70
Pryt. IX, 2	Munichion 17	Lines 71–72
Pryt. IX, 4	Munichion [1]9	Line 73
Pryt. IX, 7	Munichion 22	Line 75
Pryt. IX, 15	(Munichion 30)	Line 77
(Pryt. IX, 22)	Thargelion 7	Lines 78–79
(Pryt. X, 12)	Skirophorion 5	Lines 80–81
Pryt. X, 12	Skirophorion (5)	Line 82
Pryt. X, 23	(Skirophorion 16)	Line 86
Pryt. X, 33	(Skirophorion 26)	Line 88
(Pryt. I, 20)	Hekatombaion 20	Lines 90–91

This year was an ordinary year of twelve civil months with
which the conciliar year was coterminous. The following table
illustrates the disposition of days in the months and prytanies:[2]

[1] Cf. also Meritt, *The Athenian Calendar*, p. 97; *idem*, "Senatorial and Civil Years
in Athens," *Cl. Phil.*, XXV (1930), 238.

[2] Meritt, "Senatorial and Civil Years in Athens," *Cl. Phil.*, XXV (1930), 238.

407/6   Prytany I, 1 = Hekatombaion 1

	Days		Days
Prytany I	37	Hekatombaion	29
Prytany II	36	Metageitnion	30
Prytany III	(35)	Boedromion	(29)
Prytany IV	(35)	Pyanepsion	(30)
		Maimakterion	(29)
Prytany V	(34)	Posideion	(30)
Prytany VI	(34)	Gamelion	(29)
Prytany VII	(34)	Anthesterion	(30)
Prytany VIII	35	Elaphebolion	(29)
		Munichion	30
Prytany IX	(37)	Thargelion	(29)
Prytany X	(37)	Skirophorion	(30)
	354		354

406/5   Prytany I, 1 = Hekatombaion 1

It will be observed from the text that a payment is recorded in lines 84–85 as having been made during one of the latter days of Skirophorion — after the twentieth. This date disturbs the orderly chronological sequence of the record of payments, but need not cause concern on that account. A strict chronological sequence was not always followed, especially when there seemed to be an advantage in listing together payments made for the same purpose.[1]

It is evident from line 41 that Erechtheis held the second prytany in 407/6, and from line 92 that Erechtheis held the first prytany in 406/5.[2] The name of one other tribe, which held the ninth prytany, now appears in this inscription at the beginning of line 71. After the numeral at the end of line 70 there is an uninscribed space of one letter, which is followed by the word ἐπί. This must be restored as part of a formula of date, in con-

---

[1] Meritt, "The Departure of Alcibiades for Sicily," *A. J. A.*, XXXIV (1930), 151. Cf. *I.G.*, I², 302, lines 71–77 (p. 163, below).

[2] As Ferguson has already shown, these dispositions are sufficient to prove that *I.G.*, I², 304 B cannot be dated either in 409/8 or 408/7 (Ferguson, *The Treasurers of Athena*, p. 28). From the calendar correspondences which may be derived from the inscription it is also clear that the eighth prytany contained thirty-five days. (Meritt, *Cl. Phil.*, XXV [1930], 238). Since the eighth prytany in 408/7 contained thirty-six days, it is further apparent that *I.G.*, I², 304 B cannot be assigned to this year (Ferguson, *loc. cit.*).

nection with the enigmatic letters ΙΛΟ at the beginning of
line 71. The reading ἐπὶ [τê|s . . . ε]ἰδ̣ο[s] seems to me certain,
especially in view of the fact that the final sigma, which we have
restored, was read from the stone by Clarac and shown by him
in his transcript of the inscription.[1] The short formula thus employed, without the number or sequence of the prytany, finds
its parallel in *I.G.*, II², 1686 A, line 21, where the simple phrase
[ἐπὶ τê]s Αἰαντίδος appears. The payment recorded in line 71
of *I.G.*, I², 304 B was made on the second day of the ninth
prytany. The restoration here suggested, ἐπὶ [τê|s . . . ε]ἰδ̣ο[s],
quite appropriately introduces the accounts of this prytany and
distinguishes them from the record of the eighth prytany just
preceding. The necessary restrictions of the stoichedon order
of the inscription compel us to restore either Aigeis or Oineis.

In line 75 there appears the name [. .]ονι Κοπρείοι, without
mention of colleagues or paredroi. The name is so far separated
from the word λογισταῖ[s] in line 74 that it is impossible to assign
the official thus designated to that board, which is recorded in
the usual way as λογισταῖ[s] Ἀ[ρ]χεδέμοι [Μ]αρ[αθονίοι καὶ συνά-
ρχοσιν]. Toward the end of line 74 is preserved part of the letter
alpha in such a position on the stone as to justify the restoration
λογισταῖ[s] Ἀ[ρ]χεδέμοι [Μ]αρ[αθονίοι καὶ συνάρχοσιν καὶ ἑλλενοταμί]α-
[ι . . . . . | . .]ονι Κοπρείοι. This entry should be compared with
that given in lines 85–86, where the same name appears together
with paredroi and colleagues. The restoration here proposed is
confirmed by the reading given in these later lines.

In the entire document we have with certainty the names of
five hellenotamiai, though it is possible that - -μοι Παιονίδηι
(line 80) and - - -τοι Φαληρεῖ (line 82) should also be associated
with the hellenotamiac board. I suspect further in line 87 the
probability that the restoration [ἑλληνοταμ]ίαι Εὐαγγέλοι - - - -
is correct, in which case still another hellenotamias is mentioned.
But, leaving aside these doubtful cases, I list here with the indication of their tribal affiliation the five members who belong with
certainty to the board of hellenotamiai in 407/6:

Προτάρχοι Προβαλισίοι III
Θρασυλόχοι Θορικίοι V

[1] Cf. *I.G.*, I, 189, note. Cf. also Ferguson, *The Treasurers of Athena*, p. 17, note 3.

Ἀθενοδόροι Μελιτεῖ	VII
Λυσιθέοι Θυμαιτάδει	VIII
[. . . ⁷ . . .]ονι Κοπρείοι	VIII

The fact that there are two representatives from the eighth tribe (Hippothontis) is confirmatory evidence that the board was composed of twenty members chosen two from each tribe, as was the case also in 410/09.[1]

The accounts contained in *I.G.*, I², 304 B were based upon the Panathenaic year, instead of upon the conciliar year as before, and thus continue into the early days of 406/5 — before the festival of Athena. In lines 88–92 appear the records of payments made during the first prytany of the new year and during the month of Hekatombaion. The fact that the hellenotamias Lysitheos, whose name occurs frequently throughout the record, received with his colleagues one of these payments during the new year shows that the term of office of the hellenotamiai was the Panathenaic year, and not the civil or conciliar year, as has sometimes been claimed.[2] Since Prytany I, 1 of 406/5 must be equated with Hekatombaion 1, it follows that the dates by month and by prytany in this latter part of the inscription must be identical. The last payment of which we have record was made on the twentieth day of Hekatombaion (line 91) and on the twentieth day of the first prytany. The new item of record begun in line 92 was for some reason never completed.

The restoration proposed above for lines 69 and 70 deserves special comment and should be read in the light of Xenophon's narrative of events in the early summer of 406 (*Hellenica*, I, 5, 16–20).[3] By vote of the Athenian people, Conon was dispatched to take charge of the fleet at Samos, which he reorganized and with which he conducted plundering expeditions against the land of the enemy. In the inscription the letters ϚΤΡΑΤ appear near the end of line 69, so that six letters must be supplied before the initial ΟΝΙ preserved in line 70. The restoration

---

[1] Cf. p. 103, above.

[2] Cf. also Meritt, *The Athenian Calendar*, pp. 17–19; Bannier, "Zu attischen Inschriften," *Berl. ph. Woch.*, 1915, p. 1613; Ferguson, *The Treasurers of Athena*, p. 3, note 1.

[3] Ferguson, *Cambridge Ancient History*, V, 484.

must include some reference to an army or general for whom the loan was intended. Xenophon has listed the names of the ten generals chosen after the defeat at Notion, and that of Conon is the only one ending in ONI in the dative case. But the restoration στρατ[εγοῖ Κόν]ονι is too long by one letter to satisfy the stoichedon arrangement of letters on the stone. The word στρατ[ιᾶς] should be substituted, rather, in place of στρατ[εγοῖ] to give the reading [ἐλ]λενοταμίαι[ς καὶ] παρέ[δροις καὶ στρατεγοῖ τῆς ἐν Σάμοι] στρατ[ιᾶς Κ|όν]ονι.[1] The payment was made to Conon as he set out to reorganize the fleet and to take command at Samos. The numeral in line 70, which gives the amount of the payment, occupied nine letter spaces and ended in symbols representing two talents. If the minimum possible figure is restored, the amount of the payment would be forty-nine talents. It may, of course, have been larger. But in any case the loan represents a considerable drain on the already exhausted treasury of Athena and shows the importance attached by the Athenians to the rehabilitation of their fleet.

The date of the payment is also given as the twenty-sixth day of the (eighth) prytany, or sixth day of the month Munichion, for which the Julian equivalent (p. 179) falls in early April. The epigraphical record thus serves to fix exactly the time of an important historical event which can be ascertained only approximately from the narrative of Xenophon.

[1] Cf. Ferguson, *The Treasurers of Athena*, p. 19, note.

CHAPTER VIII

THUCYDIDES AND THE ACCOUNTS OF THE LOGISTAI

THE accounts of the logistai for the years 426/5 to 423/2, as preserved in *I.G.*, I², 324, have been made the subject of a special study in my book on the Athenian Calendar.[1] I do not propose to give again the arguments by which the text of this important document has been reconstructed, nor to elaborate in more detail the reasons for restorations already proposed. In several parts of the inscription, however, there are improvements in the text which must be noted, although they do not affect in any vital way the earlier determinations. These new restorations and some of the problems connected with them are discussed in the present chapter.

In the *Corpus* we find for lines 26–27 the following restoration: *ℎελλενοταμίαις ℎένοις Δ[ιονυσίοι ʼΑχαρνεῖ καὶ χσυνάρχοσιν καὶ παρέδροις] Χαροπίδει Σκ[αμβ]ονίδει καὶ χσυνάρχοσι[ν]* – –. It is evident that the board — or boards — which received the first payment during the conciliar year 424/3 belonged in fact to the Panathenaic year 425/4, and this passage in the inscription is one of the items of evidence that the hellenotamiai held office from Panathenaia to Panathenaia.[2] The payment first made in this year must, therefore, be dated earlier than Hekatombaion 28; it falls, consequently, in the first prytany. In my publication of this inscription I made no restoration in the lacuna of lines 26–27, because at best, it seemed to me, the name of the hellenotamias Dionysios was but a conjecture. I am now more than ever skeptical about the restoration proposed in the *Corpus*, because of the unusual mention made of the paredroi along with

---

[1] Meritt, *The Athenian Calendar in the Fifth Century*, 1928.

[2] Meritt, *The Athenian Calendar*, pp. 17–19, 95. Cf. also West, in a review of Meritt, *The Athenian Calendar*, in *Classical Weekly*, XXIII (1929), 62; Dinsmoor, *The Archons of Athens*, p. 334; Bannier, "Zu attischen Inschriften," *Berl. ph. Woch.*, 1915, p. 1612; cf. p. 126, above.

the hellenotamiai. The first certain reference to the paredroi of the hellenotamiai is in 418/7 (*I.G.*, I², 302, line 4; cf. text on p. 160, below). It seems rather that in *I.G.*, I², 324 the two boards mentioned are both of hellenotamiai, the board of the previous year being listed first, with the modifier *hέvois* and the board of the current year listed next, possibly with some such designation as τετίνοις. The four payments of the year were made to both boards, the first loan going to the hellenotamiai of 425/4 and the last three loans to the helllenotamiai of 424/3. I suggest here that the lines in question should be restored: *hελλενο-ταμίαις hέvois* Δ[. . . . . .¹⁷. . . . . *καὶ χσυνάρχοσι καὶ τετίνοις*] Χαροπίδει Σκα[μβ]ονίδει καὶ χσυνάρχοσι[ν].

Further restorations must be made of lines 37–38 as a result of studies by H. T. Wade-Gery in the Athenian *strategia*.¹ In particular he shows that the name Eurymedon must be restored in line 38 and suggests the reading – – *ἐγρ[αμμάτευε στρατεγο|ῖς ἐπὶ Ἰονίας Εὐρυμέδοντι Μυρρ]ινοσίοι καὶ – – – – –*, with the possibility of substituting *ἐς Σκιόνεν* for *ἐπὶ Ἰονίας*. This restoration seems to me eminently sound, and I accept it without question in place of my earlier suggestion. Nevertheless, I differ with Wade-Gery in the correlation of the payments made during the year 423 with the narrative of Thucydides, in that I believe all the payments made during this year were for operations in the Thracian district, and that there were no campaigns in Ionia or about Samos. The evidence for a campaign against Samos comes entirely from the traditional restoration of *I.G.*, I², 324, line 42 ([πρὸς] Σαμ[ίος]); Thucydides says nothing of operations in the eastern part of the empire during this year. Professor West has called my attention to the possibility of restoring this phrase in such a way as to indicate the source from which the money was drawn rather than the campaign for which it was spent. The words [παρὰ] Σαμ[ίον] are, epigraphically, a satisfactory substitute for [πρὸς] Σαμ[ίος], and they relieve us of the embarrassment of reconciling extensive campaigns in Ionia and against Samos with the silence of Thucydides about such operations.²

¹ Wade-Gery, "The Year of the Armistice, 423 B.C.," *Cl. Quart.*, XXIV (1930), 33–39.

² Cf. Wade-Gery, *op. cit.*, p. 37.

The money received from Samos in 410/09 is listed as τὰ ἐχ Σάμο in *I.G.*, I², 304, lines 20 and 34. This relatively late parallel may be cited here to show that such a special designation of source in these records is entirely possible, just as we find in *I.G.*, I², 324, line 20, the indication of source given by the phrase [ἐχς Ὀπισθ]οδόμο.

In earlier records I suspect the existence of the phrase [παρὰ Σα]μίον in *I.G.*, I², 297, line 16, where the letters ΜΙΟΝΓΑΡΕ are now preserved on the stone.[1] The restoration of any such phrase as [παρὰ τα]μιôν or [παρὰ ἡελλενοτα]μιôν is out of place in the formulae of this inscription, though it is quite appropriate to restore [παρὰ Σα]μίον. The passage here in question must be correlated with that in *I.G.*, I², 324, line 42, where I now propose that we read [παρὰ] Σαμ[ίον]. I believe also that we may restore in the same sense another difficult passage which has so far baffled attempts at restoration or interpretation. Lines 18–19 of *I.G.*, I², 302 (cf. text on p. 160) should read τô ἐχ Σ|[άμο κατὰ τὸν ἐνιαυτὸν ἐ]πελθόντος, again giving the source from which the money was drawn. The phrase appears in close juxtaposition to the verb παρέδομεν, as does the similar [παρὰ Σα]μίον in *I.G.*, I², 297, line 16, and is justified in substance by the reference τὰ ἐχ Σάμο ἀνομολογέθε of *I.G.*, I², 304, line 20.[2]

In my earlier study of the calendar I had assumed a close connection between the restorations that should be made in lines 38 and 56 of *I.G.*, I², 324.[3] Wade-Gery has called attention to the possibility of change in his discussion of these lines and his new text for line 38 shows that the connection is not at all necessary. At the same time I have been endeavoring to eliminate some of the irregularities in the text I had proposed for the entire paragraph from lines 54 to 59, dealing with matters not directly connected with the name of the general who received

---

[1] Cf. p. 89, above.

[2] I am indebted to Allen West for this suggestion. Cf. West, "Cleon's Assessment and the Athenian Budget," *Trans. Am. Phil. Assoc.*, LXI (1930), 219, note 8. West suggests the restoration τô ἐχ Σ|[άμο καθ' ἡομολογίαν ἀ]πελθόντος for *I.G.*, I², 302, lines 18–19; but this phrase is too short by two letters to agree with the stoichedon arrangement of the line.

[3] Meritt, *The Athenian Calendar*, p. 79.

the money. In many respects this text was not satisfactory, and for purposes of comparison I quote it here in full.[1]

54 [τάδε ἐλογίσα]ντο [ℎοι] λογιστ[αὶ ὀφελόμ]ε̣ν[α τοῖς ἄλλοις θεοῖς ἐν τοῖς τέττ]αρσιν ἔτ[εσιν ἐκ Παν]

55 [αθεναίον ἐς Παναθέν]αι̣α̣ [ℎόσα παρέδοσ]αν ℎ[οι ταμίαι τὸν ἄλλον θεὸν Γόργο]ινος Ο[ἰνείδο Ἰκαρι]

56 [εὺς καὶ χσυνάρχοντες ἐκ τὸν ἑκάστο χ]ρεμάτο[ν ℎελλενοταμίαις καὶ στρατ]εγοῖ[ς . . . . καὶ χσυν]

57 [άρχοσιν ᵛ ἐπὶ τῆς βολῆς ℎε̑ι Δεμέτρι]ος προ̑τ[ος ἐγραμμάτευε ἐπὶ τῆς Ἀκαμαντ]ίδ[ος πρυτανείας]

58 [πρότες πρυτανευόσες ℎεκατομβαιο̑]νος ὀγ[δόει φθίνοντος τετάρτει καὶ εἰκοστε̑ι τῆς πρυταν]

59 [είας τάδε παρέδοσαν Ἀρ]τέμι[δος Ἀγρ]οτέρα[ς – – – – – –].

The customary usage of this inscription requires properly the word τάδε instead of ℎόσα in line 55, giving the reading τάδε παρέδοσαν ℎοι ταμίαι – – –, which also appears in the introductory formulae of the other parts of the document (lines 2, 16, 25, 36). In this case the phrase τάδε παρέδοσαν will not be repeated in line 59. In this latter instance the phrase is also too long by one letter to fulfill satisfactorily the requirements of the restoration. A blank space of one letter should be left before the name Ἀρτέμιδος in line 59 just as before the same name in line 79. Furthermore, we miss in the text as given above the date by archon (ἐπὶ Ἀμενίο ἄρχοντος). Although the words ℎελλενοταμίαις καὶ στρατεγοῖς in line 56 fulfill all the physical requirements of the stone for restoration, I question the propriety of inserting here any reference to the hellenotamiai, especially since the board is not represented by any proper name. Since this is the appropriate place for the date by archon in the introductory formula, I suggest here that instead of the words ℎελλενοταμίαις καὶ we should read ἐπὶ Ἀμενίο ἄρχοντος. This phrase satisfies all the epigraphical requirements of the stone and gives an eminently superior reading. It is improbable also that the name of the general contained only four letters and that an uninscribed space of one letter was left after the word χσυνάρχοσιν in line 57.

[1] For a discussion of this text, cf. Meritt, op. cit., pp. 78–79.

I propose here a restoration for these lines which obviates all of the objections just enumerated that may be brought against the earlier reading, and which is, I believe, substantially correct.

54 [τάδε ἐλογίσα]ντο [ηοι] λογιστ[αὶ ὀφελόμ]εν[α τοῖς ἄλλοις θεοῖς ἐν τοῖς τέττ]αρσιν ἔτ[εσιν ἐκ Παν]

55 [αθεναίον ἐς Παναθέν]αια·[τάδε παρέδοσ]αν η[οι ταμίαι τὸν ἄλλον θεὸν Γόργο]ινος Ο[ἰνείδο Ἰκαρι]

56 [εὺς καὶ χσυνάρχοντες ἐκ τὸν ἑκάστο χ]ρεμάτο[ν ἐπὶ Ἀμενίο ἄρχοντος στρατ]εγοῖ[ς Νικίαι καὶ χσ]

57 [υνάρχοσι ἐπὶ τῆς βολῆς ηῆι Δεμέτρι]ος πρῶτ[ος ἐγραμμάτευε ἐπὶ τῆς Ἀκαμαντ]ίδ[ος πρυτανείας]

58 [πρότες πρυτανευόσες ηεκατομβαιῶ]νος ὀγ[δόει φθίνοντος τετάρτει καὶ εἰκοστῆι τῆς πρυταν]

59 [είας ἐσελελυθνίας ᵛ Ἀρ]τέμι[δος Ἀγρ]οτέρα[ς – – – – – –].

My earlier difficulties in restoring this passage were caused by inability to find a date by prytany long enough to fill the required space between ὀγ[δόει φθίνοντος] and [Ἀρ]τέμι[δος]. It seemed evident that the date was actually the twenty-fourth day of the prytany and the words τάδε παρέδοσαν were restored in line 59 to fill the lacuna after the formula of date τετάρτει καὶ εἰκοστῆι τῆς πρυτανείας. The restoration now given, however, indicates that no such assumption was necessary. The formula of date by prytany τετάρτει καὶ εἰκοστῆι τῆς πρυτανείας ἐσελελυθυίας fulfills exactly the epigraphical requirements of the stone and may be paralleled in its phraseology by other formulae from this same inscription (lines 19, 21–22).

In line 56 I have restored the name of the general as Νικίαι. The absence of patronymic and demotic is paralleled by the simple name Δεμέτριος for the first secretary of the Council in line 57, and there is authority in this same inscription for the omission of the final nu-movable in the phrase Νικίαι καὶ χσυνάρχοσι. Both of these instances are in the record of the year 423/2. Since Nicias was one of the generals operating in the summer of 423 against Mende and Skione (Thuc. IV, 129, 2), it is a reasonable supposition that the first payment made from the treasure of the Other Gods was used to defray in part the expense of his expedition.

The payments for 423 as recorded in *I.G.*, I², 324 may now be listed as follows:

Line	Prytany date	Amount	Destination
31	Pryt. VII, 2	6 tal., 1200 dr.	Unspecified
32	Pryt. VIII, 30	100 tal.	Unspecified
37	Pryt. I, 11	59 tal., 4720 dr.	[Eurymedon] and his colleagues
56	Pryt. I, 24	30 tal., 5990 dr.	[Nicias and his colleagues]
40	Pryt. III, 11	2 tal., 5500 dr.	Unspecified
41	Pryt. IV, 4	11 tal., 3300 dr.	Unspecified! (not against Samos)
51	Pryt. IV, 4	6 tal.	Unspecified

Wade-Gery has argued that the payment of 100 talents appropriated on Prytany VIII, 30 was for the campaign of Nicias against Mende mentioned by Thucydides (IV, 129) and that the smaller payment of 6 talents, 1200 drachmae, made on Prytany VII, 2 was probably for some preparations for this campaign (cf. Thuc. IV, 129, 2: ὥσπερ παρεσκευάζοντο).[1] But it must be borne in mind that the truce between Athens and Sparta in the spring of 423 was not ratified until Prytany VIII, 7 (Elaphebolion 14).[2] After this date, though perhaps by only a few days, the Athenian Aristonymos and the Spartan Athenaios set forth with a trireme to carry the news of the truce to their soldiers in the field. They found that Skione was in revolt and that Brasidas was unwilling to deliver the city to the Athenians, although in fact it had revolted two days after the truce was ratified.[3] Aristonymos immediately reported to Athens, and the Athenians were at once eager to undertake military operations against Skione. We may estimate that the Athenians received news of the revolt about two weeks after the ratification of the truce, on or near Prytany VIII, 20. They can hardly have heard sooner, unless we assume that the heralds with Aristonymos traveled with extraordinary speed on both their outward and return journeys. The Spartan offer of arbitration was then received and rejected, and the Athenians, on Cleon's motion, voted to dispossess by force of arms and put to death the Skionaeans.[4] For these overtures from Sparta, even though they were rejected,

[1] Wade-Gery, "The Year of the Armistice, 423 B.C.," *Cl. Quart.*, XXIV (1930), 36.
[2] Thuc. IV, 118. Cf. Meritt, *The Athenian Calendar*, p. 88.
[3] Thuc. IV, 122.
[4] Thuc. IV, 122.

we must postulate a still further lapse of time, so that Cleon's motion cannot have been carried many days, if at all, before Prytany VIII, 30, when the payment of one hundred talents was made from the treasury of Athena. Even so the Athenian expedition did not set forth at once, for preparations were necessary. Then came the news of the revolt of Mende, and with greater zeal than before the Athenians continued their preparations against both cities.

With these time relationships in mind I am inclined to question the propriety of assuming that the one hundred talents granted on Prytany VIII, 30 were given to Nicias specifically for his expeditions against Skione and Mende. The grant must have been made before final action against these cities had been decided upon, and I prefer to interpret the loan merely as a blanket appropriation to the generals, for their use in maintaining the fleet and armies overseas. We note that similar grants of one hundred talents each were made also at the beginning of the campaigning seasons in 425, 424, and 422,[1] a further indication that in 423 as well we are dealing with a financial transaction which reflects a general administrative policy, rather than with a specific necessity caused by the revolt of Mende and Skione. We do not know the purpose of the small payment on Prytany VII, 2. It can have no connection with the expedition of Nicias against Skione, for the grant was made forty-four days before the revolt.

It is my assumption that Nicias was at Potidaea, which he was to make his base of operations,[2] when word was definitely brought to him to proceed against the rebel cities. The preparations at Athens of which Thucydides speaks (IV, 122–123) indicate that he received reinforcements before the campaign started. And in fact, he must have drawn heavily on the one hundred talents given to him on Prytany VIII, 30 during the campaign, even though the money had not been originally voted for this purpose.

After the Athenian conquest of Mende, we hear next of siege operations before Skione. This siege lasted through the summer (Thuc. IV, 132), and when the investment was complete (Thuc.

[1] Meritt, *The Athenian Calendar*, p. 55.
[2] Thuc. IV, 129, 3.

IV, 133, 4) the Athenians left only a small detachment and departed with the rest of their forces. I assume that Eurymedon, with reinforcements, left Athens shortly after he received his grant of money on Prytany I, 11 to help in the preparation of siege works at Skione, and that a further payment was made also to Nicias, who was still in the field, on Prytany I, 24. Then, late in the summer, we have a composite payment of 17 talents, 3300 drachmae, which I suggest was granted toward the maintenance of the besieging garrison that remained before Skione after the greater part of the army had withdrawn. The one small payment made on Prytany III, 11 is too insignificant to play any part in our present considerations.

The epigraphical record of moneys borrowed from Athena in the year 423 is thus coördinated with the known military operations of the year as given by Thucydides, and we need not assume extensive operations against Samos or in Ionia, of which Thucydides says nothing. The evidence for such otherwise unrecorded campaigns disappears when we restore $[\pi\alpha\rho\grave{\alpha}]\ \Sigma\alpha\mu[\iota\text{ο}\nu]$ in place of $[\pi\rho\grave{o}\varsigma]\ \Sigma\alpha\mu[\iota\text{ο}\varsigma]$ in *I.G.*, I², 324, line 42.

A brief note should be added here on the text of fragment *h* of *I.G.*, I², 324, which is now lost but which I reproduced from Dodwell's copy [1] in the facsimile plate accompanying my volume on the Athenian Calendar. This fragment contains portions of the concluding lines of the inscription. I found, however, that the necessities of restoration demanded a slight change from the arrangement as shown by Dodwell in the relative position between the first two and the later lines of this fragment. My facsimile copy allows the later lines to extend only one letter space to the left of the margin as determined by the first two lines, although Dodwell indicates a divergence of two letter spaces in this regard.

It happens that Sir William Gell also copied this fragment in 1805. I have recently acquired a photograph of that page of his notebook, now preserved in the library of the British School of Archaeology at Athens, on which this inscription was copied. Gell's copy justifies the alteration in the arrangement of letters represented by Dodwell. I give in Figure 19 a photograph of the page in question, which may be compared with the facsimile

[1] E. Dodwell, *A Classical and Topographical Tour through Greece*, I (1819), 372.

plate (XII).¹ On the basis of Gell's very clear transcript, I have also changed the numeral in line 113 from [⊢ – –]ΔΔΔΠΙΙC to [⊢ – –]ΔΔΔΗΙΙC.

For purposes of convenient reference in connection with the study of other inscriptions included in this volume, the present text of *I.G.*, I², 324 is given here. It embodies the changes outlined above and also one other change in line 71, which is discussed in the following pages.²

I.G., I², 324 (426/5–423/2 B.C.)

[τάδε ἐλογίσαν]το ℎοι λογιστα[ὶ ἐν τοῖς τέτ]ταρσιν ἔτεσιν ἐκ Παναθεναίον ἐς [Παναθέναια ὀφελ]

[ὀμενα τάδε ℎο]ι ταμίαι παρέδοσ[αν Ἀνδρο]κλês Φλυεὺς καὶ χσυνάρχοντες ℎελλ[ενοταμίαις . . . .]

[. . . . . . . .¹⁰. . . .]ει καὶ χσυνάρχοσι[ν στρατ]εγοῖς ℎιπποκράτει
Χολαργεῖ καὶ χσυ[νάρχοσιν ἐπὶ τês]

[Κεκροπίδο]ς πρυτανείας δευτέ[ρας πρυ]τανευόσες τέτταρες ἐμέραι
ἐσαν [ἐ]σελ[ελυθυῖαι ἐπὶ τê]

5 [ς βολês ℎêι] Μεγακλείδες πρôτο[ς ἐγραμ]μάτευε ἐπὶ Εὐθύνο ἄρχοντος
ΔΔ τόκος τ[ούτοις ἐγένετο]

[⊠⊓ΗⒻΔΔ]ΔΔΠⱵ: ᵛ δευτέρα δόσις ἐπ[ὶ τês Κ]εκροπίδος δευτέρας πρυτανευόσες λοι[παὶ ἐσαν ℎεπτὰ ἐ]

[μέραι] τêι πρυτανείαι ⒻⒻ τόκος τ[ούτον ᵛ] ΤΤΧⒻΗΗΗΗⒻΔΔ
ᵛ τρίτε δόσις ἐπὶ τês Παν[διονίδος πρυτα]

[νείας] τετάρτες πρυ[τ]ανευόσες [ἐσελελ]υθυίας πέντε ἐμέρας τês
πρυτανείας Δ[ΔⒻΤΤΤ⊠ⒻΗΔΙΙΙC ᵛ τ]

[όκος τ]ούτον ᵛ ΤΧⒻΗΗΔΠⱵⱵⱵΙΙ ᵛ τ[ετάρτ]ε δόσις ἐπὶ τês Ἀκαμαντίδος πρυτανεία[ς ὀγδόες πρυταν]

10 [ευόσ]ες πέντε ἐμέρας ἐσελελυθ[υίας τê]ς πρυτανείας ΔΔΔΔ[Τ]-
ΤΤΤΧΧΧ τόκος τούτο[ν ᵛ ΤΧΧΧΧⒻΗΗΗⱵ ᵛ]

[πέμπ]τε δόσις ἐπὶ τês Ἀκαμαν[τίδος πρ]υτανείας ὀγδόες πρυτανευόσες ἐσελελ[υθυίας δέκα ἐμέ]

¹ I am indebted to the director of the British School, Dr. Humfry Payne, for his kind permission to reproduce this photograph here.

² Inasmuch as the name of the tribe Oineis must be restored in lines 3 and 34 of *I.G.*, I², 63 (see p. 13), it is necessary to supply the name Oineis also in lines 18–19 of *I.G.*, I², 324. The same tribal name must be restored in both documents. Cf. Meritt, *The Athenian Calendar*, pp. 26, 91.

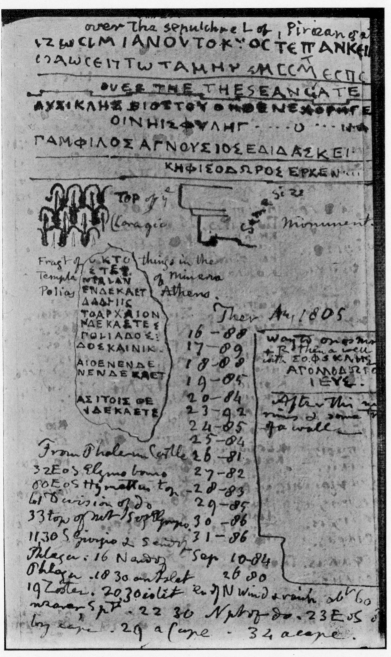

FIG. 19.   Gell's copy of fragment *h* of *I.G.*, I², 324

[ρας τ]ε̑ς πρυτανείας Ͱ τόκος τ[ούτον ᵛ]ΤΤΤⵗ𐅄ͰͰͰͰΔΔΔ
　ᵛ ʰέκτε δόσις ἐπὶ τε̑ς Ἐρε[χθεῖδος πρυταν]

[είας] δεκάτες πρυτανευόσε[ς ἐσελελ]υθυίας ʰεπτὰ ἐμέρας τε̑ς πρυτανείας ⵗ𐅗Τ[ΤΤΧΧΧ τόκος τού]

[τοις] ἐγένετο ΧΧΧΧͰ𐅄ΔΔΔͰΙ[ΙΙΙ ᵛ ᵛ κεφ]άλαιον τὸ ἀρχαῖο
ἀναλόματος ἐπὶ τε̑ς Ἀνδρ[οκλέος ἀρχε̑ς κα]

15　[ὶ χσυ]ναρχόντον ͰͰ𐅄𐅗ⵗΤⵗ𐅗Η[ΔΙΙΙϹ ᵛ τ]όκο κεφάλαιον το̑ι
ἀργυρίοι το̑ι ἀναλοθέντ[ι ἐπὶ τε̑ς Ἀνδροκ]

[λέος] ἀρχε̑ς καὶ χσυναρχόντο[ν ⵗΤΗ]𐅗ΔΔΔΔⵓͰͰͰͰ ᵛᵛᵛᵛᵛᵛ
τάδε παρέδοσαν ʰοι τα[μίαι Φοκιάδες ἐ]

[χς Οἴ]ο καὶ χσυνάρχοντες ἐπὶ Σ[τρα]τοκλέος ἄρχοντος καὶ ἐπὶ τε̑ς
βολε̑ς ʰε̑ι Πλ[ειστίας προ̑τος ᵛ]

[ἐγραμ]μάτευε στρατεγοῖς περ[ὶ Πε]λοπόννεσον Δε[μ]οσθένει Ἀλκι-
σθένος Ἀφιδ[ναῖοι ἐπὶ τε̑ς Οἰν]

[εΐδος] πρυτανείας τετάρτες [πρυτα]νευόσες τρίτει ἐ[μέ]ραι τε̑ς
πρυτανείας ἐσ[ελελυθυίας ἐχς]

20　[ὀπισθ]οδόμο 𐅄𐅄𐅄 τόκος τούτο[ις ἐγέ]νετο ⵗ𐅗ͰͰͰͰΔ ᵛ ᵛ
ʰετέρα δόσις στρατεγοῖς [Νικίαι Νικεράτ]

[ο Κυδα]ντίδει καὶ χσυνάρχο[σιν ἐπὶ] τε̑ς Πανδιονίδος πρυτανείας
ἐνάτες πρυτ[ανευόσες πέμπτ]

[ει καὶ] δεκάτει ἐμέραι τε̑ς π[ρυταν]είας ἐσελελυθυίας Ͱ τόκος τούτοις
ἐγένε[το ΤΤΧΧΧ𐅗ͰͰ𐅗Δ ᵛ]

[κεφάλ]αιον τὸ ἀρχαῖο ἀναλόμ[ατος] ἐπὶ τε̑ς Φοκιάδο ἀρχε̑ς καὶ
χσυναρχόντον Ͱ[𐅄𐅄𐅄 ᵛ τόκο κεφάλα]

[ιον το̑ι ἀ]ργυρίοι το̑ι ἀναλοθ[έντι] ἐπὶ τε̑ς Φοκιάδο ἀρχε̑ς καὶ
χσυναρχόντον Τ[ΤΤΧΧΧ𐅗Η𐅗Δ ᵛᵛᵛᵛ]

25　[τάδε παρέδ]οσαν ʰοι ταμίαι Θ[οκυ]δίδες Ἀχερδόσιος καὶ χσυνάρχοντες ἐπὶ Ἰσ[άρχο ἄρχοντος κα]

[ὶ ἐπὶ τε̑ς βολε̑ς] ʰε̑ι Ἐπί[λ[υ]κος [προ̑]τος ἐγραμμάτευε ʰελλενοταμίαις ʰένοις Δ[. . . . . . ¹⁴ . . . .]

[. . . καὶ χσυνάρχοσι καὶ τετίνοις] Χαροπίδει Σκα[μβ]ονίδει καὶ
χσυνάρχοσιν [ἐπὶ τε̑ς ʰιπποθον]

[τίδος πρυτανείας πρότες πρυταν]ευόσες ʰέκτει καὶ εἰκοστε̑ι τε̑ς
πρυτανεί[ας στρατεγοῖς ἐς]

[τὰ ἐπὶ Θράικες 𐅄𐅄𐅄ΤΤΤ𐅗𐅗 τόκος το]ύτοις ἐγένετο ΧΧΧΧ𐅗-
Η𐅗ΔⵓΙΙΙΙ ᵛ δευτέρα δ[όσις ἐπὶ τε̑ς . . ⁵ . .]

30　[. ίδος πρυτανείας τρίτες πρυταν]ευόσες δοδεκάτει τε̑ς πρυτανείας
𐅄𐅄ΤΤΤ[ΧΧΧΧͰͰ𐅗 τόκος τού]

[τοις ἐγένετο ΧΧΧ𐅃ΓΗΙΙΙΙ ᵛ τρίτε δ]όσις ἐπὶ τε͂ς Ἐρεχθεΐδος
   πρυτανείας ℎε[βδόμες πρυτανευόσ]

[ες δευτέραι τε͂ς πρυτανείας 𐅄ΤΧ]ΗΗ τόκος τούτοις ἐγένετο
   𐅄ΗΔΔΔΗΗΙϹ ᵛ τε[τάρτε δόσις ἐπὶ τε͂ς]

[Ἀκαμαντίδος πρυτανείας ὀγδόες] πρυτανευόσες τριακοστε͂ι τε͂ς
   πρυταν[είας Η τόκος τούτοις]

[ἐγένετο ΤΧΧ𐅄ΗΗΗΗ ᵛᵛ κεφάλαιον] το͂ ἀρχαίο ἀναλόματος ἐπὶ
   τε͂ς Θοκυδίδο [ἀρχε͂ς καὶ χσυναρχόν]

35 [τον ΗΙ𐅅ΔΤΤΤ ᵛ κεφάλαιον τόκο το͂ι] ἀργυρίοι το͂ι ἀναλοθέντι ἐπὶ
       τε͂ς Θοκυδ[ίδο ἀρχε͂ς καὶ χσυναρ]

[χόντον ΤΤ𐅅ΗΗ𐅄ΓΙΙΙΙϹ ᵛᵛᵛ τάδε παρ]έδοσαν ℎοι ταμίαι Τιμο-
   κλε͂ς Εἰτεαῖος κ[αὶ χσυνάρχοντες ἐπὶ]

[Ἀμενίο ἄρχοντος καὶ ἐπὶ τε͂ς βολ]ε͂ς ℎε͂ι Δεμέτριος Κολλυτεὺς προ͂τος
   ἐγρ[αμμάτευε στρατεγο]

[ῖς . . . . .⁹. . . . Εὐρυμέδοντι Μυρρ]ινοσίοι καὶ χσυνάρχοσι ἐπὶ τε͂ς
   Ἀκαμα[ντίδος πρυτανείας π]

[ρότες πρυτανευόσες ℎενδεκάτε]ι τε͂ς πρυτανείας 𐅅𐅅ΤΤΤΤΧΧΧΧ-
   𐅄ΗΗΔΔ τό[κος τούτοις ἐγένετο]

40 [ΧΧΧΧΗΗΔΔΔΔΗΗΗΙΙΙϹ ᵛ δευτέρ]α δόσις ἐπὶ τε͂ς Πανδιονί-
       δος πρυτανεί[ας τρίτες πρυτανευό]

[σες ℎενδεκάτει τε͂ς πρυτανείας] ΤΤ𐅅𐅅 τόκος τούτοις ἐγένετο Η𐅄Δ-
   ΗΗΗΙΙΙΙϹ ᵛ τρίτε δόσι]ς [ἐπὶ τε͂]

[ς . . . .⁶. . . ίδος πρυτανείας τετά]ρτες πρυτανευόσες τετάρτει τε͂ς
   πρυτα[νείας παρὰ] Σαμ[ίον ΔΤ]

[ΧΧΧΗΗΗ τόκος τούτοις ἐγένετο] 𐅄𐅅ΔΔΔΗΗ ᵛ τετάρτε δόσις
   ἐπὶ τε͂ς Αἰαντ[ίδος πρυτ]ανεί[ας ὀγδ]

[όες πρυτανευόσες πέμπτει καὶ] εἰκοστε͂ι τε͂ς πρυτανείας Η τόκος
   τούτο[ις ἐγέν]ετο Χ𐅄Η[Η ᵛ τελ]

45 [ευταία δόσις ἐπὶ τε͂ς Λεοντίδο]ς πρυτανείας δεκάτες πρυτανευόσες
       τ[ε͂ι τρίτ]ει τε͂ς πρ[υτανεί]

[ας Δ 𐅅ΤΤΤΗΔΔΗΗΙϹ τόκος τούτον] ΗΔΔΗΗΙϹ ᵛ κεφάλαιον
   το͂ ἀρχαίο ἀναλό[ματος] ἐπὶ τε͂ς Τι[μοκλέο]

[ς ἀρχε͂ς καὶ χσυναρχόντον Η𐅄ΔΔ]ΔΔΤΤΧ𐅄ΗΔΔΔΔΗΗΙϹ ᵛ
   κεφάλαιον τόκο τ[οῖς ἀ]ναλοθε͂σι χρ[έμασι]

[ἐπὶ τε͂ς Τιμοκλέος ἀρχε͂ς καὶ χσυ]ναρχόντον Τ𐅄ΗΗΗΔΗΗΙϹ ᵛ
   κεφάλαι[ον ἀν]αλόματος χσύ[μπαντ]

[ος Ἀθεν]αίας ἐν τοῖ[ς] τέ[τταρσιν ἔ]τεσιν ἐκ Παναθεναίον ἐς Πανα-
   θέν[αια 𐅅]ΗΗΔΔΔΔ𐅅ΤΤΧ[ΗΗ𐅄ΗΗ]

50 [κεφά]λαιον τόκο χσύμπαν[τος Ἀθε]ναίας ἐν τοῖς τέτταρσιν ἔτεσιν
ἐ[κ Παν]αθεναίον ἐς Πα[ναθέν]

[αια ⟊]⊢ΤΤΤΧΧΧ⊏ΗΗΗΗΔΔΔΓ[⊢⊢⊢ΙΙ ᵛ τάδε] Ἀθεναίας
Νίκες ἐ[πὶ τῆς . . . . .¹⁰ . . . .]s πρυτανείας [τετάρ]

[τες πρ]υτανευόσες τετάρτε[ι τῆς πρυτα]νείας Τιμοκ[λῆς Εἰτεαῖος καὶ
χσυ]νάρχοντες πα[ρέδοσα]

[ν ⊢Τ τόκος] τούτοις ἐ[γ]ένετο Η[ΗΗⱵⱵΙ]   vacat

[τάδε ἐλογίσα]ντο [ℎοι] λογιστ[αὶ ὀφελόμ]εν[α τοῖς ἄλλοις θεοῖς
ἐν τοῖς τέττ]αρσιν ἔτ[εσιν ἐκ Παν]

55 [αθεναίον ἐς Παναθέν]αι̣α̣ [τάδε παρέδοσ]αν ℎ[οι ταμίαι τῶν ἄλλον
θεῶν Γόργο]ινος Ο[ἰνείδο Ἰκαρι]

[εὺς καὶ χσυνάρχοντες ἐκ τῶν ἑκάστο χ]ρεμάτο[ν ἐπὶ Ἀμενίο ἄρχοντος
στρατ]εγοῖ[ς Νικίαι καὶ χσ]

[υνάρχοσι ἐπὶ τῆς βολῆς ℎῆι Δεμέτρι]ος πρῶτ[ος ἐγραμμάτευε ἐπὶ τῆς
Ἀκαμαντ]ίδ[ος πρυτανείας]

[πρότες πρυτανευόσες ℎεκατομβαιῶ]νος ὀγ[δόει φθίνοντος τετάρτει
καὶ εἰκοστῆι τῆς πρυταν]

[είας ἐσελελυθυίας ᵛ Ἀρ]τέμι[δος Ἀγρ]οτέρα[s . . . .
. . . . . . .⁴⁰ . . . .]

60 [. . . . . .¹⁸ . . . . τό]κος τ[ούτο ΗΗ]Η⊏Δ[. . . . .
. . . . .⁴² . . . .]

[. . . . . .²⁹ . . . .] Η̣ τό[κος τούτο . . .
. . . . .³⁵ . . . .]

[. . . . . .¹⁷ . . . . Ποσειδῶν]ος ἐπὶ Σο[υνίοι . . . . . . .¹³ . . .
. . . τόκ]ος τού[το . . . . .¹⁵ . . . .]

[. . . . . .²¹ . . . . τόκο]s τούτο [. . . .⁶ . . . . Ἀρτέμιδος
Μουνιχί](a)s (Τ)ΤΧΧΧΧΓⱵ[. . . . . . .¹³ . . . .]

[. . . . . .⁵²
. . . .]ΗΗΔΔΓⱵΙ τόκο[s τούτο . . .⁶ . . .]

65 [. . . .]ο ΧⱵΗΗΗΗⱵⒺΔΔΓⱵΙΙ[. . . . . .³⁶ . . . . . .
. . . .]ΔⱵⱵⱵΙΙΙΙ τόκο[s τούτο . . .⁵ . .]

[. . . .]ΙΙC Ἀφροδίτες ἐν ℎιππολυ[τείοι . . . . .²⁴ . . . . .
. . . . . .]ⱵⱵⱵΙΙΙΙIC ᵛ Μοσ[ῶν . .⁵ . . τόκο]

[s τού]το ΓⱵΙΙ ᵛ Ἀπόλλονος Ζοστῆ[ρος . . . . .²¹ . . . .
. . . Ἀδρασ]τείας ⊏ΔΔΔΓⱵ τ[όκος τούτο Ⱶ]

[Βενδ]ῖδος ⊏ΔΔΔΓⱵ τόκος τού[το Ⱶ . . . . .²⁹ . . . .
. . . .]ΙC) ᵛ Ἀπόλλον[ος . . . .⁸ . . . .]

[. . . .] τούτο τόκος ΓⱵⱵⱵ ᵛ [. . . . . .³⁶ . . . .
. . . .] ℎερακλέος ἐν [Κυνοσάργε]

70 [ι ΔΔ τ]ούτο τόκος ΙＣ^ν hε[. . . . . .²² . . . . Δε-
μ]οφôντος [. . .⁶. . .] τόκος τούτ[ο . . . .⁹. . . .]

['Αθενα]ί[ας ἐπὶ] Παλλ[ενίδι ΤⅪΗΗΗⴲΔΓ⊦⊦⊦ΙΙΙＣ τόκο]ς
τούτο ΗΔΔΓ⊦⊦⊦ΙΙΙＣ)^ν 'Απόλλο[νος . . . .⁸. . . .]

[. . . . . . . .²⁰ . . . . 'Αρτέμιδος Βραυρονία]ς ΧΗΗΗ-
ⴲΔΔΔΔΓ⊦ΙΙΙΙ τόκος τούτο Δ[. . . . .¹¹. . . . .]

[. . . .⁹. . . .]ΧΗΔ[. . . . . . . .²⁴ . . . . 'Αθ]ε-
ναίας ἐπὶ Παλλαδίοι Δεριον[έ]οι [. . . .⁹. . . .]

[τόκος το]ύτο Δ⊦[. . . . .¹¹. . . . .Χ]ⴲΗ[. . . .⁹. . . . τό]κος
τούτο ΔΔＣ^ν Ποσειδôνος Καλαυρε[άτο . .⁵. .]

75 [τόκο]ς τούτο [. . . . κεφάλαιον τ]ô ἀ[ρχαίο ἀναλό]ματος τôν ἄλλον
θεôν τês πρότες [δ]όσεο[ς τês ἐπὶ]

[Γοργ]οίνο [ἄρχοντος ꝐꝐꝐⅪⴲΗΗ]Ḥ Ḥ ⴲ[ΔΔΔΔ ^ν κεφάλ]αιον
τόκο τούτοι τôι ἀναλόματι ΧΧΗΔΔ [. . . .⁷. . . .]

[δευτ]έρ[αν δόσιν παρέδοσαν] hοι τα[μίαι τôν ἄλ]λον θεôν Γόργοινος
Οἰνείδο 'Ικαριεὺς [καὶ χσυν]

[ἄρχοντες καθ' ἕκαστον θεὸν] ἀπὸ τô[ν χρεμάτον] ἐπὶ τês Λεοντίδος
πρυτανείας δεκάτε[ς πρυταν]

[ευόσες Σκιροφοριôνος ὀγ]δόει φθ[ίνοντος εἰ]κοστêι τês πρυτανείας ^ν
'Αρτέμιδος 'Αγρ[οτέρας]

80 [ΤΤΤΤΧⴲΗΗΗΗⴲ τόκος τούτο] Δ⊦⊦⊦ΙΙ[ΙＣ^ν 'Αφροδί]τες ἐν
Κέποις ΤΤⅪΗⴲΔΔΓΙ τόκος τούτο Γ⊦[⊦⊦ΙΙΙＣ]

[. . . . . . . .¹⁶ . . . . .ΧΧⴲΗ]ΗΗΔΔΔΔ[. .⁵. . τούτο] τόκος ⊦ΙΙΙＣ)^ν Διονύσο ΗΗΗⴲΓ⊦ι τόκος το[ύτο . . .]

[. . . . . . . .¹⁹ . . . . τ]όκος το[ύτο . .^ν Ποσε]ιδôνος ἐπὶ
Σουνίοι ΤΤΤΤΧⴲΔΔΓ⊦⊦ΙΙΙＣ τό[κος τού]

[το Δ⊦⊦⊦ΙΙΙ ^ν . . .⁶. . . ΧΧ]ΧΧⴲΗΗΔΔ[ΔΔΓ⊦⊦⊦ΙΙΙΙ τ]ό-
κος τούτο ⊦⊦ΙΙΙＣ ^ν 'Αρτέμιδος Μονιχίας [. . .⁷. . .]

[. . . . . . . .¹⁷ . . . .]⊦ΙΙ ^ν Θεσέο[ς ⴲΗΗΗΓ⊦⊦⊦]ΙΙΙＣ τόκος τούτο ΙΙＣ)^ν hιλισô ΗΗΗΗ⊦ι τόκ[ος τούτο]

85 [ΙＣ . . . . . . .¹⁴ . . . . . . τ]όκος τού[το . ^ν hεφαίσ]το ΤΧⴲΗΗ-
ΔΔΔΔΓ⊦⊦⊦ τόκος τούτο ⊦⊦⊦⊦ΙＣ ^ν 'Αφ[ροδίτε]

[ς ἐν hιππολυτείοι . .]⊦ΙΙ τόκο[ς τούτο . .⁵. .]^ν Μοσôν ⴲΔΔ⊦ τόκος
τούτο ΙＣ)^ν θεô χσενικô [. .⁵. .]

[. . . . . . . .¹³ . . . . τόκο]ς τούτ[ο . . .^ν hερακλέ]ος ἐν Κυνοσάργει
ⴲΔΔΔ τόκος τούτο Ｃ^ν Δεμο[φôντο]

[ς . . . . .¹⁷ . . . .]^ν 'Αθε[ναίας ἐπὶ Παλλ]ενίδι ΧΧΧ-
ΗΗΗΗΔΓ⊦⊦⊦Ι τόκος τούτο ⊦ΙΙΙΙＣ ^ν 'Α[πόλλο]

[νος . . . . .¹⁵ . . . . τ]όκο[ς . . .⁶. . .ᵛ 'Αρτέ]μιδος Βραυ-
ρονίας ΗΗΗ𝈷ΗΗΗΙC τόκος τούτο Ι[C ᵛ . . .]

90 [. . . . . .³⁴. . . . .])ᵛ ᵛ 'Αθεναίας
ἐπὶ Παλλαδίοι ΗΗΙC τόκος τούτ[ο . . . .]

[. . . . . .³⁴. . . . .]ΔΗΗΗΙΙΙ
τόκος τούτο C ᵛ Μετρὸς ἐν "Αγρας ΗΗ[. . .⁶. . .]

[. . . . . .³⁵. . . . .]ΗΗ   τούτο
τόκος C ᵛ 'Αθεναίας Ζοστερίας Η[. . .⁷. . .]

[. . . . . .³⁴. . . . .]ΔΔΓΗΗ τόκος τούτο ΙC ᵛᵛᵛ κεφάλαιον τὸ ἀρχ[αίο ἀνα]

[λόματος τὸν ἄλλον θεὸν τῆς δευ]τέ[ρας δόσε]ος ἐπὶ Γοργοίνο ἄρχοντος
ᵛ 𐅄𐅄ΤΤΤ𐅅𐅃ΗΗΗΗ[𐅅ΔΔΔ]

95 [ΓΗΗ ᵛᵛᵛᵛ κεφάλαιον τόκο τού]τοι [τῶι ἀργ]υρίοι 𐅅ΔΔΔΗΗ ᵛᵛ
κεφάλαιον ἀναλόματος τὸ ἀ[ρχαίο]

[ἐπὶ Γοργοίνο ἄρχοντος ᵛ 𐅆ΤΤ]ΤΤ𐅅[𐅃ΗΗΗΗ]𐅅ΔΔΔΓΗΗ ᵛᵛ
κεφάλαιον τόκο χσύμπαντος το[ύτοι]

[τῶι ἀργυρίοι ΧΧΗΗΗΗ – – –]   vacat

[τάδε ἐλογίσαντο hοι λογιστ]αὶ ἐν τ[οῖς τέτ]ταρσιν ἔτεσιν τόκον τοῖς
τῆς θεὸ hὰ hοι πρό[τεροι]

[λογισταὶ λελογισμένα παρέ]δοσαν [ἐν τοῖς hε]πτὰ ἔτεσιν τόκον
τετρακισχιλίοις ταλά[ντοις]

100 [ταλάντοι τετρακισχιλίαι]ς πεντα[κοσίαις εἴ]κοσι δυοῖν δραχμαῖν
τούτοις τόκος ἐγέ[νετο]

[– – – – – – – – –]   vacat

[τάδε ἐλογίσαντο τοῖς ἄλ]λοις θεο[ῖς ἐν τοῖς τέ]τταρσιν ἔτεσιν hὰ hοι
πρότεροι λογι[σταὶ]

[λελογισμένα παρέδοσαν ἐ]ν τοῖς hεπ[τὰ ἔτεσιν πε]ντακοσίοις ταλάντοις διακοσίοις τ[αλάντ]

[τοις hεχσέκοντα ταλάντοι]ς hὲχς ταλ[άντοις χιλί]αις ἐνενέκοντα
δραχμαῖς πέντε δραχ[μαῖς π]

105 [έντε ὀβολοῖς τόκον ἐν τοῖ]ς τέτταρσ[ιν ἔτεσιν 𐅄]𐅄𐅄𐅆ΤΤΧΧΗΗΗ-
ΔΔΔΓΗΗΙC   vacat

[τάδε ἐλογίσαντο τόκο τοῖ]ς 'Αθεναία[ς Νίκες hοι ἐ]ν τοῖς τέτταρσιν
ἔτεσιν hὰ hοι πρότ[εροι]

[λογισταὶ λελογισμένα π]αρέδοσαν ἐ[ν τοῖς hεπτὰ] ἔτεσιν εἴκοσι
ταλάντοις δυοῖν ταλ[άντο]

[ιν τρισχιλίαις ἐνενέκον]τα δραχμ[αῖς] ὀκτὸ [δραχ]μαῖς δυοῖν ὀβολοῖν
Τ𐅆𐅅ΔΔΔΗΗΙΙ[ΙΙΙ   vacat   ]

[τάδε ἐλογίσαντο καὶ τοῖς] *h*ερμô ἐν [τοῖ]ς τέτ[ταρσι]ν ἔτεσιν *h*ὰ *h*οι πρότεροι λογισταὶ λ[ελογι]

[σμένα παρέδοσαν ἐν τοῖς *h*ε]π̣[τὰ ἔ]τ[εσι]ν ταλάν[τοι τ]ετρακοσίαις ἐνενέκοντα δραχμαῖς [τόκος]

[τούτοις ἐγένετο – – – – – –] *vacat*

['Αθεναίαι Νίκει ἀρχαῖον ὀφέλοσιν ἐν] ἕνδεκα ἔτεσιν ⁝𐅉𐅉𐅈TTT-XXX(𐅄)ΔΔΔΔΓ⊢⊢⊢II *vacat*

['Αθεναίαι Νίκει τόκον ὀφέλοσιν ⁝𐅈 . .]ΔΔΔ⊢IIC *vacat*

['Αθεναίαι Πολιάδι ἐν ἕνδεκα ἔτεσιν] τὸ ἀρχαῖον [ὀ]φέλοσιν ⁝𐅍𐅍𐅍𐅍-𐅌𐅋𐅋𐅉𐅉𐅉𐅉𐅈TTT𐅆𐅅H[H𐅄ΔΔΓ]

['Αθεναίαι Πολιάδι τόκον ὀφέλοσιν ἐν] ἕνδεκα ἔτεσ[ιν ⁝]𐅍𐅋𐅋𐅉𐅉𐅉𐅉-TTTXXX𐅅HHHH⊢⊢⊢⊢ *vacat*

[ἐν ἕνδεκα ἔτεσιν 'Αθεναίας Νίκες καὶ] Πολιάδος ⁝[𐅍𐅍𐅍𐅍]𐅌𐅋𐅋𐅊-𐅉𐅉𐅈TTXXXHH[HΔΔ⊢⊢⊢II *vacat*]

[ἐν ἕνδεκα ἔτεσιν καὶ 'Αθεναίας Πολιά]δος καὶ Νίκ[ες τόκ]ο ⁝𐅍𐅋𐅋-𐅉𐅉𐅉𐅉𐅈TTT – – – –

vacat

[τάδε τοῖς ἄλλοις θεοῖς ὀφέλοσιν ἀρχ]αίο ἐν ἕνδεκα [ἔτεσιν ⁝ – – – – – – – – –]

[. . . . . .25. . . . . τόκο ἐ]ν ἕνδεκα ἔτεσ[ιν ⁝ – – – – – – – – – –]

vacat

[ἐν ἕνδεκα ἔτεσιν ὀφέλοσιν ἀρχαίο ἄπ]ασι τοῖς θε[οῖς ⁝ – – – – – – –]

[. . . . . .28. . . . . ἐν] ἕνδεκα ἔτεσ[ιν – – – – – – – – –]

vacat

This text gives two equations between the conciliar year and the civil year in 423/2:

Pryt. I, 24 = [*h*εκατομβαιô]νος ὀγ[δόει φθίνοντος] (line 58)
Pryt. X, 20 = [Σκιροφοριôνος ὀγ]δόει φθ[ίνοντος] (line 79)

The twenty-fourth day of Prytany I fell 342 days before the end of the conciliar year, and the twentieth day of Prytany X fell 17 days before the end of the conciliar year.[1] The interval thus determined between the two dates of payment (342 − 17) is 325 days, which allows also a normal reconstruction of the civil year from Hekatombaion to Skirophorion.[2] But inasmuch

[1] Meritt, *The Athenian Calendar*, p. 76; also p. 71.

[2] Meritt, *op. cit.*, p. 77; Dinsmoor, *The Archons of Athens*, pp. 324, 334.

as Aristophanes, in the *Clouds* (615–626), refers to some mal-adjustment in the civil calendar and since this play was first produced in 423, it will be useful to see whether the dates given above by prytany are necessarily correct. There can be no question about the date Prytany X, 20, for the record of this date is preserved on the stone and does not depend on restoration. The date Prytany I, 24 is restored. So far as epigraphical possibilities are concerned, the number of the day within the prytany may be δευτέραι καὶ εἰκοστêι, or perhaps ἡεβδόμει καὶ εἰκοστêι, either of which conforms to the stoichedon arrangement of the line just as satisfactorily as the accepted τετάρτει καὶ εἰκοστêι given in the text.

If we assume for a moment that the first payment was made on Prytany I, 27, it follows that the interest was reckoned on this payment for a period of 339 days. This is mathematically impossible, because the figures preserved for the sums total of principal and interest in line 76 show that the payment was outstanding for at least 342 days.[1] But a restoration of these amounts is possible with an interest period of 344 days, such as would be indicated by the date Prytany I, 22.

Fortunately, one can test this alternative by considering the possible restorations of the amount of principal borrowed from Athena at Pallenis (line 71). The amount of interest on this payment is preserved entire as ΗΔΔΓΗΗΗΙΙΙC), or 129 5/8 drachmae. If this interest was reckoned over a period of 342 days, we may easily compute the amount of the principal. The rate was: 5 talents in one day yields 1 drachma.

30,000 dr. in 342 days yields 342 dr.
x dr. in 342 days yields 129 5/8 dr.
Algebraically, $342 x = 129 \ 5/8 \times 30,000 = 3,888,750$;
$x = 11,370.6$ dr. (approximate principal).

The numeral, written in Greek monetary signs, occupies fifteen letter spaces on the stone and may be restored, correct within an obol or two, as ΤⵁΗΗΗℙΔΓΗΗΗΙΙΙC. In this part of the document the signs representing two obols were regularly written in one letter space.

---

[1] Meritt, *op. cit.*, p. 77.

When the mathematical computation is reversed, we find the amount of interest that would accumulate on this principal in 342 days:

> 30,000 dr. in 342 days yields 342 dr.
> 11,369 3/4 dr. in 342 days yields x dr.
> Algebraically, $30,000 x = 342 \times 11,369\ 3/4 = 3,888,454.5$;
> $x = 129.615 + $ dr.

This figure may be written in Greek numerical signs as HΔΔ-ΠΗΗΗΙΙΙC), which is actually the number preserved on the stone in line 71. With 342 days a restoration is therefore possible.

In the same way we may consider a possible interest period of 344 days:

> 30,000 dr. in 344 days yields 344 dr.
> x dr. in 344 days yields 129 5/8 dr.
> Algebraically, $344 x = 129\ 5/8 \times 30,000 = 3,888,750$;
> $x = 11,304.5$ dr. (approximate principal).

When this figure is written out in Greek monetary signs it appears as TⅩHHHΗΗΗⅠⅠ, occupying only eleven letter spaces instead of the requisite fifteen. As it stands, the figure is obviously impossible. It must have been either slightly larger or slightly smaller, even if we assume that the supposed interest period is correct. The next possible larger figure is TⅩHHHΠ-ΗΗΗΙΙΙΙC), assuming a separate letter space for each of the last three symbols. A more probable restoration would be TⅩHHHΔΠΗΗΗΙΙΙΙC). In either case the interest accrued is slightly more than 129 2/3 drachmae, to be written as HΔΔΠ-ΗΗΗΙΙΙΙ +, giving an amount larger than that preserved on the stone. If we choose the next possible smaller figure of principal, the restoration is TⅩHHⅠΖΔΔΔΔΠΗΗΗΙΙ.

Interest on this amount may be computed algebraically as follows:

> 30,000 dr. in 344 days yields 344 dr.
> 11,300 dr. in 344 days yields x dr.
> $30,000 x = 344 \times 11,300 = 3,887,200$
> $x = 129.573 + $ dr.

This amount should be written in Greek monetary signs as HΔΔΠΗΗΗΙΙΙC and is less by 1/4 obol than the figure preserved on the stone. A similar result is obtained even if the computation is not made with the use of the algebraic method and decimal notation.[1]

1 tal., 5250 dr. in	1 day yields	$2\frac{1}{4}$ ob.	
	in 344 days yields		129 dr.
50 dr. in	1 day yields $50/1250 \times \frac{1}{4}$ ob. $= 1/100$ ob.		
	in 344 days yields		$3\frac{1}{2}$ ob.
1 tal., 5300 dr. in 344 days yields			129 dr., $3\frac{1}{2}$ ob.

If we concede that the reckoning would have been made without an undue margin of error on the part of the logistai, it may be assumed with a high degree of probability that the interest period was not 344 days. It is important to obtain some assurance on this point, for it shows that the suggested restoration of the date of the first payment as Prytany I, 24 is correct, and that the other two epigraphical possibilities, Prytany I, 22 and 27, are not mathematically sound. Whatever the irregularity in the civil calendar that caused the complaint voiced by Aristophanes in the *Clouds*, it was not a disturbance in the regular progression of months in 423/2.

At this point we turn our attention once again to Thucydides. I wish to consider the dates which he gives for the ratification of the truce in 423 (IV, 118–119) and for the Peace of Nicias in 421 (V, 19). Both events were dated not only by the Athenian calendar, but by the Spartan calendar as well. There can be no doubt that the Spartan and Athenian dates for the Peace of Nicias refer to the same day, and Artemisios 26/27 may be equated with Elaphebolion 24/25. On the other hand, there is some possibility of doubt as to the exact correspondence between the two dates given for the truce of 423. I have recorded elsewhere my belief that the dates are not identical,[2] though I have since come to believe that the exact correspondence is highly probable. Writers on Athenian chronology have expressed themselves now for, and now against, the identification.[3] I can only suggest here that an unprejudiced reading of Thucydides IV, 118–119 is the best approach to an understanding of the ques-

[1] For this method of reckoning interest, cf. Meritt, *op. cit.*, pp. 30–37, especially 33.

[2] Meritt, *The Athenian Calendar*, p. 111, note 1.

[3] E.g., for the identification, A. Schmidt, *Handbuch der griechischen Chronologie*, p. 222; against the identification, A. Mommsen, *Chronologie*, pp. 395–396.

tion. The Athenian decree ratifying the truce was passed on Elaphebolion 14 (IV, 118), and the formal ceremonial ratification, which included the libations of the plenipotentiaries of the states concerned, was dated by the Spartan calendar on Gerastios 12 (IV, 119). We learn from Thucydides that the Lacedaemonians and their allies had previously assembled at Sparta and agreed upon the terms of the truce which they were to propose to the Athenians (IV, 118, 1–10). Ambassadors with full power (IV, 118, 10) carried these terms to Athens and laid them before the people (IV, 118, 11). On the basis of these proposals the Athenians voted to declare a truce for one year, beginning with that very day, the fourteenth of Elaphebolion. The embassies which were present representing the Lacedaemonians and their allies were to pour the libations at once before the assembly to abide by the terms of the truce for one year (IV, 118, 11–14). And then the text of Thucydides continues: ταῦτα ξυνέθεντο Λακεδαιμόνιοι [καὶ ὤμοσαν] καὶ οἱ ξύμμαχοι Ἀθηναίοις καὶ τοῖς ξυμμάχοις μηνὸς ἐν Λακεδαίμονι Γεραστίου δωδεκάτῃ.[1] It does not greatly concern our present problem whether Thucydides is here speaking in his own person or quoting from an official document. The matter has been much discussed. The important point is that we have the date of the covenant between Athens and Sparta in terms of the Spartan calendar.[2] It is my conviction, however, that we have still a part of the documentary record of the truce, however imperfect the transmission of the text may have been. The fact of the ratification [and the taking of the oaths], with the verbs ξυνέθεντο [and ὤμοσαν] in the aorist tense, properly formed part of the inscribed record of the document.[3] The next, and concluding, paragraph certainly bears the stamp of epigraphical au-

[1] I give the reading of the Oxford text. The passage has suffered much in transmission and still more at the hands of various editors. For a reasonable analysis cf. Kirchhoff, *Thukydides und sein Urkundenmaterial*, pp. 18–21.

[2] Mommsen, *Chronologie*, pp. 395–396, argues that these lines refer to the preliminary negotiations among the Spartan allies at Sparta and that the ambassadors then left Sparta on Gerastios 12, arriving in Athens four days later on Elaphebolion 14! But Mommsen admits — as well he may — that the words ξυνέθεντο τοῖς Ἀθηναίοις (sic) are hardly suitable for the agreement reached between the Lacedaemonians and their allies at Sparta.

[3] Cf. *I.G.*, I², 116, lines 24–27; *I.G.*, I², 63, line 58; also Kirchhoff, *Thukydides und sein Urkundenmaterial*, pp. 18–19.

thority, listing the names of the high contracting parties and introduced by the verbs ξυνετίθεντο δὲ καὶ ἐσπένδοντο in the imperfect tense.[1] Following immediately after the provisions of the Athenian decree, the consummation of the truce recorded in IV, 119 can be dated only *after* the authorization given by the decree. The ambassadors were to pour the libations immediately (αὐτίκα μάλα) and before the assembly (ἐν τῷ δήμῳ). While it is possible that "immediately" may have turned out to be "on the following day," there is no good reason to postulate such delay. The assembly was already in session, the ambassadors were present with plenipotentiary power, their proposals had been made and accepted, and the pouring of the libations authorized. A reasonable analysis of the situation leads us to believe that the truce was consummated on the same day that this action was authorized by the assembly. In other words, the Spartan date Gerastios 12 is to be equated with Elaphebolion 14. We merely strain the interpretation of Thucydides and add to the discrepancy already existing between the civil calendars of Athens and Sparta when we assume that Gerastios 12 should be equated with some later date.

It is now known that 423/2 and 422/1 were both ordinary years in the Spartan calendar and that one of these years (422/1) was intercalary in the Athenian calendar. The month Gerastios at Sparta preceded Artemisios, and the interval between the truce of 423 and the Peace of Nicias was twenty-five months.[2] With the two equations Gerastios 12 = Elaphebolion 14 in 423 and Artemisios 26/27 = Elaphebolion 24/25 in 421 it is impossible to reconstruct the civil calendars both at Athens and at Sparta in such a way that neither shows any irregularity with reference to the true lunar cycle. Dinsmoor's scheme (*op. cit.*, p. 424) gives Elaphebolion in 423 as full and Elaphebolion in 421 as full. With 355 days in the civil year 423/2 (*op. cit.*, pp. 331, 424) we may reckon the interval of time between the truce and the Peace of Nicias from his tables as $(16 + 88) + 355 + (265 +$

---

[1] Cf. Thuc. V, 19, 2 and V, 24; *I.G.*, I², 50 (p. 49, above). Cf. also *I.G.*, I², 71, lines 78 ff. (Davis, "Two Attic Decrees of the Fifth Century," *A.J.A.*, XXX [1926], 179–188).

[2] Meritt, *The Athenian Calendar*, pp. 111–112; Dinsmoor, *The Archons of Athens*, p. 335.

25) = 749 days. If there was a similar succession of 29- and 30-day months at Sparta during the same period we obtain a maximum of 18 + 708 + 27 = 753 days, if the first and last months were both full, or a minimum of 17 + 709 + 26 = 752 days if the first and last months were both hollow. The latter reckoning gives the closer approximation, though even here we find that in 423 the beginning of the Spartan month was two days later than the beginning of the Athenian month and that in 421 the beginning of the Spartan month was 1 (or 2) days earlier than the beginning of the Athenian month. I see no escape from the conclusion that in either Athens or Sparta, or in both, the actual civil year showed variations from the astronomical lunar year. The divergence is most pronounced in the spring of 423.

The significance of these observations can be fully realized only when they are taken in connection with the complaints about the calendar made by Aristophanes in the *Clouds* (lines 615–626).

615　ἄλλα τ' εὖ δρᾶν φησιν. ὑμᾶς δ' οὐκ ἄγειν τὰς ἡμέρας
　　　οὐδὲν ὀρθῶς, ἀλλ' ἄνω τε καὶ κάτω κυδοιδοπᾶν.
　　　ὥστε ἀπειλεῖν φησιν αὐτῇ τοὺς θεοὺς ἑκάστοτε,
　　　ἡνίκ' ἂν ψευσθῶσι δείπνου, καὶ ἀπίωσιν οἴκαδε
　　　τῆς ἑορτῆς μὴ τυχόντες κατὰ λόγον τῶν ἡμερῶν.
620　κᾆθ', ὅταν θύειν δέῃ, στρεβλοῦτε καὶ δικάζετε.
　　　πολλάκις δ' ἡμῶν ἀγόντων τῶν θεῶν ἀπαστίαν,
　　　ἡνίκ' ἂν πενθῶμεν ἢ τὸν Μέμνον' ἢ Σαρπηδόνα,
　　　σπένδεθ' ὑμεῖς καὶ γελᾶτ', ἀνθ' ὧν λαχὼν Ὑπέρβολος
　　　τῆτες ἱερομνημονεῖν καὶ ἔπειθ' ὑφ' ἡμῶν τῶν θεῶν
625　τὸν στέφανον ἀφῃρέθη. μᾶλλον γὰρ οὕτως εἴσεται
　　　κατὰ Σελήνην ὡς ἄγειν χρὴ τοῦ βίου τὰς ἡμέρας.

This portion of the *Clouds* belongs to the original version of the play, which was produced at the Greater Dionysia in 423,[1] and

---

[1] There is no reason for believing that these lines belong to the revised version. The mention of Hyperbolos (623–624) as having been chosen Hieromnemon offers no evidence for the later date. He was sufficiently in the public eye to draw the fire of Aristophanes in 425 (*Acharnians*, 846) and also in 424 (*Knights*, 739, 1304–15). Certainly it cannot be argued that he was too inconspicuous a man to be chosen Hieromnemon (Mommsen, *Chronologie*, pp. 416–417, note 1). Even the fact that the scholiast on line 624 says that there was no record of Hyperbolos as Hieromnemon in

so falls at exactly that time when we have evidence from Thucydides that there were irregularities of some sort in the calendar, either at Athens or at Sparta. Naturally, Aristophanes was not concerned with the civil calendar at Sparta; nor will his text allow such an interpretation. Since he specifies clearly that the irregularity in the calendar was at Athens, we must also seek the solution to the problem offered by the divergent dates in Thucydides by recognizing that the necessary adjustment to allow the synchronism must be made in the Athenian, rather than in the Spartan, calendar. It follows that *the actual civil calendar of Athens from 423 to 421 cannot be equated with the true astronomical lunar calendar.*

In this important particular I disagree with Dinsmoor in his reconstruction of the Athenian civil calendar during the fifth century. His contribution to our knowledge of Athenian chronology in this period is an epoch-making achievement, a full appreciation of which can be gained only by reading his careful and brilliant analysis of Meton's nineteen-year cycle. There can be no question that Meton had calculated in advance the lunations for the nineteen years beginning with the summer solstice of 432 B.C., arranging also the sequence of full and hollow months according to a predetermined scheme. Meton did not name his months, but left the distribution of names to the Athenian officials who controlled also the necessary intercalation of extra months at appropriate times. Dinsmoor's argument on these points seems to me unassailable, and his Metonic cycle has been constructed, in consequence, with astronomical exactness.

It is a far different matter, however, to assume that the Athenians always made their civil months agree, in actual practice, with Meton's determinations. Meton's schedule gave the correct days for new moon, but I cannot believe, as Dinsmoor

424/3 cannot be used as evidence against this date for the lines in question. Aristophanes merely says that Hyperbolos was chosen, not that he served. In fact he implies that actually he did not hold the office: λαχὼν Ὑπέρβολος τῆτες ἱερομνημονεῖν – – – – – – – ὑφ' ἡμῶν τῶν θεῶν τὸν στέφανον ἀφηρέθη. The earlier date agrees well also with the fact that the *epirrhema* (575–594) must be dated in 424/3. Besides the abuse of Cleon, we have the evidence of the scholiast on line 584, who records the eclipse of the moon during the previous year when Stratokles was archon (Oct. 9, 425). The eclipse of the sun on March 21, 424, was probably the occasion for the reference in lines 584–586.

argues, that the first day of each civil month agreed with the Metonic date. In far the greater number of cases the correspondence may well have been exact, as Meton doubtless intended that it should be, but the evidence we have just examined from Aristophanes and Thucydides shows that in 423, at least, Meton's scheme, for whatever reason, was not rigorously applied to the civil calendar. Dinsmoor has not considered the evidence of the equations between the Spartan and Athenian calendars in this connection,[1] nor has he given sufficient weight to the complaints of Aristophanes. He dismisses them with the suggestion that "it seems unnecessary to seek . . . a definite basis for these Aristophanic jests." I urge that they are not even acceptable jests unless they have some basis in fact.[2]

While Dinsmoor's reconstruction of the sequence of full and hollow months may be applied to the civil calendar with a sufficient degree of accuracy for all practical purposes, we must still recognize the possibility of slight error in thus determining the initial dates of the Athenian civil months. I thus distinguish between the civil month and Meton's (lunar) month. They may have been in most cases identical, but we know that at times there was a divergence between them.[3]

[1] Except to imply that the irregularity should all be attributed to Sparta, *op. cit.*, pp. 334, 343.

[2] Dinsmoor, *op. cit.*, pp. 335–336. I withdraw my claim (*The Athenian Calendar*, pp. 103–104) that there is evidence in the *Peace* (406–415) for a disturbed condition in the Athenian calendar in 421. On this question I have had the valuable help and advice of Dr. J. K. Fotheringham, who has convinced me that the reference in the *Peace* may possibly deal solely with eclipses. If, however, lines 414–415 should refer to calendar irregularities, is it possible that they refer to irregularities of the past (e.g. 423) which have now been corrected? The verbs are in the imperfect tense.

[3] The reference in Thucydides II, 28 to an eclipse νουμηνίᾳ κατὰ σελήνην has been interpreted by me (*The Athenian Calendar*, p. 104) as showing that the lunar and civil months in 431 were not identical. On the other hand Dinsmoor (p. 314, note 7; p. 317) argues that this passage proves the civil month to have begun at the astronomical new moon. The passage is ambiguous, and I concede that it proves nothing one way or the other except as we give our own subjective interpretations to it.

CHAPTER IX

THE CONCILIAR YEAR

In the exact identification of the Metonic lunar months with the months of the civil calendar which were actually observed by the Athenian people, we have found that Dinsmoor's calendar scheme does not make allowance for the variation which at times existed between the two systems. Another assumption which Dinsmoor has made in his study of the calendar in the fifth century is that the Metonic solar year should be equated with the conciliar year (Pryt. I, 1 to Pryt. X, *ultimo*).[1] In fact, Dinsmoor argues that the conciliar year as we know it during the greater part of the Peloponnesian war was introduced by Meton in 432 and that before this date the civil and prytany years were coterminous, as they were after 409/8.[2]

But so far as we know, Meton's work was not connected in any way with the conciliar year. He obtained his great reputation by the publication of the nineteen-year cycle, in which he demonstrated how nineteen solar years, reckoned from the time of the summer solstice, might be equated with nineteen lunar years, containing 235 months. Though not ultimately perfect, this scheme marked so great an advance over the earlier cycles of eight or sixteen years, and the movements of the moon, the sun, and the stars were predicted with such accuracy, that even so late a writer as Diodorus Siculus (XII, 36) could speak with enthusiasm of Meton's astronomical observations. But it does not follow that the political year of Athens, the so-called conciliar year, was also an invention of Meton. The very fact that it was abandoned within twenty-five years after the publication of the nineteen-year cycle argues against the assumption that it formed any part of Meton's scheme.

[1] Dinsmoor, *The Archons of Athens*, p. 329, note 1.

[2] Dinsmoor, *op. cit.*, p. 327, note 1. Cf. also p. 108, above. Dinsmoor disallows the evidence which I have adduced from the formulae of official records to show that the separate conciliar year must have been in existence at least as early as the commencement of work on the Parthenon (447/6). Cf. Meritt, *The Athenian Calendar*, pp. 124–126; *idem*, "Senatorial and Civil Years in Athens," *Cl. Phil.*, XXV (1930), 243; Glotz, in a review of Meritt, *The Athenian Calendar*, in *Rev. arch.*, XXIX (1929), 196.

Whatever Meton's contribution in teaching the Athenians the true length of the solar year may have been, it is certain that the approximate length of this solar year was known long before Meton's cycle was introduced; we are under no obligation to credit Meton with the invention of the conciliar year of ten prytanies, which was the equivalent of this year. The evidence of official formulae in public records indicates the introduction of the conciliar (solar) year at least as early as 447 B.C. I have argued [1] that this special administrative year was introduced by Cleisthenes, at the time of the creation of the council representing the ten tribes. Ferguson calls this "a very considerable assumption," [2] and his criticism may perhaps be justifiable. I still maintain, however, that there is evidence for this separate type of administrative year as early as 447, and I can think of no more probable date for the original introduction than the era of the reforms of Cleisthenes. I know of no evidence from the first half of the fifth century which can decide the issue.

Dinsmoor's identification of the conciliar year with the Metonic solar year has, however, a number of very embarrassing consequences, which suffice, in my opinion, to show that the identification cannot be correct.

If we suppose that the first conciliar year of this type began at the time of the summer solstice in 432 on Skirophorion 13, we find that the first ten such years must have contained 3660 days, in order to satisfy the known equation Prytany I, 1 = Hekatombaion 10 = July 5 in 422 B.C. [3] The same true solar years comprised only 3652 days, and we are forced at once to the conclusion that in any case the application of the Metonic norm to the administrative year was only approximate. The divergence had grown to the very considerable figure of eight days in the first ten years after the adoption of the conciliar year.

If the comparison is carried further, we find that the first thirteen years of the cycle must have contained 4758 days, in order to satisfy the equation which is implicit in Antiphon's

---

[1] Meritt, *The Athenian Calendar*, p. 72.

[2] Ferguson, in a review of Meritt, *The Athenian Calendar*, in *A.J.A.*, XXXIII (1929), 341; Dinsmoor, *The Archons of Athens*, p. 326. But cf. Cavaignac, "Note sur la chronologie attique," *Rev. des ét. anc.*, XXXI (1929), 213.

[3] Cf. Dinsmoor, *op. cit.*, Table VII, p. 331.

speech περὶ τοῦ χορευτοῦ for 419/8: Prytany I, 1 = Hekatombaion 16.[1] By this time the divergence had grown to ten days.
But the first cycle of Meton came to an end on Skirophorion 13
in 413 B.C., which date must be equated with the Julian June 27.
In order to correct the divergence of ten days which existed in
419, Dinsmoor assumes that two of the six remaining years of
the cycle in the conciliar year contained only 364 days,[2] whereas
three of the remaining six years contained only 363 days. This
is in itself not a convincing reconstruction of the conciliar year,
in view of the fact that the first fourteen years of the cycle aver-
aged 366 days. The sequence of five short years comes at that
point where Dinsmoor claims no evidence for the length of the
years other than the necessities of his cycle.

It is true, however, that the conciliar year did vary at times
from the length of the true solar year. A formal proof of this
fact is given by the record of interest on the moneys borrowed
by the state from 426 to 422 (I.G., I², 324), from which it is evident that the four years in question contained 1464 days and
that one year (425/4) contained 368 days.[3] Such a variation
seems to me easier to explain if we interpret the conciliar year
as representing a long-standing tradition of approximation to
the solar year, than if we assume that Meton first instituted it
as the equivalent of the solar year after his careful observations
and calculations of the length of this year.

But these are not the major objections to Dinsmoor's scheme.
It is much more significant that, after the equation Prytany I,
1 = Skirophorion 14 = June 28 has been established for the
beginning of the second Metonic cycle in 413, there is no possibility of utilizing the equation given in Aristotle's Constitution
of Athens (32, 1) for the correspondence between the civil and
conciliar years in 411 (Prytany I, 1 = Skirophorion 14). By no
device of calendar reconstruction can the two intervening years
in the Metonic-solar-prytany calendar be made equal in length
to the two intervening years in the lunar-civil calendar, no matter

[1] Cf. Dinsmoor, loc. cit.; Meritt, The Athenian Calendar, pp. 121–122.

[2] Dinsmoor, op. cit., Table VII, p. 331. The observation of the solstice in 432 had
been one day too early, so that the amount of correction necessary between 419 and
413 was actually nine, instead of ten, days.

[3] Meritt, The Athenian Calendar, pp. 70–71.

whether the civil years have twelve or thirteen months each. But instead of abandoning the assumed identification of the Metonic-solar and conciliar years, Dinsmoor here rejects the evidence of Aristotle as "null and void," with the suggestion that "Aristotle apparently knew nothing of the prytany-solar year."[1] There is no need to dwell long upon the validity of this rejection; Dinsmoor has saved his calendar scheme by attributing to Aristotle a blunder which could have arisen only through gross ignorance of Athenian political institutions in the fifth century — and that too in the very treatise which Aristotle had composed upon the history of these institutions. Nor is this all. Even so, the equation Prytany I, 1 = Skirophorian 14 in 413 can be maintained only by the further assumption that one of the last few months of the civil year 414/3 was omitted.[2]

I do not consider valid any hypothesis which rejects the Aristotelian equation Prytany I, 1 = Skirophorion 14 in 411 B.C. Not only have we every reason to believe that Aristotle understood the nature of the conciliar year in the fifth century, but when this equation is compared with the epigraphical correspondence Prytany I, 1 = Hekatombaion 10 in 422, we find that the eleven conciliar years so determined average 365 5/11 days.[3] Since the conciliar year is known to have been approximately equivalent in length to the solar year, the average thus determined suffices to reinforce the validity of Aristotle's data, if we wish to search for such additional support.

We should reject, not Aristotle's equation in 411, but the equation which Dinsmoor has proposed as Prytany I, 1 = Skirophorion 14 = June 28 in 413. It follows that the conciliar year was not identified with the Metonic-solar year at the end of the first cycle, and also — since we relieve Meton of all responsibility for the conciliar year — that there is no longer any compelling reason for accepting the equation Prytany I, 1 = Skirophorion 13 in 432 B.C. at the beginning of Meton's first cycle.

Dinsmoor has proposed three fundamental equations for the reconstruction of the calendar in the fifth century:

[1] Dinsmoor, op. cit., pp. 328–329.

[2] Dinsmoor, op. cit., p. 342, suggests that perhaps there was no month of Munichion in this year, and he cites a possible parallel from 167/6 B.C.

[3] Cf. Meritt, The Athenian Calendar, p. 118.

1. 432 B.C. Prytany I, 1 = Skirophorion 13 = June 27
2. 422 B.C. Prytany I, 1 = Hekatombaion 10 = July 5
3. 413 B.C. Prytany I, 1 = Skirophorion 14 = June 28

Of these, the first and the third are based only upon the assumption that Meton's solar year was the same as the conciliar year, and the third is further incompatible with the evidence of Aristotle.[1] I propose to reject these two equations and to consider as fundamental only the following, taken from *I.G.*, I², 324 and from Aristotle:

1. 422 B.C. Prytany I, 1 = Hekatombaion 10 = July 5 [2]
2. 411 B.C. Prytany I, 1 = Skirophorion 14 = July 7 [2]

We have seen the difficulties which were involved in the attempt to bring the conciliar year into conformity with the Metonic-solar year at the end of the first cycle. In particular, it was evident that certain rather impressive evidence had to give way before a rigid interpretation of an assumed calendar scheme. In general, it is my conviction that no rigid system can be applied either to the prytany calendar or to the civil calendar of Athens in the fifth century. We expect at the end of the first Metonic cycle to find that the nineteen civil years, in which the months corresponded to the astronomical Metonic months, will have been brought to completion. Since the summer solstice, with an error of one day because of incorrect observation, fell on Skirophorion 13 in 432, it is reasonable to suppose that in 413 the date of the solstice will fall on Skirophorion 14. Dinsmoor's calendar scheme has been so constructed as to give the necessary correspondence between the civil calendar and the Julian calendar, where we find that in this latter year Skirophorion 14 is the same as June 28, the day of the solstice. There is evidence, however, that in the year 414/3 both the seventh and the twenty-fifth of Gamelion must have fallen within the seventh prytany

---

[1] Dinsmoor (*op. cit.*, p. 343) cites Plutarch (*Nicias*, 28) as supporting evidence for his dating of Athenian civil months in 413. But the correspondence which Plutarch gives between the Doric Karneios and the Attic Metageitnion is a general equation, not specifically applicable to 413. Cf. Meritt, "The Spartan Gymnopaidia," *Cl. Phil.*, XXVI (1931), 79.

[2] In giving the Julian equivalents I follow Dinsmoor, rather than my earlier publication (*The Athenian Calendar*, p. 118).

of the conciliar year (*I.G.*, I², 328).[1] The necessary consequence is that the ensuing civil year can have commenced only at the second new moon after the solstice in 413, and that the month of Skirophorion in 414/3 was not the last month of the first Metonic cycle, but rather the first month of the second Metonic cycle. Dinsmoor considers this an "incredible condition of affairs,"[2] and effects a remedy by omitting the month of Munichion from 414/3, so that Skirophorion 14 may actually fall on the solstice instead of a month later.[3]

According to his scheme the year 415/4 was intercalary, containing a second Hekatombaion by virtue of the provisions of the Eleusinian Tax Decree (*I.G.*, I², 76), which he dates in the eighth prytany of 416/5.[4] In the addition of this extra month the orderly sequence of years whereby Skirophorion 14 in 413 should have come at the summer solstice was disturbed. All succeeding months, after Hekatombaion in 415, were thrown one month later, so that without a correction the final Skirophorion of 414/3 must inevitably have been crowded over into the second Metonic cycle. It so happens, however, that the year 414/3 had been determined as an intercalary year, and Dinsmoor assumes that it actually did contain a second Posideion.[5] Now the natural way to correct the error introduced into the calendar by the addition of a second Hekatombaion in 415/4 was to omit the second Posideion of 414/3. It was within the province of the Archon Basileus to decide whether any given year should have twelve or thirteen months. But, according to Dinsmoor's argument, instead of perceiving that the year would not end properly with the Metonic cycle in 413, when there was still time to omit the superfluous Posideion, the Athenians realized only too late that the civil year would extend into the second Metonic cycle unless something drastic should be done to correct the error. They omitted, consequently, one of the regular last months of the year, possibly Munichion.

[1] Meritt, *The Athenian Calendar*, p. 93; *idem*, "The Spartan Gymnopaidia," *Cl. Phil.*, XXVI (1931), 71; Dinsmoor, *op. cit.*, p. 342.

[2] Dinsmoor, *op. cit.*, p. 328.

[3] Dinsmoor, *op. cit.*, p. 342, and Table IX, p. 424.

[4] Dinsmoor, *op. cit.*, p. 340.

[5] Dinsmoor, *op. cit.*, p. 342, and Table IX, p. 424.

I cannot bring any formal proof to show that Munichion was not omitted from the year 414/3, and yet I consider such an omission here highly improbable. To my mind we should have a state of affairs much more incredible than if we allow one month of 414/3 to lap over into the beginning of Meton's second cyclic period. Our interpretation must be subjective, but once granted that the Athenians could become sufficiently concerned to omit almost any month in order to make their civil year come out even with an artificial cycle, we are impressed by the fact that they knew the trouble which lay ahead of them as early as Hekatombaion of 415, and yet made no plans during that year or the first six months of the next to do the easiest thing that could be done to avoid the difficulty.

Since it seems evident that they could not have been so much concerned over the approaching misfit of the calendar as the last-minute omission of Munichion would imply, I draw the conclusion that they did nothing more to remedy the misfit in the last six months of 414/3 than they had done in the previous eighteen. In other words, I do believe, not that a month was omitted from 414/3, but that this year contained its full complement of twelve regular months, plus the extra Posideion, which should have been omitted if any month at all were to be left out.

This implies, of course, that the Athenians did not have the respect for Meton's cycle which Dinsmoor claims, even though he has to suppose that they did not always realize their obligations until some last-minute surgery was necessary to make the civil calendar conform. We have already observed that in the individual civil months the Athenians allowed some variation from the astronomical norm laid down by Meton.[1] It is probable also that they occasionally borrowed a day from one month to add to the month preceding or following.[2] It is just as easily conceivable that they borrowed a month from the beginning of the second Metonic cycle to add to the end of the first Metonic cycle, so that the normal progression of civil months in 414/3 might be undisturbed. In fact, this would hardly be so much of an irregularity as the borrowing of a single day, because the

[1] Cf. p. 151, above.
[2] Cf. Dinsmoor, *op. cit.*, p. 424, note.

civil months would still correspond to the true lunar periods. The whole adjustment, or lack of adjustment, would merely be a matter of giving names to the months, and Meton's scheme did not attempt to dictate the names that should be given to the months in his cycle.

I still prefer to see in *I.G.*, I², 328 the indication that the civil year 413/2 began at the second new moon after the solstice, and I give the calendar correspondences for this year as follows:

413 B.C. Prytany I, 1 = Thargelion 23 = July 7

The first day of the civil year was brought back to the time of the first new moon after the summer solstice during the early years of the second Metonic cycle by the simple expedient of omitting the extra month Posideion from the first year which would normally have been intercalary.[1]

Dinsmoor and I are in agreement that the civil year 414/3 began with the new moon of July 27, though my interpretation of the conciliar year gives a different equation for the complete set of correspondences:

414 B.C. Prytany I, 1 = Skirophorion 11 = July 7

In the study of the year 415 there are more serious complications, for the evidence of events which occurred after the mutilation of the herms must be brought to bear on the problem and combined in some intelligible way with the epigraphical records preserved for this year in *I.G.*, I², 302. I have made elsewhere a special study of this year[2] and so refrain from giving all the arguments again. Dinsmoor's work on the calendar, however, has necessitated some changes in my previous analysis, which I wish to discuss here in the light of his contribution. A revised facsimile of *I.G.*, I², 302, embodying the necessary corrections in restoration, is given in Plate XIII. The new text, as illustrated in the facsimile plate, is here transcribed. References throughout are to the lines as numbered in the present transcript.

[1] Cf. reviews of Meritt, *The Athenian Calendar*, by Ferguson, in *A.J.A.*, XXXIII (1929), 341, and by Fotheringham, in *Cl. Rev.*, XLIII (1929), 20–21.

[2] Meritt, "The Departure of Alcibiades for Sicily," *A.J.A.*, XXXIV (1930), 125–152.

I.G., I², 302 (418/7–415/4 B.C.)

[Θ   ε   ο]   ι

['Αθεναῖοι ἀνέλοσαν ἐπὶ 'Αντιφο͂ντος ἄρχοντος καὶ ἐπὶ τῆς βολῆς ῆ̔ει

. . . .⁷. . . . προ͂τος ἐγραμμάτευε τ]αμίαι ῾

[ιερὸν χρεμάτον τῆς 'Αθεναίας Πυθόδορος 'Αλαιεὺς καὶ συνάρχοντες

ηο῀ις Φορμίον 'Αριστίονος Κ]υδαθεναιε

[ὺς ἐγραμμάτευε παρέδομεν ηελλενοταμίαις 'Εργοκλεῖ 'Αριστείδο

Βεσαιεῖ καὶ συ]νάρχοσι καὶ παρέδροις ῾

5   [ιεροκλεῖ 'Αρχεστράτο 'Αθμονεῖ καὶ συνάρχοσι ἐπὶ τῆς . . .⁶. . . . ίδος

πρότες πρυτα]νευόσες καὶ ηεμέραι δευτ

[έραι καὶ τριακοστε͂ι τῆς πρυτανείας ᵗᵘᵐᵐᵃ ⁶ ᵖᵉᶜᵘⁿⁱᵃᵉ· . . . . . ηόστε δο͂ναι τριε-

ράρχοις ἐπὶ 'Εϊόν]ος τοῖς μετὰ Δεμοσθένος ἔ

[δοχσεν τῆι βολῆι καὶ το͂ι δέμοι .]ιο[. . . .⁹ . . . . εἶπε τὸ ἀργύ-

ριον τοῦτο παραδο͂να]ι τὸς ηελλενοταμίας καὶ [τ]

[ὸς παρέδρος τοῖς ταμίαις τῆς] θεο͂ Πυθ[οδόροι 'Αλαιεῖ καὶ χσυνάρχοσι

καὶ τὸς τα]μίας τῆς θεο͂ πάλιν παραδο͂[ν]

[αι τοῖς ηελλενοταμίαις κ]αὶ τοῖς παρέδ[ροις τούτος δὲ δο͂ναι στρατε-

γοῖς ἐπὶ Θ]ράικες Εὐθυδέμοι Εὐδέμο [ν]

10   [– – – – – – – – – – – – – – – –] vacat

[ἐπὶ τῆς . . .⁶. . . .ίδος πρυτα]νείας δευτέρας [πρυτανευόσες ηελλενο-

ταμίαις 'Ερ]γοκλεῖ 'Αριστείδο Βεσαιεῖ[ν]

[. . . . . . . .¹⁷ . . . . Αἰχ]σονεῖ καὶ συνάρχο[σι καὶ παρέδροις

ηιεροκλεῖ 'Αρχε]στράτο 'Αθμονεῖ καὶ συν[ά]ρχ[ο]

[σι _ _ ⁶ ᵛᵉˡ ⁸ _ _ καὶ _ _ ⁴ ᵛᵉˡ ² _ κοστε͂]ι τῆς πρυτανείας π[αρέδομεν ᵗᵘᵐᵐᵃ ⁹

. . . . ᵖᵉᶜᵘⁿⁱᵃᵉ τε καὶ χρυσί]ο Κυζικενο͂ στατε͂ρας 𐅷𐅷𐅷𐅷 [. .]

[_ _ ±⁴ _ _ καὶ ηέκτας _ _ _ _ ±⁸ _ _ _ _] ἀργύριον τούτον [γίγνεται

. . . . .ᵗᵘᵐᵐᵃ ²⁰ ᵖᵉᶜᵘⁿⁱᵃᵉ. . . . .]|| τοῦτο τὸ χρυσίον παρέδομ[ε]

15   [ν τοῖς τριεράρχοις ἐπὶ ῎Α]ργος τοῖς μετὰ Δεμ[οσθένος φσεφισαμένο

το͂ δέμο τὲν] ἄδειαν vacat

       ——————¹⁴——————→

[ἐπὶ τῆς – – – –ίδος – – – –]ες πρυτανευόσες ὀ[γδόει εἰκοστε͂ι

ηεμέραι τῆς πρυ]τανείας στρατεγοῖς παρέδομ

[εν 'Αλκιβιάδει Σκαμβονί]δει Αὐτοκλεῖ 'Αναφλ[υστίοι – – – – – –

– – – – – – – – –] vacat

[ἐπὶ τῆς . . . . .¹³ . . . . . . .ά]τες πρυτανευόσες τ[ρίτει καὶ δεκάτει

ηεμέραι τῆς π]ρυτανείας παρέδομεν τὸ ἐχ Σ

[άμο κατὰ τὸν ἐνιαυτὸν ἐ]πελθόντος ηελλενοτ[αμίαις 'Εργοκλεῖ

'Αριστείδο Βεσ]αιεῖ καὶ χσυνάρχοσι καὶ παρ

20 [ἕδροι ἑλλ]ενο[ταμιôν ℎι]εροκλεῖ ᾿Αρχεστράτο [᾿Αθμονεῖ . . ℎοῦτοι

δὲ ἔδοσαν στρ]ατ[[ρατ]]εγοῖς Νικίαι Νικεράτ

[ο Κυδαντ]ίδει Κ̣α̣λ̣[λιστρ]άτοι ᾿Εμπέδο ℎοêθεν Κ[_ _ _ _ _ _ _ nomen,

_ _ _ _ _ _ _ _ _ _ _ _ _ _ _ _ _ _] vacat
  nomen patris,   demoticum

[Κ ε] φ ά λ α [ι] ο ν ἀ ν α λ [ό μ α τ ο ς τ ô] ἐ π ὶ τ ê ς

[ἀ] ρ χ ê ς ⟐ ⟐ Τ Χ ⟐ Η Η Ι⫽[. . . . 8. . . .] ⎟⎟ vacat

᾿Αθεναῖοι ἀνέλοσαν ἐ[πὶ Εὐφέμο ἄρ]χοντος καὶ [ἐπὶ τês βολês ℎêι

. . . . .9. . . . πρ]ôτος ἐγραμμάτευε ταμίαι ℎιε

25 ρôν χρεμάτον τês ᾿Α[θεναίας ᾿Αναχσικράτες Λαμπτρεὺς καὶ χσυνάρ-

χοντες ℎοῖς] Εὔχσενος Εὐφάνος Προσπάλτ

ιος ἐγραμμάτευε π[αρέδομεν . . . . 28. . . . .

στρατεγοῖς ἐς] τὰ ἐπὶ Θράικες κα[ὶ] ῾Ρίνονι Χ

αρικλέος Παιανιε[ῖ ἐπὶ τês . . .είδος . . .6. . . πρυτανευόσες καὶ

ℎεμέραι δευτέ]ραι καὶ εἰκοστêι τês πρυτα

νείας [φ]σεφισαμέν[ο τô δέμο τὲν ἄδειαν - - - - - - - - - -

- - - - - - - - - -] vacat

ἐπὶ τês Αἰαντίδο[ς . . .6. . . πρυτανευόσες παρέδομεν στρατεγοῖς ἐς

Μέλον Τεισί]αι Τεισιμάχο Κεφαλêθεν ᵛ

30 Κλεομέδει Λυκο[μέδος Φλυεῖ . . . . .18. . . . . τês πρυτα-

νείας φσεφισαμέν]ο τô δέμο τὲν ἄδειαν ⟑ᵛᵛᵛᵛ

ἐπὶ τês ᾿Αντιοχί[δος _2-3_άτες πρυτανευόσες ℎελλενοταμίαις παρέ-

δομεν _ _ _ 8-7_ _ _ _]οι Α[ὐρ]ίδει Τιμάρχοι Παλ

λενεῖ καὶ στρα[τεγοῖς ἐς Μέλον Τεισίαι Τεισιμάχο Κεφαλêθεν

Κλεομέδει Λυκομέδ]ος Φλυεῖ τρίτει καὶ δεκ

άτε̣[ι τê]ς̣ [πρυτανείας φσεφισαμένο τô δέμο τὲν ἄδειαν - - - - - -

- - - - - - - - - - - - -] vacat

[Κ ε φ ά λ α ι ο ν ἀ ν α λ ό μ α τ ο ς τ ô ἐ] π ὶ τ ê ς

35 [ἀ ρ χ ê ς _ _ _ _ _ _ _ _ _ _ _ _ summa pecuniae _ _ _ _ _ _ _ _ _ _ _ _] vacat

[᾿Αθεναῖοι ἀνέλοσαν ἐπὶ ᾿Αριμνέστο ἄρχοντος καὶ ἐπὶ τês βολês ℎêι

. . . . .8. . . .πρôτος] ἐγραμμάτευε ταμίαι [ℎ]

[ιερôν χρεμάτον τês ᾿Αθεναίας Δεχσίθεος Φυλάσιος καὶ χσυνάρχοντες

ℎοῖς Λυσικλês Δ]ρακοντίδο Βατêθ[εν]

[ἐγραμμάτευε . . . . 61. . . . . . .

. . . .] Παλλενεῖ . .5. . .

[- -

- -]

lacuna

45 [- -

- - - - - - - - - - - - - - - - - - - -]

[. . . . . .¹³. . . . . .]ΔΔ *vacat*

[ἐπὶ τῆς Κεκρο]πίδος [– – – – – – – – – – – – – – – – – –

– – – – – – – – – – – – – – – – – –]

[. . . . .¹¹. . . . .]ονει[. . . . . .⁴⁵. . . . . .

. . . .]οι[. . . . . .²³. . . . .]

[ἐπὶ τῆς Κεκροπ]ίδος [ὀγδόες πρυτανευόσες _ _ _⁶ ᵛᵉˡ ⁸ _ _ _ καὶ _ _ _ _¹⁰ ᵛᵉˡ ⁸_ _

– – – – ἡεμέραι] τῆς πρυτανεία[ς στρατε]γο[ῖς Ἀλ]

50   [κιβιάδει Κλειν]ί[ο Σκαμβονίδει Λαμάχοι Χσενοφάνος ℎοέθεν Νικίαι

N]ικεράτο Κυδαντίδει καὶ παρέδρο[ις]

[. . . . .*nomen et demoticum,* 29 *nomen et demoticum*. . . . . Ἀντιμάχοι ℎερμείοι

. . . .⁹. . . .] ⊦⊦⊦ *vacat*

[ἐπὶ τῆς – – – – – ἐνάτες πρυτανευόσες – – – – – ℎεμέραι στρ]ατεγοῖς

ἐς Σικελίαν Ἀλκιβιάδει Λαμάχο[ι]

[Νικίαι καὶ παρέδροις. . . . . .*nomen et demoticum.* 29 *nomen et demoticum*. . . . .

Ἀντ]ιμάχοι ℎερμείοι ⊿[⊿]⊿ *vacat*

[ἐπὶ τῆς – – – – – ἐνάτες πρυτανευόσες – – – – – ℎεμέρα]ι στρατεγοῖς

ἐς Σικελί[α]ν Ἀλκιβιάδει Λαμάχοι

55   [Νικίαι καὶ παρέδροις. . . . .*nomen et demoticum,* 29 *nomen et demoticum*. . . . . . .]

Ἀντιμάχοι ℎερμείοι ⊿ΤΤΤΤΧ[.]ΗΗΗ   *vacat*

[ἐπὶ τῆς . . . . .¹¹. . . . δεκάτες πρυτανευόσες ὀγδόει ℎεμέρ]αι

στρατεγοῖς ἐς Σικελίαν Ἀλκιβιάδει Λαμάχο[ι]

[Νικίαι καὶ παρέδροις. . . . . .*nomen et demoticum,* 29 *nomen et demoticum*. . . . . . .]

Ἀντιμάχοι ℎερμείοι χρυσίο Κυ[ζ]ικενῶ στατῆρ

[ας . . . . .⁴⁴. . . . .]

⊦⊦⊦||Ⅽ *vacat*

[Κ ε φ ά λ α ι ο ν ἀ ν α λ ό μ α]τ ο ς τ ῶ ἐ π ὶ τ ῆ ς

60   [ἀ ρ χ ῆ ς . . . . .¹¹. . . . .]ΔΓ⊦|||| *vacat*

[Ἀθεναῖοι ἀνέλοσαν ἐπὶ Χαρίο ἄρχοντος καὶ ἐπὶ τῆς βολῆς ℎεῖ. .⁵. .]

ίδες πρõτος ἐγραμμάτευε ταμίαι ℎιερõν χρεμάτονᵛ

[τῆς Ἀθεναίας Λεοχάρες . . . . .¹¹. . . . . καὶ χσυνάρχοντες ℎοῖς

Τελέα]ς Τελενίκο Περγασῆθεν ἐγραμμάτευε παρέδοσαν στρ

[ατ]εγοῖς Τελεφόν[οι . .⁵. . . καὶ χσυνάρχοσι καὶ ℎελλενοταμίαι καὶ]

παρέδροι Φερεκλείδει Πειραιεῖ φσεφισαμένο τõ δέμ

[ο] τὲν ἄδειαν ἐπὶ τῆς Αἰαντίδος τρί[τες πρυτανευόσες . . .⁶. . . ℎεμ]-

έραι τῆς πρυτανείας ⊿ΤΧΧΧ⋢[Η]Η⋤ΔΔΔΓ⊦⊦||||Ⅽ τε καὶ

χρυσίο

65   Κυζικενõ ⊦⊦⊿⊿⊿⊿⊿⋤ΣΣΣ τιμὲ τούτον γίγν[εται . . . . .¹⁶. . . . .

. . . . .] *vacat*

ℎελλενοταμίαις καὶ παρέδροις ἐδανείσα[μεν . . . . .¹⁵. . . . . . .]

ʼΑριστοκράτει Εὐονυμεῖ καὶ χσυνάρχοσι Ⲫ Τ Τ Τ Τ οὗτοι δ

ἐ ἔδοσαν ἀθλοθέταις ἐς Παναθέναια ʼΑμέμπτο[ι . . . . . ¹¹. . . . . καὶ]

χσυνάρχοσι ἐπὶ τῆς ʼΕρεχθεΐδος δευτέρας πρυτανευόσε

ς εἰκοστῆι ℎεμέραι τῆς πρυτανείας *vacat*

ἐπὶ τῆς Κεκροπίδος τετάρτες πρυτανευόσες ℎέ[κτει ℎεμέραι τ]ῆς

πρυτανείας ℎελλενοταμίαις καὶ παρέδροις ʼΑριστοκρ

70 άτει Εὐονυμεῖ καὶ χσυνάρχοσι στρατιόταις ἐ[μ Μέλοι. . .⁷. . .]

ΔΔ *vacat*

ἐπὶ τῆς ʼΑντιοχίδος ὀγδόες πρυτανευόσες δεκά[τει ℎεμέραι τῆς]

πρυτανείας ℎελλενοταμίαις καὶ παρέδροις ʼΑριστοκρ[ά]

τει Εὐονυμεῖ καὶ χσυνάρχοσι στρατιόταις ἐμ Μ[έλοι . . . .⁹. . . .]

// // *vacat*

ἐπὶ τῆς ʼΑντιοχίδος ὀγδόες πρυτανευόσες τρίτε[ι ℎεμέραι τῆς πρυ]τα-

νείας ℎελλενοταμίαις καὶ παρέδροις ʼΑριστοκρ[άτ]

ει Εὐονυμεῖ καὶ χσυνάρχοσι ⲎⲎⲎ ℎοῦτοι δ' ἔδοσαν [τῆι ἐν Σικελίαι

σ]τρατιᾶι *vacat*

75 ἐπὶ τῆς ʼΑντιοχίδος ὀγδόες πρυτανευόσες εἰκοσ[τῆι ℎεμέραι τῆς πρ]υτα-

νείας ℎελλενοταμίαις καὶ παρέδροις ʼΑριστοκρ[ά]

τει Εὐονυμεῖ καὶ χσυνάρχοσι ἐς τὰ(ς) ναῦς τὰς ἐς Σι[κελίαν ἐσκομισά-

σα]ς τὰ χρέματα Τ Τ Τ Τ Χ Χ *vacat*

ἐπὶ τῆς ʼΑντιοχίδος ὀγδόες πρυτανευόσες δευτέ[ραι ℎεμέραι τῆς

πρυτα]νεία[ς] ℎελλενοταμίαι καὶ παρέδροι Φιλομέ[λοι Μ]

αραθονίοι καὶ στρατεγοῖ ἐν τῶι Θερμαίοι κόλπο[ι . . . . . ¹⁸. . . . . .

. . . . . καὶ τ]ῆι αὐτῆι ℎεμέραι ℎελλενοταμίαι κ[αὶ παρέ]

δροι Φιλομέλοι Μαραθονίοι καὶ στρατεγοῖ ἐν ʼΕφ[– – – – – – – –

– – – – – – –] *vacat*

80 Κ ε φ ά λ α ι ο ν   ἀ ν α [λ ό μ α τ ο ς   τ] ῶ   ἐ π ὶ   τ [ῆ ς]

ἀ ρ χ ῆ ς   Ⲏ Ⲏ Ⲏ Ⲫ Τ Τ Τ – – – – – – –

vacat

The changes in restoration for lines 18–19 and 63 have already
been discussed above (pp. 90, 130). To Kirchner I am indebted
for pointing out that [.]ιο[. . .⁷. . . εἶπε· τὸ δὲ ἀργύριον – –] is not
a satisfactory restoration for line 7. The particle δέ must be
omitted, to give the reading [.]ιο[. . . .⁹. . . . τὸ ἀργύριον – – –].
Ferguson's suggestion that the restoration of lines 53, 55, and
57 might be [Νικίαι καὶ τῶι ταμίαι τῶι χσυμπλέοντι μετὰ τῆς στρατιᾶς]

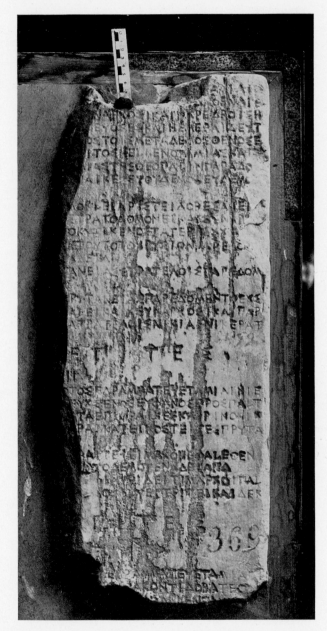

FIG. 20.   Fragment *c* of *I.G.*, I², 302

Ἀντίμαχοι hΕρμεῖοι should also be noted.[1] A renumbering of the lines in the upper part of the inscription has been made necessary by the discovery that the first line should be restored [Θεο]ί. The final iota is preserved on the stone in fragment *c* (cf. Figure 20).[2]

For our present discussion the important part of the document is the record of four payments made to the generals in

FIG. 21. Fragments *a* and *b* of *I.G.*, I², 302

charge of the expedition to Sicily in the early summer of 415. I had originally assumed that the first payment was made in the ninth prytany, and that the last three payments were made in the tenth prytany.[3] The final payment was undoubtedly made in the tenth prytany, for the expedition set sail for Sicily in midsummer (Thuc. VI, 30, 1), and the final payment to the

[1] Ferguson, *The Treasurers of Athena*, p. 23, note 1.

[2] A similar invocation occupied the first line of the record for 432/1 (*I.G.*, I², 296; cf. p. 80).

[3] Meritt, "The Departure of Alcibiades for Sicily," *A.J.A.*, XXXIV (1930), 140.

fleet must have been made later than Prytany IX, 20, the last date which can be restored on the stone for the ninth prytany.[1] Dinsmoor observed, however, that the second and third payments may well be assigned to the ninth prytany, while at the same time

Fig. 22. Fragment *d* of *I.G.*, I[2], 302

relegating the first payment to the eighth prytany.[2] This possibility cannot be denied, and I must change accordingly the restorations which I have proposed for the records of these payments.

[1] Meritt, *op. cit.*, p. 134.
[2] Dinsmoor, *op. cit.*, p. 340.

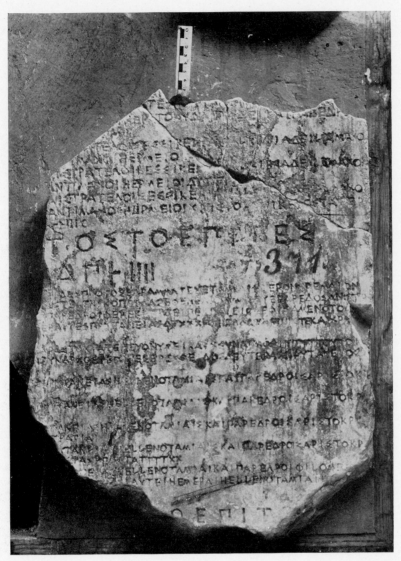

Fig. 23. Fragment *e* of *I.G.*, I², 302

It is, in fact, extremely probable that the new fragment of this inscription (E.M. 6742*b*; cf. Figure 24), which I assigned tentatively to lines 40–44,[1] should be lowered so that the lines till now numbered 43 and 44 may form the beginning of lines 49 and 50.[2] The text as thus restored reads as follows:

49 [ἐπὶ τῆς Κεκροπ]ίδος [ὀγδόες πρυτανευόσες _$\overset{6\ or\ 8}{-----}$_ καὶ _$\overset{10\ or\ 8}{------}$_
hεμέραι] τῆς πρυτανεία[ς στρατε]γο[ῖς Ἀλ]

50 [κιβιάδει Κλειν]ί[ο Σκαμβονίδει Λαμάχοι Χσενοφάνος hοῖθεν Νικίαι
Ν]ικεράτο Κυδαντίδει καὶ παρέδρο[ις]

The date to be restored in line 49 must lie between the twenty-second and the thirty-sixth days of the prytany, whether the prytany be restored as the eighth or ninth of the conciliar year. I follow Dinsmoor here in restoring the date as of the eighth prytany,[3] in order that the first payment to the generals may come as close in point of time as possible to the decision reached by the assembly authorizing the expedition at the beginning of spring.[4]

Line 52 probably records a payment made during the ninth prytany, though we have no way of determining the name of the prytanizing tribe or the date within the prytany. The restoration of line 54 depends on the text which we determine for line 56, to which we now turn our attention.

Dinsmoor reads in line 56: [ἐπὶ τῆς . . . .ίδος δεκάτες πρυτανευόσες δοδεκάτει hεμέρ]αι – – –, a restoration which from the epigraphical point of view is just as satisfactory as my earlier proposal [ἐπὶ τῆς . . .ντίδος δεκάτες πρυτανευόσες εἰκοστῖι hεμέρ]αι – – –. He then equates this conciliar date Prytany X, 12 with the civil date June 7, and so discovers that the last payment of money for the departing fleet was made on the very day before the mutilation of the herms, that is, before the night of June 7/8.[5] The sacrilege itself is then explained as nothing more than a drunken frolic on the part of the soldiers who were about to

[1] Meritt, "The Departure of Alcibiades for Sicily," *A.J.A.*, XXXIV (1930), 150 and Plates I and II. A new facsimile of the document is given in Plate XIII.

[2] Cf. Dinsmoor, *op. cit.*, p. 340.

[3] Dinsmoor, *op. cit.*, p. 340.

[4] Thuc. VI, 8; VI, 26.

[5] Dinsmoor, *op. cit.*, p. 338.

leave for Sicily. Dinsmoor then continues: "This immediate juxtaposition of the events, as determined by independent epigraphical and astronomical sources, seems so logical that it furnishes welcome confirmation of my calendar scheme."

But let us reflect a moment. The astronomical evidence on which the equation Prytany X, 12 = June 7 depends is nothing more than Dinsmoor's assumption that the conciliar year and the Metonic solar year had to end together at the summer solstice of 413. The equation here given for 415 depends directly on Dinsmoor's other equation Prytany I, 1 = Skirophorion 14 =

Fig. 24.   New fragment of *I.G.*, I², 302   (E.M. 6742*b*)

June 28 in 413. But we have found that this latter equation is irreconcilable with the evidence for 411 given by Aristotle, and that it necessitates also other irregularities in the reconstruction of the sequence of conciliar years between 422 and 411.[1]

When we determine the calendar correspondences in 415 on the basis of the fundamental equations for 422 and 411 given on p. 156, we find that Prytany X, 12 must be equated with June 11,[2] and that the close juxtaposition of events which Dinsmoor claims in support of his scheme is at once dissipated. So far as the epigraphical requirements of *I.G.*, I², 302 are concerned, we may

[1] Cf. pp. 153–154.   [2] Cf. table, p. 176.

also substitute for the restoration suggested by Dinsmoor in line 56 the formula [ἐπὶ τῆς . . .⁷. . . ίδος δεκάτες πρυτανευόσες ὀγδόει ἡεμέρ]αι, etc., thereby bringing the date of the last payment to the generals to June 7 and obtaining for an entirely different calendar scheme all the advantages which Dinsmoor claims that the close juxtaposition of events confers upon his own reconstruction of the calendar. We thus discover that the equation Prytany X, 12 = June 7 cannot be used to justify a hypothesis which rejects the evidence of Aristotle, for an entirely different equation, equally possible epigraphically (Prytany X, 8 = June 7), can be constructed so as to harmonize with the Aristotelian dates in 411 and at the same time represent the same sequence of events in Athens in 415 as the other.

I suggest that the restoration in *I.G.*, I², 302, line 56, should be [ἐπὶ τῆς . . .⁷. . . ίδος δεκάτες πρυτανευόσες ὀγδόει ἡεμέρ]αι- - . It is probable that both the payments listed in lines 52 and 54 were made in the ninth prytany. The possibilities of restoration are numerous, and neither the prytany nor the date can be exactly determined.[1]

The events which occurred in Athens just prior to the departure of the fleet may now be outlined somewhat differently from the manner described in my earlier study. We assume that the last payment of money was made to the generals on June 7, with full expectation that the fleet was to depart at once for Sicily. During the following night (June 7/8) occurred the outrage of the mutilation of the herms, which may have been merely the result of a drunken revel or may have been a last-minute attempt on the part of the opposition to prevent the expedition. Plutarch tells us that it was taken as an evil omen by many who were usually above such superstitions (*Alcibiades*, XVIII). At any rate there was a temporary delay, during which the Council and the assembly met frequently to learn the truth of the matter (*loc. cit.*) and during which a special commission was appointed to investigate, while rewards were offered to any informers who wished to give evidence concerning this or any other act of sacrilege (Andocides, I, 27).

[1] My former contention that the tenth prytany was either Leontis or Aiantis must be abandoned (Meritt, "The Departure of Alcibiades for Sicily," *A.J.A.*, XXXIV [1930], 140).

We may well believe that the generals in charge of the expedition, which was ready for departure (Diodorus, XIII, 2; Plutarch, *Alcibiades*, XVIII), chafed at what seemed to reasonable people an unnecessary and useless delay. They soon convinced the assembly that the fleet should be held at Athens no longer, but should sail at once for Sicily. This is the interpretation which I give to the passage from Andocides (I, 11) in which he describes the meeting of the assembly called for the benefit of the generals when the flag-ship of Lamachos was already riding at anchor outside the harbor.

But there was destined to be still further delay. At this special meeting of the assembly the charge of sacrilege in connection with the Eleusinian mysteries was brought against Alcibiades. We may see in this accusation a last-minute attempt to discredit Alcibiades — possibly also a desperate hope that the whole undertaking might yet be abandoned. Alcibiades offered to stand trial at once, but his political enemies urged with malicious intent that his departure should not be delayed. They were planning even then to recall him at their pleasure to face the indictment when he could not have the support of the army on which to rely (Thuc. VI, 29).

Perhaps we may allow an interval of ten days between the mutilation of the herms and the accusation of Alcibiades. The actual departure of the fleet can hardly have been postponed more than another three days. I propose the following chronological table to replace that given in my earlier study: [1]

Last payment to the generals (*I.G.*, I², 302, line 56)	Prytany X, 8 = June 7
Mutilation of the herms	Prytany X, 9 = June 7/8
Accusation of Alcibiades (Cf. Andocides, I, 11)	Prytany X, 18 = June 17
Departure of the fleet (Thuc. VI, 29, 30–32)	Prytany X, 21 = June 20

In giving this sequence of events I am in substantial agreement with Dinsmoor, whose account I follow in preference to the one which I had myself proposed before his publication ap-

---

[1] Meritt, "The Departure of Alcibiades for Sicily," *A.J.A.*, XXXIV (1930), 143; cf. Dinsmoor, *op. cit.*, p. 338.

peared. The dates which I have given by the conciliar year differ, of course, from those given by Dinsmoor, for reasons which have been advanced above. We must now determine these dates in terms of the Athenian civil calendar.

For the year 414 the equation Prytany I, 1 = Skirophorion 11 = July 7 has already been determined. Now, if 415/4 was a year of thirteen months, as Dinsmoor supposes, the new moon of June 8 in 415 must be equated with Skirophorion 1. Let us assume that the equation Skirophorion 1 = June 8 is correct for the year 415. It follows that this day in the conciliar calendar was Prytany X, 9.[1] Assuming that Prytany X contained thirty-seven days and that Skirophorion contained thirty days,[2] we may calculate that in the summer of 415 the new conciliar year began on Skirophorion 30. When we further postulate that Hekatombaion was a hollow month and allow 36/37 days for the first prytany of the new year, it develops that Prytany II, 20 (*I.G.*, I², 302, lines 66–68) must be equated with the twenty-sixth or twenty-seventh day of the *second* civil month. In any normal year the name given to this month would be Metageitnion, as a matter of course. But Dinsmoor has found strong arguments in favor of dating the much-disputed Eleusinian Tax Decree in 416/5, and he draws from this inscription (*I.G.*, I², 76, lines 53–54) the inevitable conclusion, if his date for the document is correct,[3] that the second month in the civil year 415/4 was not Metageitnion but rather a second Hekatombaion.

The payment to the *athlothetai* for the Panathenaic festival recorded in *I.G.*, I², 302, lines 66–68 was made, therefore, on the

---

[1] This represents the necessary correction in Dinsmoor's table, *op. cit.*, p. 331. Cf. p. 169.

[2] Dinsmoor, *op. cit.*, Table IX, p. 424.

[3] A strong argument in favor of this date is the fact that the decree was passed in the prytany of Kekropis, probably the eighth prytany of the year. We know from *I.G.*, I², 302, line 49, that Kekropis held the eighth prytany in 416/5. Another telling piece of evidence in favor of 416/5 is to be found in the provisions of Lampon's amendment (*I.G.*, I², 76, lines 54–59) respecting the Pelargikon. At the beginning of the Archidamian War the Athenians had learned to their sorrow the consequences of divine wrath because of their failure to obey the Delphic command, " τὸ Πελαργικὸν ἀργὸν ἄμεινον" (Thuc. II, 17). As the great expedition was preparing to set forth to Sicily in the spring of 415, they thought to protect themselves against a similar pestilence by taking proper precautions in their care of the Pelargikon.

twenty-sixth or twenty-seventh day of the second Hekatombaion, rather than in the month of Metageitnion.

I have argued consistently that any reconstruction of the civil and conciliar years which brought the date of this payment one complete month after the festival of Athena must be, for that very reason, incorrect.[1] The only direct evidence that we have for the time of such payments (*I.G.*, I², 305) shows that they were made before the festival date rather than later. I am all the more convinced that this is true since being able to prove that in 410/9 (*I.G.*, I², 304, lines 5–7) the payment to the athlothetai may well have been earlier than Hekatombaion 28, even though the payment itself was made during the second prytany.[2] I should still contend even here that in 415/4 we should restore a year of twelve rather than thirteen months, if the alternative were to allow the payment to the athlothetai to fall one complete month after the time of the Panathenaia.

But even with a year of thirteen months in 415/4 it is now possible, with Dinsmoor's date for *I.G.*, I², 76, to reconstruct the civil calendar in such a way that Prytany II, 20 fell before the epochal date of the festival. I assume that, for whatever reason, the lesser Panathenaia in this year were celebrated in the intercalated month, thirty days later than the normal time of celebration, but still on the third day from the end of Hekatombaion. To the best of my knowledge, this interpretation reconciles all the scattered bits of evidence for the calendar correspondences between the conciliar and civil years at this time. It also allows the requisite interval of approximately seven weeks instead of three for the events which took place between the accusations of Diokleides and the Panathenaic festival.[3] In view of these circumstances I withdraw my contention that the new moon of June 8 fell on Thargelion 1, and agree with Dinsmoor that this Julian date should be equated rather with Skirophorion 1. The tables of correspondences between the various calendar schemes have been constructed accordingly.[4]

---

[1] Meritt, *The Athenian Calendar*, p. 93; *idem*, "The Departure of Alcibiades for Sicily," *A.J.A.*, XXXIV (1930), 142–143.   [2] Cf. p. 107, above.

[3] Cf. Meritt, "The Departure of Alcibiades for Sicily," *A.J.A.*, XXXIV (1930), 142, 146–149. Cf. Dinsmoor, *op. cit.*, p. 338, note 2.

[4] Cf. p. 176.

With a normal arrangement of civil and conciliar years between 422 and 415 we are now able to satisfy the evidence of Antiphon's speech περὶ τοῦ χορευτοῦ by establishing in 419 the equation:

419 B.C. Prytany I, 1 = Hekatombaion 16 = July 7 [1]

The year 419/8 must have been intercalary, and in order to avoid exceptional irregularity in the calendar in the succession of ordinary and intercalary years between 419/8 and 415/4 we must assume that the intervening years followed in the order O I O. I have shown elsewhere that the two years 413/2 and 412/1 must have been ordinary.[2]

Dinsmoor and I are in agreement as to the succession of ordinary and intercalary years in the civil calendar before 422, though our dates by the conciliar year differ, because Dinsmoor has assumed, without sufficient reason, that the conciliar year was instituted by Meton at the summer solstice of 432.[3] I have argued that this separate administrative year was in existence even before Meton's epochal date, and it follows that the known approximate length of this year may still be used to prove that there were four intercalary years in the interval from 433/2 to 423/2, and that 433/2 was itself intercalary.[4] It is then a reasonable deduction that 432/1 should be construed as an ordinary year. As a matter of fact, there is independent evidence to support this conclusion, and I give here the outline of an argument first proposed by Cavaignac.[5]

The Milesian *parapegma* gives the equation Skirophorion 13 = June 27 for the year 433/2.[6] We may establish, therefore, the date of Hekatombaion 1 in 432/1 as the equivalent of July 15 in the Julian calendar (Dinsmoor, *op. cit.*, p. 317).

Now in the history of Thucydides (II, 28) there is recorded an eclipse of the sun which was visible in Athens on the after-

---

[1] I again follow Dinsmoor in giving the Julian date. Cf. Dinsmoor, *op. cit.*, p. 331.

[2] Meritt, *The Athenian Calendar*, pp. 93–94; p. 159, above.

[3] P. 152, above.

[4] Meritt, *The Athenian Calendar*, pp. 88–89; Dinsmoor, *op. cit.*, p. 327, note 1.

[5] E. Cavaignac, *Note sur la chronologie attique au Vᵉ siècle* (Versailles, 1908), p. 6; also *idem*, "Note sur la chronologie attique," *Rev. des ét. anc.*, XXXI (1929), 214.

[6] H. Diels and A. Rehm, "Parapegmenfragmente aus Milet," *Sitzb. Ak. Berlin*, 1904, pp. 92–100; Meritt, *The Athenian Calendar*, p. 88; Dinsmoor, *op. cit.*, p. 312.

noon of August 3, 431. Thucydides tells us that the eclipse took place νουμηνίᾳ κατὰ σελήνην, which may be interpreted either as *on* or *near* the first day of a civil month, the only time when such an eclipse could possibly occur. The month was, of course, Hekatombaion if 432/1 was intercalary or Metageitnion if 432/1 was ordinary. In the former case the civil year of the archon Euthydemos must have begun on August 3, while in the latter case the initial date of the year must have been July 5.

Cavaignac further calls our attention to the fact that the decree mentioned in Thucydides II, 24 relative to the reserve fund of one hundred talents on the Acropolis and to the one hundred triremes set aside for the defense of the city in case of extreme necessity is the same decree as that given in the famous Strasbourg papyrus (Wilcken, *Hermes*, XLII [1907], 374 ff.) and dated under the archonship of Euthydemos. The events narrated by Thucydides in II, 24–27 must all be assigned to the archonship of Euthydemos, if the correct chronological sequence of the author's narrative is to be preserved. After the passage of the decree providing for the safety of the state (II, 24), we find mention made of further activities of the Athenian fleet about the Peloponnesus (II, 25); of raids on the Lokrian coast opposite Euboea (II, 26); and of the expulsion of the Aeginetans from Aegina (II, 27). Then follows the report of the eclipse on August 3 (II, 28). If 432/1 is to be construed as an intercalary year, then all of these events here narrated, which must have occurred under the archonship of Euthydemos, must be dated on August 3. It is evident that 432/1 must have been an ordinary and not an intercalary year, and that 431/0 began, as indicated in our tables, on July 5. This interpretation allows an interval of one month, which is entirely sufficient for the events described by Thucydides (II, 24–27).[1]

[1] Dinsmoor advances still another proof to show that 432/1 was ordinary (*op. cit.*, pp. 330–331). His argument assumes that the conciliar and Metonic-solar years began on the same date in 432. This would be true only in case Meton instituted the conciliar year, or in case the conciliar year already in existence was adjusted to the Metonic-solar year at the beginning of the nineteen-year cycle (Dinsmoor, *op. cit.*, p. 332, note 4). There is no need to assume such an adjustment, but in any case the divergence between the two different types of year was hardly great enough to impair the validity of Dinsmoor's argument.

The following table illustrates the correspondences between Athenian conciliar and civil calendars and the Julian calendar during the latter part of the fifth century:

THE ATHENIAN CALENDAR FROM 432 TO 404 B.C.

	CIVIL YEAR				CONCILIAR YEAR			
	Attic inter-calation	Date of Hekatom-baion I	Number of days	Date of Prytany I, 1		Number of days	Julian inter-calation	
432/1	O	July 15	355	Skir. 18 =	July 2	365	O	432/1
431/0	(I)	July 5	384	Skir. 28 =	July 2	365	O	431/0
430/29	(O)	July 24	354	Skir. 9 =	July 2	366	I	430/29
429/8	(O)	July 12	354	Skir. 21 =	July 2	365	O	429/8
428/7	(I)	July 1	384	Hek. 2 =	July 2	365	O	428/7
427/6	O	July 20	354	Skir. 12 =	July 2	365	O	427/6
426/5	I	July 9	384	Skir. 23 =	July 2	366	I	426/5
425/4	O	July 27	355	Skir. 5 =	July 2	368	O	425/4
424/3	O	July 17	354	Skir. 19 =	July 5	365	O	424/3
423/2	O	July 6	355	Skir. 29 =	July 5	365	O	423/2
422/1	I	June 26	384	Hek. 10 =	July 5	366	I	422/1
421/0	O	July 14	354	Skir. 22 =	July 5	366	O	421/0
420/19	O	July 3	354	Hek. 4 =	July 6	366	O	420/19
419/8	I	June 22	384	Hek. 16 =	July 7	365	O	419/8
418/7	O	July 11	354	Skir. 26 =	July 7	366	I	418/7
417/6	I	June 29	384	Hek. 9 =	July 7	365	O	417/6
416/5	O	July 18	355	Skir. 19 =	July 7	365	O	416/5
415/4	I	July 8	384	Skir. 30 =	July 7	365	O	415/4
414/3	I	July 27	384	Skir. 11 =	July 7	366	I	414/3
413/2	O	Aug. 14	354	Tharg. 23 =	July 7	365	O	413/2
412/1	O	Aug. 3	355	Skir. 3 =	July 7	(365)	O	412/1
411/0	O	July 23	354	(Skir. 14) =	July 7	(...)	O	411/0
410/09	O	July 13	354	(Skir. 15) =	(June 27)	(370)	I	410/09
409/8	I	July 1	384	Hek. 1 =	July 1	384	O	409/8
408/7	O	July 20	355	Hek. 1 =	July 20	355	O	408/7
407/6	O	July 10	354	Hek. 1 =	July 10	354	O	407/6
406/5	I	June 29	384	Hek. 1 =	June 29	384	I	406/5
405/4	O	July 17	354	Hek. 1 =	July 17	354	O	405/4
404/3	..	July 6	...	Hek. 1 =	July 6	...	O	404/3

The following table is based upon Dinsmoor's study (*op. cit.*, pp. 424–425) of the order of full and hollow months after the introduction of Meton's nineteen-year cycle, revised in the light of the argument presented in the foregoing pages, particularly for the years 413–411. The 235 months of Meton's first cycle had been completed at the end of Thargelion in 413, and Skirophorion of this year must be construed as belonging to Meton's second period. This does not imply any irregularity in Meton's cycle, for he had no control over the intercalation of months or the designation of names of months in the Athenian civil calendar. I know of no way to determine the exact nature of the variation between Meton's norm and the civil calendar between 423 and 421 (above, pp. 146–151), and represent the sequence of months throughout this period, as is also done by Dinsmoor, as though no variation existed. Allowance must be made for the slight margin of error possible because of divergences of this type. The plus and minus signs indicate full and hollow months respectively.

ORDER OF MONTHS FROM 432 TO 406 B.C.

432	July	15 + He	430	Sept.	21 − Bo	428	Nov.	26 − Po
	Aug.	14 − Me		Oct.	20 + Py		Dec.	25 + Po
	Sept.	12 + Bo		Nov.	19 − Ma	427	Jan.	24 − Ga
	Oct.	12 − Py		Dec.	18 + Po		Feb.	22 + An
	Nov.	10 + Ma	429	Jan.	17 − Ga		March	24 + El
	Dec.	10 − Po		Feb.	15 + An		April	23 − Mo
431	Jan.	8 + Ga		March	16 − El		May	22 + Th
	Feb.	7 − An		April	14 + Mo		June	21 − Sk
	March	8 + El		May	14 − Th		July	20 + He
	April	7 + Mo		June	12 + Sk		Aug.	19 − Me
	May	7 − Th		July	12 − He		Sept.	17 + Bo
	June	5 + Sk		Aug.	10 + Me		Oct.	17 − Py
	July	5 − He		Sept.	9 − Bo		Nov.	15 + Ma
	Aug.	3 + Me		Oct.	8 + Py		Dec.	15 − Po
	Sept.	2 − Bo		Nov.	7 + Ma	426	Jan.	13 + Ga
	Oct.	1 + Py		Dec.	7 − Po		Feb.	12 − An
	Oct.	31 − Ma	428	Jan.	5 + Ga		March	13 + El
	Nov.	29 + Po		Feb.	4 − An		April	12 − Mo
	Dec.	29 − Po		March	5 + El		May	11 + Th
430	Jan.	27 + Ga		April	4 − Mo		June	10 − Sk
	Feb.	26 − An		May	3 + Th		July	9 + He
	March	27 + El		June	2 − Sk		Aug.	8 + Me
	April	26 − Mo		July	1 + He		Sept.	7 − Bo
	May	25 + Th		July	31 − Me		Oct.	6 + Py
	June	24 + Sk		Aug.	29 + Bo		Nov.	5 − Ma
	July	24 − He		Sept.	28 − Py		Dec.	4 + Po
	Aug.	22 + Me		Oct.	27 + Ma	425	Jan.	3 − Po

425 Feb.	1	+ Ga		422 Sept.	22	+ Py		418 May	13	+ Th
March	2	− An		Oct.	22	− Ma		June	12	− Sk
March	31	+ El		Nov.	20	+ Po		July	11	+ He
April	30	− Mo		Dec.	20	− Po		Aug.	10	− Me
May	29	+ Th		421 Jan.	18	+ Ga		Sept.	8	+ Bo
June	28	− Sk		Feb.	17	− An		Oct.	8	− Py
July	27	+ He		March	17	+ El		Nov.	6	+ Ma
Aug.	26	− Me		April	16	− Mo		Dec.	6	− Po
Sept.	24	+ Bo		May	15	+ Th		417 Jan.	4	+ Ga
Oct.	24	+ Py		June	14	+ Sk		Feb.	3	− An
Nov.	23	− Ma		July	14	− He		March	3	+ El
Dec.	22	+ Po		Aug.	12	+ Me		April	2	− Mo
424 Jan.	21	− Ga		Sept.	11	− Bo		May	1	+ Th
Feb.	19	+ An		Oct.	10	+ Py		May	31	− Sk
March	21	− El		Nov.	9	− Ma		June	29	+ He
April	19	+ Mo		Dec.	8	+ Po		July	29	+ Me
May	19	− Th		420 Jan.	7	− Ga		Aug.	28	− Bo
June	17	+ Sk		Feb.	5	+ An		Sept.	26	+ Py
July	17	− He		March	7	− El		Oct.	26	− Ma
Aug.	15	+ Me		April	5	+ Mo		Nov.	24	+ Po
Sept.	14	− Bo		May	5	− Th		Dec.	24	− Po
Oct.	13	+ Py		June	3	+ Sk		416 Jan.	22	+ Ga
Nov.	12	− Ma		July	3	− He		Feb.	21	− An
Dec.	11	+ Po		Aug.	1	+ Me		March	22	+ El
423 Jan.	10	+ Ga		Aug.	31	− Bo		April	21	− Mo
Feb.	9	− An		Sept.	29	+ Py		May	20	+ Th
March	10	+ El		Oct.	29	− Ma		June	19	− Sk
April	9	− Mo		Nov.	27	+ Po		July	18	+ He
May	8	+ Th		Dec.	27	+ Ga		Aug.	17	− Me
June	7	− Sk		419 Jan.	26	− An		Sept.	15	+ Bo
July	6	+ He		Feb.	24	+ El		Oct.	15	+ Py
Aug.	5	− Me		March	26	− Mo		Nov.	14	− Ma
Sept.	3	+ Bo		April	24	+ Th		Dec.	13	+ Po
Oct.	3	− Py		May	24	− Sk		415 Jan.	12	− Ga
Nov.	1	+ Ma		June	22	+ He		Feb.	10	+ An
Dec.	1	− Po		July	22	− Me		March	12	− El
Dec.	30	+ Ga		Aug.	20	+ Bo		April	10	+ Mo
422 Jan.	29	− An		Sept.	19	− Py		May	10	− Th
Feb.	27	+ El		Oct.	18	+ Ma		June	8	+ Sk
March	29	− Mo		Nov.	17	− Po		July	8	− He
April	27	+ Th		Dec.	16	+ Po		Aug.	6	+ He
May	27	+ Sk		418 Jan.	15	− Ga		Sept.	5	− Me
June	26	− He		Feb.	13	+ An		Oct.	4	+ Bo
July	25	+ Me		March	15	+ El		Nov.	3	− Py
Aug.	24	− Bo		April	14	− Mo		Dec.	2	+ Ma

414	Jan.	1 − Po	411	Jan.	27 + Ga	408	Jan.	24 + Ga
	Jan.	30 + Ga		Feb.	26 − An		Feb.	23 − An
	March	1 + An		March	27 + El		March	24 + El
	March	31 − El		April	26 − Mo		April	23 − Mo
	April	29 + Mo		May	25 + Th		May	22 + Th
	May	29 − Th		June	24 + Sk		June	21 − Sk
	June	27 + Sk		July	24 − He		July	20 + He
	July	27 − He		Aug.	22 + Me		Aug.	19 − Me
	Aug.	25 + Me		Sept.	21 − Bo		Sept.	17 + Bo
	Sept.	24 − Bo		Oct.	20 + Py		Oct.	17 − Py
	Oct.	23 + Py		Nov.	19 − Ma		Nov.	15 + Ma
	Nov.	22 − Ma		Dec.	18 + Po		Dec.	15 − Po
	Dec.	21 + Po	410	Jan.	17 − Ga	407	Jan.	13 + Ga
413	Jan.	20 − Po		Feb.	15 + An		Feb.	12 − An
	Feb.	18 + Ga		March	17 − El		March	13 + El
	March	19 − An		April	15 + Mo		April	12 − Mo
	April	17 + El		May	15 − Th		May	11 + Th
	May	17 − Mo		June	13 + Sk		June	10 + Sk
	June	15 + Th		July	13 − He		July	10 − He
	July	15 + Sk		Aug.	11 + Me		Aug.	8 + Me
	Aug.	14 − He		Sept.	10 − Bo		Sept.	7 − Bo
	Sept.	12 + Me		Oct.	9 + Py		Oct.	6 + Py
	Oct.	12 − Bo		Nov.	8 + Ma		Nov.	5 − Ma
	Nov.	10 + Py		Dec.	8 − Po		Dec.	4 + Po
	Dec.	10 − Ma	409	Jan.	6 + Ga	406	Jan.	3 − Ga
412	Jan.	8 + Po		Feb.	5 − An		Feb.	1 + An
	Feb.	7 − Ga		March	5 + El		March	3 − El
	March	8 + An		April	4 − Mo		April	1 + Mo
	April	7 + El		May	3 + Th		May	1 − Th
	May	7 − Mo		June	2 − Sk		May	30 + Sk
	June	5 + Th		July	1 + He		June	29 − He
	July	5 − Sk		July	31 − Me		July	28 + Me
	Aug.	3 + He		Aug.	29 + Bo		Aug.	27 + Bo
	Sept.	2 − Me		Sept.	28 − Py		Sept.	26 − Py
	Oct.	1 + Bo		Oct.	27 + Ma		Oct.	25 + Ma
	Oct.	31 − Py		Nov.	26 − Po		Nov.	24 − Po
	Nov.	29 + Ma		Dec.	25 + Po		Dec.	23 + Po
	Dec.	29 − Po						

INDEXES

GENERAL INDEX

INDEX OF GREEK WORDS IN ENGLISH TEXT

INDEX OF INSCRIPTIONS

(An asterisk signifies a restoration)

PLATES

PLATE I

I.G., I², 297 (414/3 B.C.) *I.G.*, I², 298 (411 B.C.)

```
     AΘENAIOIANEΛOΣANEΓITEIΣANΔROARXONTOΣKAIEΓITEΣBOLEΣHEI              ΓROTOΣEΛΡAMMAT       AΘHNAIOIANHΛΩΣANE
     EYETAMIAIHIERONXΡEMATONTEΣAΘENAIAΣTEIΣAMENOΣ          ΓAIANIEYΣKAIΣYNARXONTEΣHOIΣΓO       MNAΣIΛOXOYARXONTO
     ΛYMEΔEΣATENEYΣEΛΡAMMATEYEΓAREΔOMENΣTRATEΛOIΣEΣTAEΓIΘRAIKEΣEYETIONIMELEΣANΔRO
         KAIΣYNARXOΣIKAIHELLENOTAMIAIΣKAIΓAREΔROIΣ                        KEΦAΛEΘENKAI       TAMIAIIERΩNXRHMA
  5  ΣYNARXOΣIΦΣEΦIΣAMENOTOΔEMOEΓITEΣHIΓΓOΘONTIΔOΣΔEYTERAΣΓRYTANEYOΣEΣKAIHEMERAI            ΩNTHΣAΘHNAIAΣAΣ
         KAI         TEΣΓRYTANEIAΣ          EΓITEΣ          IΔOΣΓEMΓTEΣΓRYTANEYOΣHΣEIKOΣTHIT    ΓOΔΩROΣKYΔAΘH
     EΣΓRYTANEIAΣΓAREΔOMENTOIΣΣTRATEΛOIΣNIKIAIKYΔANTIΔEIKAIΣYNARXOΣIKAIHELLENOTAMIA          IEYΣKAIΣYNARXON
     IΣKAIΓAREΔROIΣ                KEΦAΛEΘENKAIΣYNARXOΣINHΔΔEΤAΣNAYΣTAΣΡOMIΙOΣAΤ             EΣOIΣEYANΔROΣI
     AXREMATATAΣMETAEYRYMEΔONTOΣΓROTAΣEKΓΛEOΣAΣEΓITEΣ               IΔOΣΓEMΓTEΣΓRYTANEYOΣEΣ    IΟAΛIΩNOΣEYΩN
 10      KAIEIKOΣTEITEΣΓRYTANEIAΣΓAREΔOMENΦΣEΦIΣAMENOTOΔEMO          HAYTAIΔEEΣΣIKELIA         EYΣEΓRAMMATEYE
     NEΛONTAXREMATATOIΣΣTRATEΛOIΣNIKIAIKYΔANTIΔEIKAIΣYNARXOΣINEΓITEΣERΕXΘEIΔOΣHEBAΣ          ΓAREΔOΣANELLH
     MEΣΓRYTANEYOΣEΣ          TEΣΓRYTANEIAΣΓAREΔOMENΣTRATEΛOIΣEΣΣIKELIANΔEMOΣΘENEIAΦI        TAMIAIΣANTIΣOΕ
     ΔNAIOI        EΓITEΣ          IΔOΣ          ΓRYTANEYOΣEΣ          TEΣΓRYTANEIAΣΓAREΔOMΕN   EIERMEΙΩIKAIΣY
                                                                      KAIHELLE               ΛRXOΣINYΨHΦIΣΑ
 15  NOTAMIAIΣ                                        ΓRYTANEYOΣEΣHEIKOΣT                     NHΣTHΣBOLHΣEKΑ
     EITEΣΓRYTANEIAΣ                                  ΓARAΣAMIONΓARE                          OMBAIΩNOΣENAΤΕ
     ΔOMEN                                            KYΔAΘENΑ                                ΦΟINONTOΣAΓOΤΘ
     IEI                                                                                      XRHMATΩNAΘHNAIA
                                                                                             ΓOΛIAΔOΣΔΔΗΤΤX
                                                                                                ΔΔΗΗΗΙΙΙΤ
                                                                                             ΣNIKHΣAΘHNAIAΣAΓ
                                                                                             TΩNXRHMATΩNΓΗΔΔ
```

Facsimile drawing of the record of accounts of 414/3, 411, and 432

⊙   Ε   Ο   Ι

Left margin (vertical): ΤΩΑΤΡΑΝΟΝΝΕΤΙΝΣΧΗΟ

```
ΑΘΕΝΑΙΟΙΑΝΕΛΟΣΑΝΕΣΜΑΚΕΔΟΝΙΑΝΚΑΙΕΣΠΕΛΟΠΟΝΝΕΣΟΝΤΑΔΕΕΠΙΠΥΘΟΔΟΡΟΑΡΧΟΝΤΟΣΚΑΙΕΠΙΤΕΣΒΟΛΕΣΗΕ
       ΔΙΟΤΙΜΟΦΕ   ΛΤΕΥΣΠΡΟΤΟΣΕΛΡΑΜΜΑΤΕΥΕΤΑΜΙΑΙΗΙΕΡΟΝΧΡΕΜΑΤΟΝΤΕΣΑΘΕΝΑΙΑΣΕΥΡΕΚΤΕΣ
    ΑΤΕΝΕΥΣΚΑΙΧΣΥΝΑΡΧΟΝΤΕΣΗΟΙΣΑΠΟΛΛΟΔΟΡΟΣΚΡΙΤΙΑΦΙΟΝΑΙΟΣΕΛΡΑΜΜΑΤΕΥΕΠΑΡΕΔΟΣΑΝΣΤΡΑΤΕΛΟ
ΙΣΤΟΙΣΕΣΜΑΚΕΔΟΝΙΑΝΕΥΚΡΑΤΕΙ          ΚΑΙΧΣΥΝΑΡΧΟΣΙΦΣΕΦΙΣΑΜΕΝΟΤΟΔΕΜΟΕΠΙΤΕΣ      ΙΔΟΣΠΡΥΤ          5
ΑΝΕΙΑΣΔΕΥΤΕΡΑΣΠΡΥΤΑΝΕΥΟΣΕΣΕΜΕΡΑΙΕΣΕΛΕΛΥΘΥΙΑΙΕΣΑΝ                    ΤΑΔΕΕΣΜΑΚΕΔΟΝΙΑ
ΝΚΑΙΠΟΤΕΙΔΑΙΑΝΠΑΡΕΔΟΜΕΝΗΕΛΛΕΝΟΤΑΜΙΑΣΙ                ΦΙΛΕΤΑΙΡΟΙΙΚΑΡΙΕΙΦΙΛΟΧΣΕΝΟΙ
  ΗΙΕΡΟΝΥΜΟΙ       ΙΔΕΙ                          ΧΑΡΙΑΙΔΑΙΔΑΛΙΔΕΙ
     ΕΙΟΛΥΜΠΙΟΔΟΡΟΙ                  ΗΟΙΣ    ΜΟΧΑΡΕΣΜΥΡΡΙΝΟΣΙΟΣΕΛΡΑΜΜΑΤΕΥΕΕΠΙΤΕ
ΣΠΑΝΔΙΟΝΙΔΟΣΠΡΥΤΑΝΕΙΑΣΤΡΙΤΕΣΠΡΥΤΑΝΕΥΟΣΕΣΕΜΕΡΑΙΕΣΕΛΕΛΥΘΥΙΑΙΕΣΑΝ                              10
ΤΑΥΤΑΕΔΟΘΕΤΕΙΣΤΡΑΤΙΑΙΤΕΙΕΣΜΑΚΕΔΟΝΙΑΝΚΑΙΠΟΤΕΙΔΑΙΑΝΔΕΥΤΕΡΑΔΟΣΙΣΗΕΛΛΕΝΟΤΑΜΙΑΣΙΕΠΙΤΕΣΛΕΟ
ΝΤΙΔΟΣΠΡΥΤΑΝΕΙΑΣΤΕΤΑΡΤΕΣΠΡΥΤΑΝΕΥΟΣΕΣΕΜΕΡΑΙΕΣΕΛΕΛΥΘΥΙΑΙΕΣΑΝ
  ΤΑΥΤΑΕΛΕΤΕΙΕΣΠΟΤΕΙΔΑΙΑΝΚΑΙΜΑΚΕΔΟΝΙΑΝΣΤΡΑΤΙΑΙΣΤΡΑΤΕΛΟΣΕΣΤΑΕΠΙΘΡΑΙΚΕΣΦΟΡΜΙΟΝΠΑΙΑΝΙΕΥΣ
ΤΡΙΤΕΔΟΣΙΣΗΕΛΛΕΝΟΤΑΜΙΑΣΙΕΠΙΤΕΣ  ΕΙΔΟΣΠΡΥΤΑΝΕΙΑΣΠΕΜΠΤΕΣΠΡΥΤΑΝΕΥΟΣΕΣΕΜΕΡΑΙΕΣΕΛΕΛΥΘΥΙΑ
ΙΕΣΑΝΔΟΔΕΚΑ:   ΤΑΥΤΑΕΔΟΘΕΤΕΙΣΤΡΑΤΙΑΙΤΕΙΕΣΜΑΚΕΔΟΝΙΑΝΚΑΙΠΟΤΕΙΔΑΙΑΝΤΕΤΑΡΤΕΔΟΣΙΣ         15
ΗΕΛΛΕΝΟΤΑΜΙΑΣΙΕΠΙΤΕΣ  ΕΙΔΟΣΠΡΥΤΑΝΕΙΑΣΗΕΚΤΕΣΠΡΥΤΑΝΕΥΟΣΕΣΕΜΕΡΑΙΕΣΕΛΕΛΥΘΥΙΑΙΕΣΑΝΔΥΟΚΑΙ
ΕΙΚΟΣΙ:ΗΠΠΔΡ ΤΑΥΤΑΕΛΕΤΕΙΕΣΜΑΚΕΔΟΝΙΑΝΚΑΙΠΟΤΕΙΔΑΙΑΝΣΤΡΑΤΙΑΙ               ΠΕΜΠΤΕΔΟΣΙΣΗΕΛΛΕ
ΝΟΤΑΜΙΑΣΙΕΠΙΤΕΣ       ΙΔΟΣΠΡΥΤΑΝΕΙΑΣΗΕΒΔΟΜΕΣΠΡΥΤΑΝΕΥΟΣΕΣΕΜΕΡΑΙΕΣΕΛΕΛΥΘΥΙΑΙΕΣΑΝ      ΚΑ
ΙΔΕΚΑ:ΔΔ: ΤΑΥΤΑΕΛΕΤΕΙΕΣΤΡΑΤΙΑΙΤΕΙΕΣΜΑΚΕΔΟΝΙΑΝΚΑΙΠΟΤΕΙΔΑΙΑΝ                ΗΕΚΤΕΔΟΣΙΣ
ΗΕΛΛΕΝΟΤΑΜΙΑΣΙΕΠΙΤΕΣΑΠΑΝΤΙΔΟΣΠΡΥΤΑΝΕΙΑΣΟΛΔΟΕΣΠΡΥΤΑΝΕΥΟΣΕΣΕΜΕΡΑΙΕΣΕΛΕΛΥΘΥΙΑΙΕΣΑΝΤΕΤΤΑ    20
ΡΕΣΚΑΙΔΕΚΑ:Τ    ΗΠΔΔ   ΤΑΥΤΑΕΔΟΘΕΜΙΣΘΟΟΣΗΙΠΠΕΥΣΙΜΑΚΕΔΟΣΙ     ΚΟΣΙΟΙΣΗΕΒΔΟΜΕΔΟΣΙΣΗΕΛΛ
ΕΝΟΤΑΜΙΑΣΙΕΠΙΤΕΣΗΙΠΠΟΘΟΟΝΤΙΔΟΣΠΡΥΤΑΝΕΙΑΣΕΝΑΤΕΣΠΡΥΤΑΝΕΥΟΣΕΣΕΜΕΡΑΙΕΣΕΛΕΛΥΘΥΙΑΙΕΣΑΝΔΕΚΑΗ
ΕΧΣ:ΔΔΔΔ:ΤΑΥΤΑΕΔΟΘΕΤΕΙΣΤΡΑΤΙΑΙΤΕΙΕΣΠΟΤΕΙΔΑΙΑΝΦΟΡΜΙΟΝΙΠΑΙΑΝΙΕΙΟΛΔΟΕΔΟΣΙΣΗΕΛΛΕΝΟΤΑΜΙΑΣ
ΙΕΠΙΤΕΣΗΙΠΠΟΘΟΟΝΤΙΔΟΣΠΡΥΤΑΝΕΙΑΣΕΝΑΤΕΣΠΡΥΤΑΝΕΥΟΣΕΣΕΜΕΡΑΙΛΟΙΠΟΙΕΣΑΝΤΕΙΠΡΥΤΑΝΕΙΑΙ
ΔΔΗΠΔΔΓ:ΤΑΥΤΑΕΛΕΤΕΙΕΣΠΟΤΕΙΔΑΙΑΝΣΤΡΑΤΙΑΙΣΤΡΑΤΕΛΟΣΕΣΤΑΕΠΙΘΡΑΙΚΕΣ                           25
ΕΝΑΤΕΔΟΣΙΣΗΕΛΛΕΝΟΤΑΜΙ  ΙΕΠΙΤΕΣΤΕΣΑΚΑΜΑΝΤΙΔΟΣΠΡΥΤΑΝΕΙΑΣΔΕΚΑΤΕΣΠΡΥΤΑΝΕΥΟΣΕΣΕΜΕΡΑΙΕΣΕΛΕ
ΛΥΘΥΙΑΙΕΣΑΝΗΕΠΤΑΚΑΙΔΕΚ:ΔΓΤΤ   ΤΑΥΤΑΕΔΟΘΕΜΙΣΘΟΟΣΗΙΠΠΕΥΣΙΜΑΚΕΔΟΣΙ     ΚΟΣΙΟΙΣΚΑΙΣΙΤΟΣ
ΗΙΠΠΟΙΣ: ΚΕΦΑΛΑΙΟΝΤΟΕΣΜΑΚΕΔΟΝΙΑΝΚΑΙΠΟΤΕΙΔΑΙΑΝΑΝΑΛΟΜΑΤΟΣ

ΤΕΙΝΑΥΦΑΡΚΤΟΙΣΤΡΑΤΙΑΙΤ  ΙΠΕΡΙΠΕΛΟΠΟΝΝΕΣΟΝΤΑΜΙΑΙΕΠΙΠΥΘΟΔΟΡΟΑΡΧΟΝΤΟΣΠΑΡΕΔΟΜΕΝΣΤΡΑΤΕΛΟΙΣ    30
ΣΟΚΡΑΤΕΙΗΑΛΑΙΕΙΠΡΟΤΕΑΙΑΝΥΣΟΝΕΙΚΑΡΚΙΝΟΙΘΟΡΙΚΙΟΙΕΠΙΤΕΣΗΙΠΠΟΘΟΟΝΤΙΔΟΣΠΡΥΤΑΝΕΙΑΣΕΝΑΤΕΣΠΡΥ
ΤΑΝΕΥΟΣΕΣΕΜΕΡΑΙΛΟΙΠΟΙΕΣΑΝΟΚΤΟΤΕΙΠΡΥΤΑΝΕΙΑΙ                ΤΑΔΕΗΕΛΛΕΝΟΤΑΜΙΑΣΙ
  ΦΙΛΕΤΑΙΡΟΙΙΚΑΡΙΕΙΦ  ΧΣΕΝΟΙ       ΗΙΕΡΟΝΥΜΟΙ        ΙΔΕΙ
    ΧΑΡΙΑΙΔΑΙΔΑΛΙΔΕΙΕΙ                 ΟΛΥΜΠΙΟΔΟΡΟΙ                          ΓΑΡΕΔΟ
ΜΕΝΕΠΙΤΕΣΗΙΠΠΟΘΟΟΝΤΙΔΟΣΕΠΙΥΤΑΝΕΙΑΣΕΝΑΤΕΣΠΡΥΤΑΝΕΥΟΣΕΣΕΜΕΡΑΙΛΟΙΠΟΙΕΣΑΝ       ΤΕΙΠΡΥΤΑΝΕΙΑΙ    35
ΤΑΥΤΑΕΔΟΘΕΚΑΡΚΙΝΟΙΟΘΟΡΙΚΙΟΙΚΑΙΧΣΥΝΑΡΧΟΣΙΤΕΙΝΑΥΦΑΡΚΤΟΙΣΤΡΑΤΙΑΙΔΕΥΤΕΡΑΔΟΣΙΣΕΠ
ΙΤΕΣΗΙΠΠΟΘΟΟΝΤΙΔΟΣΠΡΥΤΑΝΕΙΑΣΕΝΑΤΕΣΠΡΥΤΑΝΕΥΟΣΕΣΕΜΕΡΑΙΛΟΙΠΟΙΕΣΑΝ      ΤΕΙΠΡΥΤΑΝΕΙΑΙ
ΤΑΥΤΑΕΔΟΘΕΚΑΡΚΙΝΟΙΟΘΟΡΙ  ΙΟΙΚΑΙΧΣΥΝΑΡΧΟΣΙΤΡΙΤΕΔΟΣΙΣΗΕΛΛΕΝΟΤΑΜΙΑΣΙΣΤΡΑΤΕΛΟΙΣΤΟΙΣΠΕΡΙΠΕΛ
ΟΠΟΝΝΕΣΟΝΣΟΚΡΑΤΕΙΗΑΛΑΙΕΙΚΑΙΧΣΥΝΑΡΧΟΣΙΕΠΙΤΕΣΑΚΑΜΑΝΤΙΔΟΣΠΡΥΤΑΝΕΙΑΣΔΕΚΑΤΕΣΠΡΥΤΑΝΕΥΟΣΕΣΤ
ΕΤΤΑΡΕΣΕΜΕΡΑΙΕΣΕΛΕΛΥΘΥΙΑΙΕΣΑΝ                                                           40
```

PLATE II

Upper left section of the record of accounts of 410/09 B.C. (*I.G.*, I², 304 A)

PLATE III

Upper right section of the record of accounts of 410/09 B.C. (*I.G.*, I², 304 A)

PLATE IV

Lower left section of the record of accounts of 410/09 B.C. (*I.G.*, I², 304 A)

PLATE V

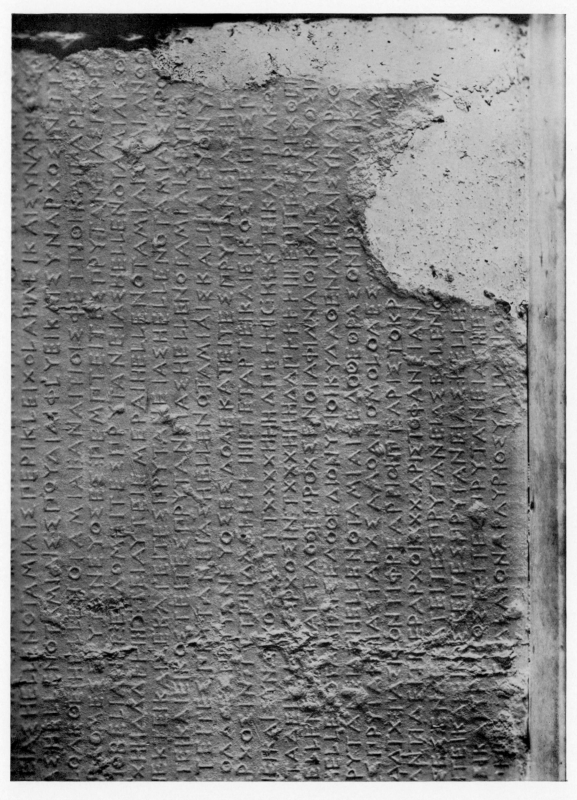

Lower right section of the record of accounts of 410/09 B.C. (*I.G.*, I², 304 A)

PLATE VI

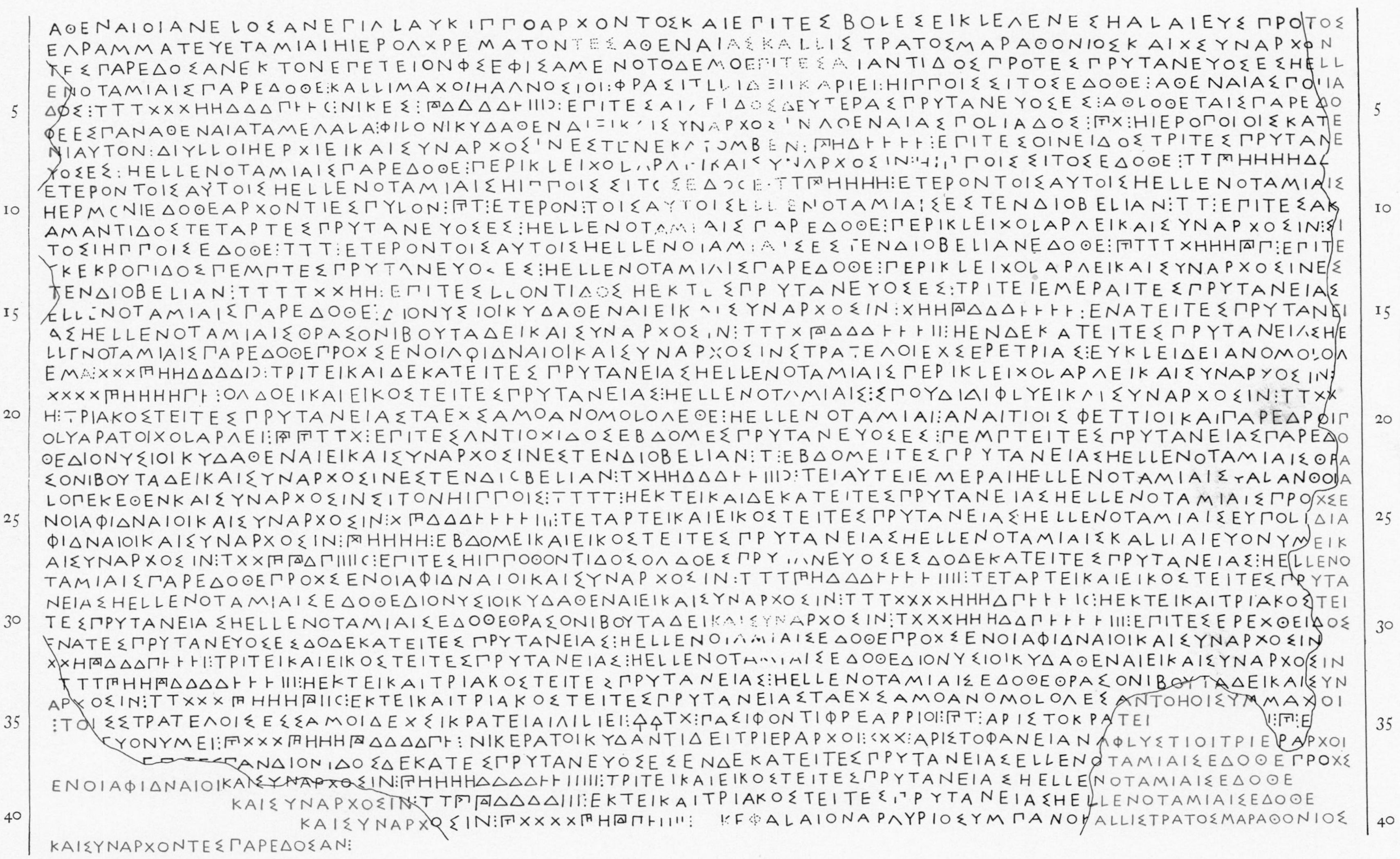

Facsimile drawing of the record of accounts of 410/09 B.C. (*I.G.*, I². 304 A), with restorations in red

PLATE VII

Upper left section of the record of accounts of 407/6 B.C. (*I.G.*, I², 304 B)

PLATE VIII

Upper right section of the record of accounts of 407/6 B.C. (*I.G.*, I², 304 B)

PLATE IX

Lower left section of the record of accounts of 407/6 B.C. (*I.G.*, I², 304 B)

PLATE X

Lower right section of the record of accounts of 407/6 B.C. (*I.G.*, I², 304 B)

Facsimile drawing of the record of accounts of 407/6 B.C. (*I.G.*, I² 304 B), with restorations in red

PLATE XI

Facsimile drawing of the record of accounts of the logistai (*I.G.*, I² 324), with restorations in red

PLATE XII

I.G., I², 324

426/5–423/2 B.C.

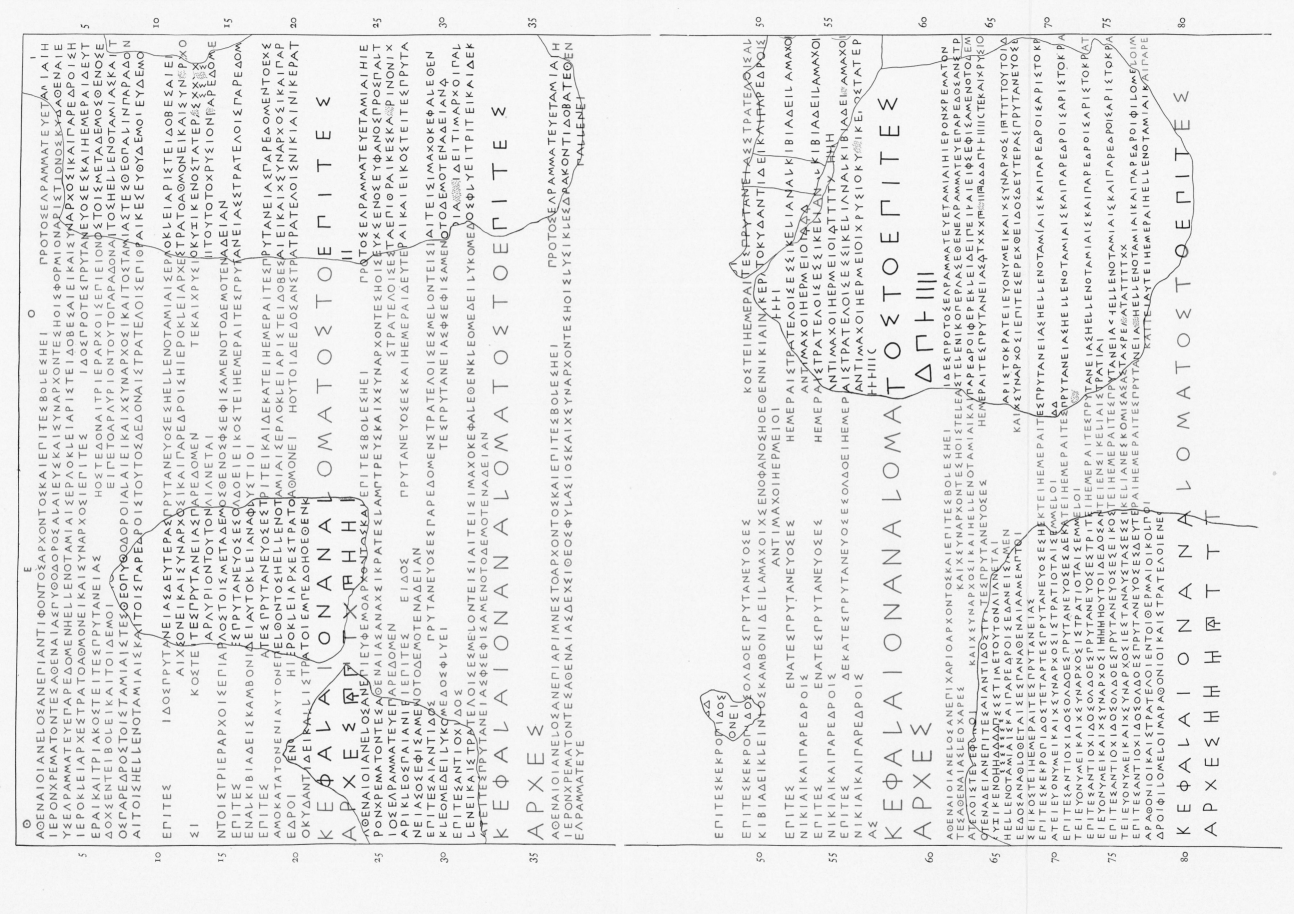

Facsimile drawing of the record of accounts of 418/7–415/4 B.C. (*I.G.*, I³, 302), with restorations in red

PLATE XIV

Upper section of the obverse face of the record of accounts of 409/8 B.C. (*I.G.*, I², 301)

PLATE XVI

Upper and lower sections of the right lateral face of the record of accounts of 409/8 B.C.
(*I.G.*, I², 301)

PLATE XVII

Facsimile drawing of the record of accounts of 409/8 B.C.
(*I.G.*, I², 301)

University of Michigan Studies

HUMANISTIC SERIES

General Editors: JOHN G. WINTER, HENRY A. SANDERS, AND EUGENE S. McCARTNEY

Size, 22.7 × 15.2 cm. 8°. Bound in cloth

VOL. I. ROMAN HISTORICAL SOURCES AND INSTITUTIONS. Edited by Henry A. Sanders, University of Michigan. Pp. vii + 402. (*Out of print.*)

VOL. II. WORD FORMATION IN PROVENÇAL. By Edward L. Adams, University of Michigan. Pp. xvii + 607. $4.00. Postage extra.

VOL. III. LATIN PHILOLOGY. Edited by Clarence Linton Meader, University of Michigan. Pp. vii + 290. (*Out of print.*)

Parts Sold Separately in Paper Covers:

Part I. THE USE OF IDEM, IPSE, AND WORDS OF RELATED MEANING. By Clarence L. Meader. Pp. 1-112. $0.75.

Part II. A STUDY IN LATIN ABSTRACT SUBSTANTIVES. By Manson A. Stewart. Pp. 113-78. $0.40.

Part III. THE USE OF THE ADJECTIVE AS A SUBSTANTIVE IN THE DE RERUM NATURA OF LUCRETIUS. By Frederick T. Swan. Pp. 179-214. $0.40.

Part IV. AUTOBIOGRAPHIC ELEMENTS IN LATIN INSCRIPTIONS. By Henry H. Armstrong. Pp. 215-86. $0.40.

VOL. IV. ROMAN HISTORY AND MYTHOLOGY. Edited by Henry A. Sanders. Pp. viii + 427. (*Out of print.*)

Parts Sold Separately in Paper Covers:

Part I. STUDIES IN THE LIFE OF HELIOGABALUS. By Orma Fitch Butler, University of Michigan. Pp. 1-169. $1.25.

Part II. THE MYTH OF HERCULES AT ROME. By John G. Winter, University of Michigan. Pp. 171-273. $0.50.

Part III. ROMAN LAW STUDIES IN LIVY. By Alvin E. Evans. Pp. 275-354. $0.40.

Part IV. REMINISCENCES OF ENNIUS IN SILIUS ITALICUS. By Loura B. Woodruff. Pp. 355-424. $0.40.

VOL. V. SOURCES OF THE SYNOPTIC GOSPELS. By Rev. Dr. Carl S. Patton. Pp. xiii + 263. $1.30. Postage extra.

Size, 28 × 18.5 cm. 4to.

VOL. VI. ATHENIAN LEKYTHOI WITH OUTLINE DRAWING IN GLAZE VARNISH ON A WHITE GROUND. By Arthur Fairbanks, Director of the Museum of Fine Arts, Boston. With 15 plates, and 57 illustrations in the text. Pp. viii + 371. $4.00. Postage extra.

Orders should be addressed to The Librarian, University of Michigan, Ann Arbor, Michigan.

University of Michigan Studies — *Continued*

VOL. VII. ATHENIAN LEKYTHOI WITH OUTLINE DRAWING IN MATT COLOR ON A WHITE GROUND, AND AN APPENDIX: ADDITIONAL LEKYTHOI WITH OUTLINE IN GLAZE VARNISH ON A WHITE GROUND. By Arthur Fairbanks. With 41 plates. Pp. x + 275. $3.50. Postage extra.

VOL. VIII. THE OLD TESTAMENT MANUSCRIPTS IN THE FREER COLLECTION. By Henry A. Sanders, University of Michigan. With 9 plates showing pages of the Manuscripts in facsimile. Pp. viii + 357. $3.50. Postage extra.

Parts Sold Separately in Paper Covers:

Part I. THE WASHINGTON MANUSCRIPT OF DEUTERONOMY AND JOSHUA. With 3 folding plates. Pp. vi + 104. $1.25. Postage extra.

Part II. THE WASHINGTON MANUSCRIPT OF THE PSALMS. With 1 single plate and 5 folding plates. Pp. viii + 105-357. $2.00. Postage extra.

VOL. IX. THE NEW TESTAMENT MANUSCRIPTS IN THE FREER COLLECTION. By Henry A. Sanders, University of Michigan. With 8 plates showing pages of the manuscripts in facsimile. Pp. x + 323. $3.50. Postage extra.

Parts Sold Separately in Paper Covers:

Part I. THE WASHINGTON MANUSCRIPT OF THE FOUR GOSPELS. With 5 plates. Pp. vii + 247. $2.00. Postage extra.

Part II. THE WASHINGTON MANUSCRIPT OF THE EPISTLES OF PAUL. With 3 plates. Pp. vii + 249-315. $1.25. Postage extra.

VOL. X. THE COPTIC MANUSCRIPTS IN THE FREER COLLECTION. By William H. Worrell, Hartford Seminary Foundation. With 12 plates. Pp. xxvi + 396. $4.75. Postage extra.

Parts Sold Separately in Paper Covers:

Part I. THE COPTIC PSALTER. The Coptic Text in the Sahidic Dialect, with an Introduction, and with 6 plates showing pages of the manuscript and fragments in facsimile. Pp. xxvi + 112. $2.00. Postage extra.

Part II. A HOMILY ON THE ARCHANGEL GABRIEL BY CELESTINUS, ARCHBISHOP OF ROME, AND A HOMILY ON THE VIRGIN BY THEOPHILUS, ARCHBISHOP OF ALEXANDRIA, FROM MANUSCRIPT FRAGMENTS IN THE FREER COLLECTION AND THE BRITISH MUSEUM. The Coptic Text, with an Introduction and Translation, and with 6 plates showing pages of the manuscripts in facsimile. Pp. 113-396. $2.50 Postage extra.

VOL. XI. CONTRIBUTIONS TO THE HISTORY OF SCIENCE. By Louis C. Karpinski and John G. Winter. With 11 plates. Pp. xi + 283. $3.50. Postage extra.

Parts Sold Separately:

Part I. ROBERT OF CHESTER'S LATIN TRANSLATION OF THE ALGEBRA OF AL-KHOWARIZMI. With an Introduction, Critical Notes, and an English Version. By Louis C. Karpinski, University of Michigan. With 4 plates showing pages of manuscripts in facsimile, and 25 diagrams in the text. Pp. vii + 164. $2.00. Postage extra.

Orders should be addressed to The Librarian, University of Michigan, Ann Arbor ,Michigan.

University of Michigan Studies — *Continued*

Part II. The Prodromus of Nicolaus Steno's Latin Dissertation on a Solid Body Enclosed by Process of Nature within a Solid. Translated into English by John G. Winter, University of Michigan, with a Foreword by William H. Hobbs. With 7 plates. Pp. vii + 169–283. $1.30. Postage extra.

Vol. XII. Studies in East Christian and Roman Art. By Charles R. Morey, Princeton University, and Walter Dennison. With 67 plates (10 colored) and 91 illustrations in the text. Pp. xiii + 175. $4.75. Postage extra.

Parts Sold Separately:

Part I. East Christian Paintings in the Freer Collection. By Charles R. Morey. With 13 plates (10 colored) and 34 illustrations in the text. Pp. xiii + 86. (*Out of print.*)

Part II. A Gold Treasure of the Late Roman Period from Egypt. By Walter Dennison. With 54 plates and 57 illustrations in the text. Pp. 89–175. $2.50. Postage extra.

Vol. XIII. Fragments from the Cairo Genizah in the Freer Collection. By Richard Gottheil, Columbia University, and William H. Worrell, University of Michigan. Text, with Translation, Notes and an Introduction. With 52 plates showing the different styles of writing in facsimile. Pp. xxxi + 273. $4.00. Postage extra.

Vol. XIV. Two Studies in Later Roman and Byzantine Administration. By Arthur E. R. Boak and James E. Dunlap, University of Michigan. Pp. x + 324. $2.25. Postage extra.

Parts Sold Separately in Paper Covers:

Part I. The Master of the Offices in the Later Roman and Byzantine Empires. By Arthur E. R. Boak. Pp. x + 160. Paper covers. $1.00.

Part. II. The Office of the Grand Chamberlain in the Later Roman and Byzantine Empires. By James E. Dunlap. Pp. 161-324. $1.00.

Vol. XV. Greek Themes in Modern Musical Settings. By Albert A. Stanley, University of Michigan. With 10 plates. Pp. xxii + 385. (*Out of print.*)

Parts Sold Separately in Paper Covers:

Part I. Incidental Music to Percy Mackaye's Drama of Sappho and Phaon. Pp. 1–68. $.90.

Part II. Music to the Alcestis of Euripides with English Text. Pp. 71–120. $.80.

Part III. Music for the Iphigenia among the Taurians by Euripides, with Greek Text. Pp. 123–190. $.75.

Part IV. Two Fragments of Ancient Greek Music. Pp. 217–225. $.30.

Part V. Music to Cantica of the Menaechmi of Plautus. Pp. 229–263. $.50.

Part VI. Attis: A Symphonic Poem. Pp. 265–384. $1.00.

Orders should be addressed to The Librarian, University of Michigan, Ann Arbor, Michigan.

University of Michigan Studies—*Continued*

Vol. XVI. Nicomachus of Gerasa: Introduction to Arithmetic. Translated into English by Martin Luther D'Ooge, with Studies in Greek Arithmetic by Frank Egleston Robbins and Louis C. Karpinski. Pp. vii + 318. (*Out of print.*)

Vols. XVII–XX. Royal Correspondence of the Assyrian Empire. Translated into English, with a transliteration of the Text and a Commentary. By Leroy Waterman, University of Michigan.

Vol. XVII. Translation and transliteration. Pp. x + 492. $4.50. Postage extra.

Vol. XVIII. Translation and transliteration. Pp. iv + 524. $4.50. Postage extra.

Vol. XIX. Commentary. Pp. x + 377. $4.00. Postage extra.

Vol. XX. Supplement and Indexes. (*In preparation.*)

Vol. XXI. The Minor Prophets in the Freer Collection and the Berlin Fragment of Genesis. By Henry A. Sanders, University of Michigan, and Carl Schmidt, University of Berlin. With 7 plates. Pp. xii + 436. $3.50. Postage extra.

Vol. XXII. A Papyrus Codex of the Shepherd of Hermas. By Campbell Bonner, University of Michigan. (*In press.*)

Vol. XXIII. The Complete Commentary of Oecumenius on the Apocalypse: Now printed for the first time from Manuscripts at Messina, Rome, Salonika and Athos. By H. C. Hoskier. Pp. viii + 260. $4.00. Postage extra.

Vol. XXIV. Zenon Papyri in the University of Michigan Collection. By C. C. Edgar. Pp. xiv + 211. With 6 plates. $3.50. Postage extra.

Vol. XXV. Karanis: Topographical and Architectural Report of Excavations during the Seasons 1924–28. By A. E. R. Boak and E. Peterson. Pp. viii + 69. With 42 plates, 19 plans, and 1 map. $2.00. Postage extra.

Vol. XXVI. Coptic Sounds. By William H. Worrell, University of Michigan.

Part I. The Main Currents of Their History. Pp. x + 59. Bound in paper. $1.50. Postage extra.

Part II. (*In preparation.*)

Vol. XXVII. Athenian Financial Documents of the Fifth Century. By B. D. Meritt, University of Michigan. Pp. xiv + 192. $3.50. Postage extra.

Orders should be addressed to The Librarian, University of Michigan, Ann Arbor, Michigan.

University of Michigan Studies — *Continued*

FACSIMILES OF MANUSCRIPTS

Size, 40.5 × 35 cm.

FACSIMILE OF THE WASHINGTON MANUSCRIPT OF DEUTERONOMY AND JOSHUA IN THE FREER COLLECTION. With an Introduction by Henry A. Sanders. Pp. x; 201 heliotype plates. The University of Michigan. Ann Arbor, Michigan, 1910.

Limited edition, distributed only to Libraries, under certain conditions. A list of Libraries containing this Facsimile is printed in *University of Michigan Studies*, *Humanistic Series*, Volume VIII, pp. 351–353.

Size, 34 × 26 cm.

FACSIMILE OF THE WASHINGTON MANUSCRIPT OF THE FOUR GOSPELS IN THE FREER COLLECTION. With an Introduction by Henry A. Sanders. Pp. x; 372 heliotype plates and 2 colored plates. The University of Michigan. Ann Arbor, Michigan, 1912.

Limited edition, distributed only to Libraries, under certain conditions. A list of Libraries containing this Facsimile is printed in *University of Michigan Studies*, *Humanistic Series*, Volume IX, pp. 317–320.

Size, 30.5 × 40.6 cm.

FACSIMILE OF THE WASHINGTON MANUSCRIPT OF THE MINOR PROPHETS IN THE FREER COLLECTION AND THE BERLIN FRAGMENT OF GENESIS, with an Introduction by Henry A. Sanders. With 130 plates. The University of Michigan. Ann Arbor, Michigan, 1927.

Limited edition, distributed only to Libraries, under certain conditions. A list of Libraries containing this Facsimile is printed in *University of Michigan Studies*, *Humanistic Series*, Volume XXI, pp. 431–434.

SCIENTIFIC SERIES

Size, 28 × 18.5 cm. 4°. Bound in cloth

VOL. I. THE CIRCULATION AND SLEEP. By John F. Shepard, University of Michigan. Pp. ix + 83, with an Atlas of 63 plates, bound separately. Text and Atlas, $2.50. Postage extra.

VOL. II. STUDIES ON DIVERGENT SERIES AND SUMMABILITY. By Walter B. Ford, University of Michigan. Pp. xi + 194. $2.50. Postage extra.

Size, 23.5 × 15.5 cm.

VOL. III. THE GEOLOGY OF THE NETHERLANDS EAST INDIES. By H. A. Brouwer. With 18 plates and 17 text figures. Pp. xii + 160. $3.00. Postage extra.

VOL. IV. THE GLACIAL ANTICYCLONES: THE POLES OF THE ATMOSPHERIC CIRCULATION. By William Herbert Hobbs. With 3 plates and 53 figures. Pp. xxiv + 198. $2.75. Postage extra.

Orders should be addressed to The Librarian, University of Michigan, Ann Arbor, Michigan.

Vols. V–VIII. Reports upon the Greenland Expeditions of the University of Michigan (1926–31).

Vol. V. Aërology, Expeditions of 1926 and 1927–29. With 23 plates and 30 text figures. Pp. xii + 262. $6.00. Postage extra.

Vol. VI. Aërology, Expeditions of 1930-31. (*In preparation.*)

Vol. VII. Meteorology. (*In preparation.*)

Vol. VIII. Geology, Glaciology, Botany, etc. (*In preparation.*)

MEMOIRS OF THE UNIVERSITY OF MICHIGAN MUSEUMS

Size, 26 × 17 cm. 4°. Bound in cloth

Vol. I. The Whip Snakes and Racers: Genera Masticophis and Coluber. By A. I. Ortenburger, University of Oklahoma. With 36 plates and 64 text figures. Pp. xviii + 247. $6.00. Postage extra.

Vol. II. Description of the Skull of a New Form of Phytosaur, with Notes on the Characters of Described North American Phytosaurs. By E. C. Case. With 7 plates and 24 text figures. Pp. vi + 56. $2.00. Postage extra.

University of Michigan Publications

HUMANISTIC PAPERS

General Editor: EUGENE S. McCARTNEY

Size, 22.7 × 15.2 cm. 8°. Bound in cloth

The Life and Work of George Sylvester Morris: A Chapter in the History of American Thought in the Nineteenth Century. By Robert M. Wenley, University of Michigan. Pp. xv + 332. $1.50. Postage extra.

Latin and Greek in American Education, with Symposia on the Value of Humanistic Studies, Revised Edition. Edited by Francis W. Kelsey. Pp. xiii + 360. $1.50. Postage extra.

Size, 18 × 12 cm. Bound in paper

The Menaechmi of Plautus. The Latin Text, with a Translation by Joseph H. Drake, University of Michigan. Pp. xi + 129. $0.60. Postage extra.

LANGUAGE AND LITERATURE

Vol. I. Studies in Shakespeare, Milton and Donne. By Members of the English Department of the University of Michigan. Pp. viii + 232. Cloth. $2.50. Postage extra.

Orders should be addressed to The Librarian, University of Michigan, Ann Arbor, Michigan.

University of Michigan Publications — *Continued*

Vol. II. Elizabethan Proverb Lore in Lyly's 'Euphues' and in Pettie's 'Petite Pallace,' with Parallels from Shakespeare. By Morris P. Tilley. Pp. x + 461. Cloth. $3.50. Postage extra.

Vol. III. The Social Mode of Restoration Comedy. By Kathleen M. Lynch. Pp. x + 242. Cloth. $2.50. Postage extra.

Vol. IV. Stuart Politics in Chapman's 'Tragedy of Chabot.' By Norma D. Solve. Pp. x + 176. Cloth. $2.50. Postage extra.

Vol. V. El Libro del Cauallero Zifar: Part I, Text. By C. P. Wagner. With 9 facsimiles. Pp. xviii + 532. Cloth, $5.00. Postage extra.

Vol. VI. El Libro del Cauallero Zifar: Part II, Commentary. By C. P. Wagner. (*In preparation.*)

Vol. VII. Strindberg's Dramatic Expressionism. By C. E. W. L. Dahlström. Pp. xii + 242. Cloth. $2.50. Postage extra.

Vol. VIII. Essays and Studies in English and Comparative Literature. By Members of the English Department of the University of Michigan. Pp. viii + 231. Cloth. $2.50. Postage extra.

Vol. IX. Toward the Understanding of Shelley. By Bennett Weaver, University of Michigan. Pp. xii + 258. Cloth. $2.50. Postage extra.

HISTORY AND POLITICAL SCIENCE

The first three volumes of this series were published as "Historical Studies" under the direction of the Department of History. Volumes IV and V were published without numbers.

Vol. I. A History of the President's Cabinet. By Mary Louise Hinsdale. Pp. ix + 355. (*Out of print.*)

Vol. II. English Rule in Gascony, 1199–1259, with Special Reference to the Towns. By Frank Burr Marsh. Pp. xi + 178. Cloth. $1.25. Postage extra.

Vol. III. The Color Line in Ohio; A History of Race Prejudice in a Typical Northern State. By Frank Uriah Quillan. Pp. xvi + 178. Cloth. $1.50. Postage extra.

Vol. IV. The Senate and Treaties, 1789–1817. The Development of the Treaty-Making Functions of the United States Senate during Their Formative Period. By Ralston Hayden, University of Michigan. Pp. xvi + 237. Cloth. $1.50. Postage extra.

Orders should be addressed to The Librarian, University of Michigan, Ann Arbor, Michigan.

University of Michigan Publications — *Continued*

Vol. V. William Plumer's Memorandum of Proceedings in the United States Senate, 1803–1807. Edited by Everett Somerville Brown, University of Michigan. Pp. xi + 873. Cloth. $3.50. Postage extra.

Vol. VI. The Grain Supply of England during the Napoleonic Period. By W. F. Galpin, Syracuse University. Pp. xi + 305. Cloth. $3.00. Postage extra.

Vol. VII. Eighteenth Century Documents relating to the Royal Forrests, the Sheriffs and Smuggling: Selected from the Shelburne Manuscripts in the William L. Clements Library. By Arthur Lyon Cross, University of Michigan. With 4 plates. Pp. x + 328. $3.00. Postage extra.

Vol. VIII. The Low Countries and the Hundred Years' War, 1326–1347. By Henry S. Lucas, University of Washington. Pp. xviii + 696. Cloth. $4.00. Postage extra.

Vol. IX. The Anglo-French Treaty of Commerce of 1860 and the Progress of the Industrial Revolution in France. By A. L. Dunham. Pp. xiv + 409. $3.50. Postage extra.

Vol. X. The Youth of Erasmus. By A. Hyma. Pp. xii + 342. With 8 plates and 2 maps. $3.00. Postage extra.

CONTRIBUTIONS FROM THE MUSEUM OF PALEONTOLOGY

Vol. I. The Stratigraphy and Fauna of the Hackberry Stage of the Upper Devonian. By Carroll Lane Fenton and Mildred Adams Fenton. With 45 plates, 9 text figures and one map. Pp. xi + 260. Cloth. $2.75. Postage extra.

Vol. II. Consisting of 14 miscellaneous papers, published between July 10, 1924, and August 3, 1927. With 41 plates, 39 text figures and 1 map. Pages ix + 240. Cloth. $3.00. Postage extra.

(A list of the titles and the prices of the separate papers of Volume II may be had upon application.)

UNIVERSITY OF MICHIGAN COLLECTIONS

Catalogue of the Stearns Collection of Musical Instruments (Second Edition). By Albert A. Stanley. With 40 plates. Pp. 276. $4.00.

Orders should be addressed to The Librarian, University of Michigan, Ann Arbor, Michigan.

University of Michigan Publications — *Continued*

PAPERS OF THE MICHIGAN ACADEMY OF SCIENCE, ARTS AND LETTERS

(containing Papers submitted at Annual Meetings)

Editors: EUGENE S. McCARTNEY AND PETER OKKELBERG

Size, 24.2 × 16.5 cm. 8°. Bound in cloth

VOL. I (1921). With 38 plates, 1 text figure and 5 maps. Pp. xi + 424. $2.00 Postage extra.

VOL. II (1922). With 11 plates and 7 text figures. Pp. xi + 226. $2.00. Bound in paper, $1.50. Postage extra.

VOL. III (1923). With 26 plates, 15 text figures and 3 maps. Pp. xii + 473. $3.00. Bound in paper, $2.25. Postage extra.

VOL. IV (1924), PART I. With 27 plates, 22 text figures and 3 maps. Pp. xii + 631. $3.00. Bound in paper, $2.25. Postage extra.

VOL. IV (1924), PART II. A KEY TO THE SNAKES OF THE UNITED STATES, CANADA AND LOWER CALIFORNIA. By Frank N. Blanchard. With 78 text figures. Pp. xiii + 65. Cloth. $1.75. Postage extra.

VOL. V (1925). With 27 plates, 26 text figures and 1 map. Pp. xii + 479. $3.00 Bound in paper, $2.25. Postage extra.

VOL. VI (1926). (This volume contains papers in botany only.) With 28 plates, 4 text figures and 3 maps. Pp. xii + 406. $3.00. Bound in paper, $2.25. Postage extra.

VOL. VII (1926). (This volume does not contain papers in botany.) With 28 plates, 17 text figures and 7 maps. Pp. xii + 435. $3.00. Bound in paper, $2.25. Postage extra.

VOL. VIII (1927). With 32 plates, 35 text figures and 2 maps. Pp. xiv + 456. $3.00. Bound in paper, $2.25. Postage extra.

VOL. IX (1928). (This volume contains papers in botany and forestry only.) With 99 plates and 29 text figures. Pp. xiv + 597. $4.00. Bound in paper, $2.25. Postage extra.

VOL. X (1928). (This volume does not contain papers in botany and forestry.) With 24 plates, 61 text figures and 13 maps. Pp. xvii + 620. $4.00. Bound in paper, $2.25. Postage extra.

Orders should be addressed to The Librarian, University of Michigan, Ann Arbor, Michigan.

University of Michigan Publications—*Continued*

VOL. XI (1929). (This volume contains papers in botany and zoölogy only.) With 55 plates, 30 text figures and 3 maps. Pp. xii + 494. $3.50. Bound in paper, $2.25. Postage extra.

VOL. XII (1929). (This volume does not contain papers in botany and zoölogy.) With 39 plates, 10 text figures and 8 maps. Pp. xii + 348. $3.00. Bound in paper, $2.25. Postage extra.

VOL. XIII (1930). (This volume contains papers in botany and zoölogy only.) With 48 plates, 46 text figures, and 8 maps. Pp. xii + 603. $4.00. Bound in paper, $2.25. Postage extra.

VOL. XIV (1930). (This volume does not contain papers in botany and zoölogy.) With 64 plates, 20 text figures, and 51 maps. Pp. xv + 650. $4.00. Bound in paper, $2.25. Postage extra.

VOL. XV (1931). (This volume contains papers in botany, forestry and zoölogy only.) With 47 plates, 18 text figures and 10 maps. Pp. x + 511. $3.50. Bound in paper, $2.25. Postage extra.

VOL. XVI (1931). (This volume does not contain papers in botany, forestry and zoölogy.) With 36 plates, 20 text figures and 43 maps. Pp. x + 521. $3.50. Bound in paper, $2.25. Postage extra.

Orders should be addressed to The Librarian, University of Michigan, Ann Arbor, Michigan.